D-DAY

COMMANDO

From Normandy to the Maas
with 48 Royal Marine Commando

D-DAY
COMMANDO

From Normandy to the Maas
with 48 Royal Marine Commando

KEN FORD

SUTTON PUBLISHING

First Published in the United Kingdom in 2003 by
Sutton Publishing Limited.
Phoenix Mill · Thrupp · Stroud · Gloucestershire · GL5 2BU

This paperback edition first published in 2005

British Library Cataloguing in Publication Data
A catalogue record for this book is available from the British Library.

ISBN 0 7509 4004 2

Typeset in 10/12pt Plantin Light.
Typesetting and origination by
Sutton Publishing Limited.
Printed and bound in England by
J.H. Haynes & Co. Ltd, Sparkford.

To my new grandson
Joseph James Buenfeld
born 3 July 2002

CONTENTS

Maps

Acknowledgements

I would like to extend my sincere thanks to all who have helped me in the preparation of this book.

I begin by giving special thanks to Hedley Phillips, who first got me interested in 48 Royal Marine Commando. It was through him that I learned of the exploits of the unit and of the men who served in the Commando. Special thanks also go to the Secretary of the 48 RM Association, Dennis Smith, who put me in touch with so many of his comrades. A particular debt is owed to these two marines and to the other real-life heroes who served with the Commando. To all of those who took the trouble to get in touch with me and to wish me well in my endeavours, I am most grateful:

Capt Percy Bream, R.E. 'Ted' Brooks, Richard Cannock, Tom Clark, Tom Clarke, Bob Coleman, John Desmond, Roy Dewar, Dr James Dick, Ralph Dye, R.D. 'Dougie' Edwards, Vic Edwards, Lt Col David Ellis, Dougie Gray, George Hawkins, Vince Horton, Bill Hudson, Trevor Ireland, Harry Lane, Capt Geoff Linnell, Andrew 'Jock' Mathieson, Ian Muir, Donald Nicholson, Tony Pratt, Ron Price, Ronald Pugh, Capt Michael Reynolds, Bert Skinner, Sir Harold Smedley, Capt John Square, Joe Stringer, Ernie Taylor, Harry Timmins, Derek Turner, Jimmy Wood, the Right Revd Maurice Wood DSC and Fred Wyatt.

I should like to thank Geoff Linnell for his kindness in allowing me to quote from his history of the unit, *48 Royal Marine Commando: The Story 1944–46*. This excellent book gives a full account of the actions fought by the Commando and was written by an officer who participated in each of them. I recommend it all who have an interest in military history. Thanks also goes to Dr James Dick, Harry Timmins, Derek Turner and Evan Thomas for permission to quote from their unpublished memoirs. I also appreciate very much the permission granted by Jimmy Dunning to quote from his book *It Had To Be Tough*, and by Jean Portugal for allowing me to quote from the D-Day experiences of Geoff Linnell, Ian Muir and Bill Aird, which are contained in her book *We Were There: The Army, Vol. 4*. I would also like to thank the Trustees of the Imperial War Museum for allowing me to use the material obtained from their reading room, photographic archive and sound recording archive in this book. The quotations from Hedley Phillips, Dennis Smith, Joe Stringer and Ralph Dye have been supplemented with details obtained from the Imperial War Museum's sound archive. Thanks also go to the Royal Marines Museum for allowing me access to its archives.

Ken Ford
February 2003
Southampton

CHAPTER ONE

The Youngest Commando

48 Royal Marine Commando was the last Commando to be formed during Second World War. It owed its existence, in an indirect way, to General Sir Bernard Montgomery, for the unit was raised as a result of the British general's criticism of the original plans for D-Day.

In late 1943, while he was still leading the British Eighth Army in Italy, Montgomery was designated as land force commander for Operation Overlord, the invasion of France. He was promoted to take charge of 21st Army Group for the landings, which included the US First Army and the British Second Army. At the end of December Monty handed over his famous desert army to Lt Gen Oliver Leese and came back to England.

The plan for the invasion of Normandy had been drawn up by Gen Sir Frederick Morgan, Chief of Staff to the Allied Supreme Commander (COSSAC). Morgan's planning team had been constrained in the scale of the operation by several factors, not least of which was the limited availability of specialised landing craft with which to get the assault troops ashore. When Montgomery was shown the outline plan for Overlord he was dismayed by the size of the assault. Morgan had proposed that the initial landings be made on a narrow front by just three divisions. The strength of the proposed attack, and the command structure that was envisaged to handle the landings, led Montgomery to believe that the plan would have to be drastically altered to have any chance of success.

When Montgomery arrived back from the Mediterranean on 3 January 1944, he immediately set about having Overlord changed. He proposed that a much larger assault be landed over a longer stretch of Normandy coastline. He suggested that a lodgement be gained by five assault divisions, each landing on a separate beach, and that these five divisions be supported by airborne landings on the outer flanks. Operations inland would expand from these beachheads, with each landing beach then being given over to the build-up of a complete corps.

Montgomery's new staff at 21st Army Group drew up a revised plan for Overlord by 1 February, encompassing all of the commander's proposals. This rearranged plan caused a myriad of new problems, each requiring a great deal of staff work and organisation to solve it. The greatest amphibious assault in history required the greatest effort by all of the services. The complexity and scale of the enterprise, together with the limited time available for the planning and execution of the operation, produced a host of almost impossible demands. One such demand was for the commitment of a number of Commandos for special tasks.

The Commandos to be used on the day of the invasion, D-Day, had a variety of roles. Their light equipment and ability to move at speed made them suitable formations to seize and hold key objectives once off the landing beaches. As the planners got to work on the detail of Overlord, these tasks began to take shape. They fell into two broad categories: first, the Commandos could take and hold the immediate flanks of each beach to enable the main assaulting troops to move inland without having to worry about the enemy in the areas adjacent to them, and second, they could travel fast and light to bring relief to the exposed airborne troops who were to land behind the enemy lines. When the details of these requirements were finally resolved, it became clear that 21st Army Group was one Commando short; there were just not enough Commandos in England to carry out all of the tasks allocated to them.

Officers of 48 RM Commando, taken in Camp C19 on Southampton Common prior to leaving for Normandy. Back row: Capt Godkin, Lts Curtis, Goodlet, Aldworth, Ford, Square and Yates. Second row: Lts Mackenzie, Smedley, Grant, McLean and Fouché, Capt Lennard, Lt Winser, Capt Hoare, Lts Rubinstein and Rigby. Front row: Capts Linnell and Reynolds, Majs de Stacpoole and Sanders, Lt Colonel Moulton, Capt Flunder, Revd Armstrong, Maj Freeman and Capt Perry. (*John Square*)

This need for another Commando was raised at the next Chief of Staffs' Committee. The First Sea Lord, Admiral of the Fleet Sir Andrew Cunningham, saw few problems with the demand and said that the Royal Marines could provide the new Commando. This edict was passed down to the Commandant General of the Royal Marines, Gen Sir Thomas Hunton, and he in turn told the commander of the Commando Group, Maj Gen Robert Sturges, that he would have to create another Commando in time for the invasion, which was then set for May 1944. Hunton also told Sturges that men from the soon to be disbanded 7th Battalion Royal Marines could form the nucleus of the new Commando when it arrived back in England from Italy on 10 February, and any shortfall in numbers could be made up with the marines of the Second Mobile Naval Base Defence Organisation (MNBDOII), which was also on its way back from the Mediterranean to be broken up. This left Sturges and his team just three months to raise, equip and train the new Commando before it saw action at the sharp end of the invasion. It was a very tall order.

When the original concept of raising Commandos to raid enemy-occupied territory was implemented early in the war, it was the Army that provided the necessary troops, even though the Corps of Royal Marines, Britain's seagoing soldiers, had been carrying out amphibious warfare for centuries. This was eventually remedied in August 1943 when the RM Division, the RM brigades and most of the RM battalions were disbanded and converted into Commandos. 1st, 2nd, 3rd, 5th, 9th and 10th RM Battalions became 42, 43, 44, 45, 46 and 47 RM Commandos respectively, with 8th RM Battalion becoming 41 RM Commando in October 1943. Those personnel of battalions that did not wish to transfer to the commandos, or failed to meet the high standards of fitness and competence required, were sent for training on landing craft. The HQ staff of the RM Division became the HQ of the Special Service Group and the division's commander, Maj Gen Bob Sturges, became responsible for the new commando brigades.

In contrast to many of the RM battalions, 7th RM Battalion had a long and chequered career. It was not disbanded in August 1943 like the others, for at that time it was abroad, in action with the enemy. MNBDOII was similarly in the Mediterranean and had been there since earlier in the year. As its name suggests, the Second Mobile Naval Base Defence Organisation was designed to defend, and partly operate, a captured naval base following an invasion. In the event, the unit was not used in action in this role as a complete group, but it did send anti-aircraft and coastal artillery units to Sicily to defend the ports of Augusta and Syracuse after the landings. The Royal Marines had raised two MNBDOs during the war, neither of which was ever successfully employed in its designated role. However, they were both often asked to provide sub-units to carry out specific tasks as and when the need arose. For instance, part of MNBDOI was used as infantry during the Crete fiasco, with most of its personnel going into captivity when the island fell to the Germans. Other units were taken away from it for service in Ceylon and on fortified island bases in the Indian Ocean. Eventually the whole of MNBDOI moved to Ceylon where it remained until it was disbanded in mid-1944.

The man picked to command 48 RM Commando was an inspired choice on the part of Commando Group Headquarters. James Moulton was called at his home in Devon in late January 1944 and given the news. He was elated. Jim Moulton had narrowly missed getting one of the earlier Royal Marine Commandos when they were raised the previous year and he had been languishing in a staff appointment as Senior Liaison Officer at Combined Operations Headquarters ever since, hoping fervently that he might break out of his desk-bound job before the war was over. He was now given an opportunity to do just that.

James Louis Moulton, the son of a naval captain, was born on 3 June 1906. He enlisted in the Royal Marines as a probationary subaltern in 1924. Three years later he joined the new battleship *Rodney* on her first commission. A tour in *Revenge* followed in 1929, but Moulton later decided that he had had enough of capital ships and volunteered for the Fleet Air Arm. As a flying officer, he served in 460 and 462 Flights in the carrier *Glorious* in the Mediterranean in 1931 and with 824 and 825 Squadrons on the carrier *Eagle* in 1935. When he came back to England he left the Fleet Air Arm and rejoined the Royal Marines. At the outbreak of war he was sent to France as GSO3 in the operations section of the British Expeditionary Force (BEF). The next year he played an important part in the evacuation of the BEF at Dunkirk, being among the last to get away before the Germans arrived. In May 1942 he took part in the assault on Diego Suarez and the occupation of the Vichy French island of Madagascar as GSO1 with Force 121. Moulton was then a lieutenant-colonel and dropped a rank so that he could become a battalion second-in-command, hoping to eventually command his own unit. In the large reorganisation of the Royal Marines in August 1943, when the RM battalions were disbanded and their men sent to either Commandos or landing craft, Moulton was passed over and did not get the command he was hoping for. It was a sickening blow for him as he later admitted in his memoirs. He desperately wanted to command a fighting unit.

When Lt Col Moulton reported to Commando Group Headquarters to receive his orders, he was told to raise a new Commando, styled 48 RM Commando, and train it ready to take part in the invasion. For personnel he was to have the pick of the men from 7th RM Battalion and those of MNBDOII. Moulton was told that after the men he chose had been given disembarkation leave, he and his fledgling new unit were to report to Commando Basic Training Centre at Achnacarry to begin commando training on 12 March. After this initial training, the Commando would join the 4th Special Service Brigade and begin specialised training for the landings in France.

Moulton was fortunate in that he could hand-pick his team from scratch. He had full authority to select and reject any officer or marine that he chose, without having to give any reasons. The number of men available to him meant that the Commando could be assembled for the most part from volunteers. As far as possible, no man would have to be with him unless he chose to be. Moulton was also empowered to deal directly with Special Service Group Headquarters on any matter, giving him a fast track to decision making. To give them their due, in an age of reaction, red tape and 'Colonel Blimps,' those in higher authority were determined to go all out to make it possible for Moulton to achieve his objectives.

CHAPTER TWO

7th RM Battalion and the MNBDOII

The 7th RM Battalion was originally formed in late 1940, joining with 8th RM Battalion to form 103rd Royal Marine Brigade, part of the Royal Marine Division. Throughout the whole of its existence, the 7th RM Battalion, like all of the other Royal Marine battalions, Royal Marine brigades and the Royal Marine Division, never had a clear role during the early years of the war. Seagoing marines saw a great deal of action manning the guns of the capital ships, but land-based units seemed to spend the first few years of the conflict organising and reorganising. Two of the RM brigades were deployed and sent to South Africa during the Dakar operation between August and October 1940, but other than this the Royal Marine Division spent the first three years of the war at home training.

For the early part of its life 7th Battalion struggled to form its identity. Drafts were taken from the battalion to help raise other units, most notably when 300 men were sent to the newly formed Mobile Naval Base Defence Organisation. It took a very long period before the battalion was brought up to strength. This was also true for some other Royal Marine battalions, for their growth was equally slow and disjointed. By May 1941, the 7th's commander, Lt Col Sandall, had the responsibility for two other battalions, the 8th and 9th RM battalions, and all three units had a combined strength of only 28 officers and 797 other ranks.

One of the first marines allocated to the battalion was Colin Travers, a pre-war regular who was later to become the RSM of 48 Commando. 'The 7th Battalion was formed at Exton and later went into camp at Dalditch, not far from Exmouth. There was nothing much there when we arrived, but it was a fine training ground. It was a tented camp at first, then made permanent by the addition of Nissen huts. Here we trained and marched, marched and trained.'

Harry Timmins came straight to the 7th Battalion from the training camp at Exton after he had completed his six weeks basic training.

We left Exton in full marching order, with our greatcoat, spare boots and other articles in our large pack. At the main entrance the guard turned out and presented arms. We marched past to attention with 'eyes right'. After going down a few streets we turned across muddy fields and for the next two or three hours staggered along in the mud. We finally arrived at an isolated and unwelcoming looking camp full of Nissen huts. By this time we were wet, miserable and tired. Our boots were muddy and we were very bedraggled after walking so far in marching order. We duly lined up on the parade ground and came to attention as the adjutant walked up to inspect us. He was a horrible looking fellow with a great long waxed moustache, a good two inches either side of his mouth. He inspected us with a nasty sneer on his face. 'This is Dalditch Camp,' he said, 'And you are now in the 7th Battalion Royal Marines, a fighting unit already well trained and so you will have to work very hard to catch up and, by God, you will work hard.' He then turned to the sergeant in charge of us. 'Give them two extra parades because their boots are filthy.' With that he turned and stamped away.

In June 1942, things began to settle down and the unit had been found a role in South Africa, guarding naval stores dumps. Lt Col Dewhurst was appointed to command the battalion and to take it overseas. 'Dewhurst was an old pre-war style officer,' recalls Percy Bream. 'He always had to have a horse and wherever he was someone had to find him one. People went all over the shop to find one so that he could ride it on parade. In Plymouth he used to ride a horse into a barrack room and, with his stick, he would knock your stuff off the shelves, telling you to tidy it up. You might say he was a little bit eccentric and rather pompous.'

In September 1943, the battalion embarked for South Africa in the troopship *Empress of Russia*. The ship was full of other units as well as the 7th Battalion, so the marines manned the ship's guns and helped on various duties, including security and keeping order, during the passage. When the battalion arrived in Durban it was put into a transit camp while a tricky political problem was sorted. The South African government had decided that they did not want foreign troops guarding any of their sensitive installations, so the intended role of the battalion was made redundant. Five weeks later, 7th Battalion was sent round Africa to Egypt and landed at Suez on 1 January 1943.

In Egypt the battalion was involved in preparations for the invasion of Sicily, helping to run the Combined Training Centre in Kabrit. It was then given a specific role in the operation. It was ordered to organise the development of what was called a 'beach brick' for the invasion of Sicily. This was an organisation that would handle the logistics of landing stores and troops across a newly captured beach after an invasion. The 7th Battalion formed the core of No. 31 Beach Brick – though there were no other beach bricks at this time, it was numbered 31 so as to imply that there were many others. The battalion provided the HQ Company, HQ Defence Company and three rifle companies for the brick. The remainder of the organisation, which numbered 2,700 men, was made up of specialist engineering groups, transport groups, administration and nine companies of working parties from various other units, including three companies of the Baluchi Rifles.

No. 31 Beach Brick arrived in Sicily on 10 July behind the assault troops of 231st Brigade Group on the eastern tip of Cape Passero. The marines landed immediately after the beach had been made secure to prepare the landing site to receive supplies and reinforcements. The Defence Company cleared snipers from the beach area and mopped up pockets of resistance

Capt John Square at the end of the war. He joined the Royal Marines aged seventeen by lying about his age. He served with MNBDOII in the Middle East before returning to England to join 48 RM Commando. (*John Square*)

bypassed by the assaulting troops. For the next seven days the Beach Brick received a continuous supply of men and *matériel* through the landing area, feeding it on to the whole of British XXX Corps for its advance inland. During that period No. 31 Beach Brick was dive-bombed and machine-gunned from the air, but had no other contact with enemy troops. On 17 July, the defence commitment to the Beach Brick was finished and 7th Battalion moved inland to Buccheri to help with occupation duties. Lt Col Dewhurst becoming Military Governor of the area.

The battalion's main duties were to organise the civic authorities and to enforce the curfew. A few days later it moved further up the line to take over the defence of XXX Corps HQ. Then something happened which came as a shock to all those involved; the Battalion was ordered further forward into the front line to make an attack across the River Dittaino.

The 7th Battalion had been trained and had landed in Sicily as a beach defence organisation. It had no supporting arms of its own, two of its 3-inch mortars had been lost and it had no transport other than four carriers. It had not trained as infantry since leaving England ten months previously and none of its men had yet seen action in the field.

Since arriving in Sicily, British Eighth Army had been meeting increasingly stiff resistance. It had tried to advance up the coastal route to Messina, but had been stopped on the Catania plain. Montgomery had attempted to get round this hold-up by moving through the foothills on the western side of Mount Etna. It was here that the 51st Highland Division had crossed the Dittaino but could not advance out of its bridgehead. The 7th Battalion was to try to cross the river farther to the west in an attempt to outflank the enemy.

Maj de Courcy-Ireland, the second-in-command, was given orders for the attack to start that evening when he arrived at 51st Division's HQ at 1400 hours on 19 July. The rest of the battalion was strung out along the road on its march forward and the major requested that it be given 24 hours to complete its move and organise itself for the attack, reminding the divisional commander that the battalion lacked recent infantry training. The request was refused.

The 7th Battalion made the attack that evening and got across the river but could not hold on to the gains. Enemy fire forced the troops back to their start line on the slopes of Massa Parlato and inflicted heavy casualties among the attacking companies. The battalion was left in position on this exposed high ground for the next nine days, sending out patrols and suffering three or four casualties a day from shelling. During the night, they moved on to the face of Massa Parlato, but withdrew on to the reverse slopes in daylight. On 28 July the battalion was pulled out of the line. In this short action it lost 76 men, 14 of whom were killed. Shortly after the action, Lt Col Dewhurst was replaced as battalion commander by Lt Col Kenneth Hunt.

After the River Dittaino the 7th Battalion was given the task of maintaining order in the town of Catania. In September it moved over to Italy as a local protection force in the naval base in Taranto. Then, in November 1943, came the news that the battalion was being returned to Britain for disbandment.

MNBDOII had a similar odyssey to the 7th Battalion in the Mediterranean. It had been formed in January 1941 and sailed for Egypt in February 1943. In Egypt MNBDOII served with Eighth Army's supply echelons and its heavy and light anti-aircraft regiments were moved to Malta to provide air defence. Immediately after the invasion of Sicily, MNBDOII landed and carried out its intended role of defending the naval bases at Syracuse and Augusta. The unit remained in Sicily, mainly in the Augusta area, for six more months until January 1944 when it was posted back to Britain for disbandment.

Both the 7th Battalion and MNBDOII arrived back in Scotland in February 1944. There to meet them in their transit camps in Paisley was Lt Col Moulton. He had come north to start the selection process for 48 RM Commando. He met the two commanding officers and explained what he was hoping to achieve, asking them to nominate their most suitable men to give him some indication as to who he might choose for the Commando. The whole of both units were first given a thorough medical examination and a 'weeding out' process began. Almost 65 per cent of these men were rejected; they were either too old, medically unfit or generally unsuitable. Many of them were suffering from malaria and jaundice. Most of MNBDOII had had no infantry experience, other than during basic training several years previously, but those that had served in the Air Defence Brigade and in the Coastal Artillery Regiment were suitable, as were drivers from the Supply Unit and signallers from the Signals Unit.

Preference was given to those who put themselves forward for commando duties, for Moulton still wanted to adhere as closely as possible to the tradition of having a Commando made up of volunteers. It was certainly important that all of the officers selected for 48 Commando were volunteers, but this was not practical for the numbers of NCOs and men who were needed. The bulk of these other ranks had to be drafted into the unit, for the 7th Battalion and the MNBDOII were being disbanded and all of their men had to go somewhere. It was just not possible to get volunteers for all the specialisms that were required, as George Hawkins explains: 'I was one of a number of drivers assigned to the Commando. It was a case of you, you and you and then we were in; we did not volunteer. We felt good about it later because we knew that we were joining the elite and each man prayed that he could meet the challenge and get his green beret.'

Some men went against their better nature and put themselves forward, such as one lieutenant from MNBDOII, Harold Smedley:

A circular came round, a bit like when I joined the Royal Marines, asking for men to transfer to the RM Commandos and once again I did the thing that you are not supposed to do in the forces, I volunteered! Myself and a couple of other officers put down our names. When we arrived in England we were given leave and then I joined the Commando as a troop officer, my friend was appointed Intelligence Officer. He was very well equipped for the job being a good linguist, but soon developed trouble with his feet, which was not a very good start to the campaign for him, so the CO said he was sorry but he had to go. I replaced him.

Maj Sanders was the Commando's second-in-command and he was the first appointment made by Moulton. He was a veteran of MNBDOI in Ceylon and had served with the unit in the Middle East. While the CO was in Scotland selecting the main officers of the Commando, Sanders began the planning and administration work necessary to get the unit going. Many of the young officers from the 7th Battalion who had been in the disastrous action in Sicily were obvious choices for Moulton; men such as Linnell, de Stacpoole, Perry, Flunder, Aldworth and Curtis all had valuable battle experience. Linnell, de Stacpoole and Perry were all made troop commanders and Aldworth and Curtis were both made second-in-command of troops. Dan Flunder became the Adjutant.

The Heavy Weapons Troop, S Troop, was equipped with two very different weapons and was formed from marines from two different backgrounds. The medium machine gun sub-unit was manned by highly-trained machine-gunners from 15 Machine Gun Battalion RM, while the men who joined the Mortar sub-unit mainly came from the 7th RM Battalion, most of whom had very little experience of mortaring.

The Commando's Medical Officer, Lt David Winser, was a remarkable man, as the unit's second padre, Revd Maurice Wood, recalls: 'Dr David Winser stroked for the Oxford Boat in 1938, won a scholarship to Yale, won the Newdigate Prize for poetry and had written several novels under the name of John Arey. He was one of the finest doctors I have known.' At the start of the war, Winser trained to be a pilot in the RAF, but was rejected due to colour blindness. He spent the whole of the Blitz working with medical teams in Charing Cross Hospital in London. As soon as he qualified as a doctor, he joined the Royal Army Medical Corps and volunteered for the Commandos. He was later to win the Military Cross for his work with the Commando during the invasion.

When 48 RM Commando was formed it did not have a chaplain. The senior chaplain of the commando group, Revd John Armstrong, therefore wrote to Moulton offering to look after the unit himself part-time, and volunteering to land with the Commando on D-Day. In preparation for this, he also suggested that he would do the basic training course at Achnacarry. The men were impressed.

When the main body of the Commando first met together in Deal on 2 March, it was 250 strong. A further 170 men arrived later from MNBDOII and joined the Commando in Scotland on 14 March when it started its basic training at Achnacarry. The men from MNBDOII, for the most part, had no current knowledge of infantry tactics or of modern infantry weapons. A few selected officers and senior NCOs were sent on War Office and command courses so that they could act as unit instructors when they returned. One of these officers was Lt John Square:

Moulton came north to interview us and I was selected and told to report to Deal after some leave. When I arrived at Deal the newly formed Commando was put into strict training for a week and then dispatched to Achnacarry for commando training. I did not go, however, for I was selected to attend a foreign weapons course. When I got back to the Commando it had returned from Scotland and was at Gravesend. The marines were still doing commando training and I got through that with no problems, so I still got my green beret.

Not all of the volunteers for 48 RM Commando came from 7th Battalion and MNBDOII. Many were seagoing marines who had served a good part of their service manning the big guns on capital ships and cruisers. Capt Mike Reynolds, who commanded A Troop, had spent all of his service at sea with the Royal Marines. Bert Skinner was another seagoing marine, who joined the Corps in January 1942 as a Boy Bugler and received the King's Shilling, a practice that he thought had disappeared with the First World War. He later served on the brand-new Colony Class Cruiser *Gambia* and the battleship *Resolution* before requesting to join the RM Commandos. Several other marines, including Ron Price, came from the cruiser *Newfoundland*, which had been torpedoed in the Mediterranean. Jimmy Wood also transferred from seagoing service to the Commandos and joined

Nan Red Beach taken on D-Day during the late morning. The landing place of the Commando is shown in the bottom left. The sea wall around the large house can be seen jutting out into the beach. The assembly area is the dark field on the mid-left. The rockets fired during the pre-landings barrage have left a mosaic of white shell holes all over the picture.
(*Imperial War Museum, MH 24332*)

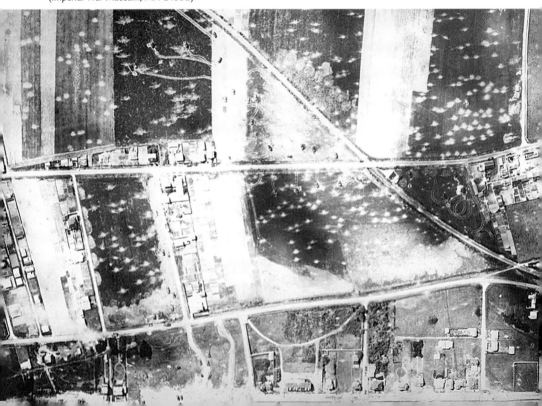

the unit later in the war. He was fed up with losing his ships and wanted a change after being torpedoed in the cruiser *Bonaventure* in the Mediterranean and sunk by midget Italian submarines while on board the battleship *Valiant*.

Ernie Taylor had served with 11th RM Battalion in Ceylon, guarding oil stocks in Colombo, and became trained in jungle warfare. Another 11th Battalion volunteer was Vince Horton and he was with that battalion during its abortive attack on Tobruk in 1942. Horton was captured during the operation by the Germans and handed over to the Italians, but was later released in Italy during an exchange scheme with some of their prisoners. It was his second time as a POW, for he had also been captured by the Germans in Crete while serving there with MNBDOI. A few months after Crete had fallen, he managed to escape from the island by submarine with a group of Australians. Being twice made a prisoner of war is an unusual event and this feat came to the attention of the security forces in England. When he arrived back in the UK, Horton was summoned to MI5 for interrogation. They suspected him of being a plant by the Nazis!

Tony Pratt arrived from a different background altogether as he explains:

I joined the Royal Naval Air Service (RNAS) when I was seventeen and trained to be a rear gunner. After a while I thought that this could be a bit dangerous and was looking for a way out. After one Sunday church parade we were all lined up and they asked for volunteers to join the Royal Marine Commandos. I thought that this would be even worse and so of course did not volunteer. The sergeant came along the ranks with his stick and began saying 'You, you and you,' and passed me by. I thought 'Thank goodness for that,' but the sergeant then turned and came back and said 'And you,' pointing to me. The next thing I knew was that I was in the Commandos.

CHAPTER THREE

Training the Commando

The bulk of the Commando arrived at Achnacarry as one group and were put through a shortened course because of the lack of time available. Normally a volunteer at the Commando Training Centre would attend a six-week course, but this was reduced to eighteen days for 48 RM Commando. Everyone possible had to attend the commando training, although a few officers and NCOs who were away on specialised instruction courses managed to avoid this rigorous initiation into the brotherhood of the green beret. Moulton brought his men north on 13 March and they reached the camp after a 25-hour train journey, tired and exhausted.

George Hawkins recalls his arrival in Scotland:

> We got to Spean Bridge station, got off the train the wrong side and then climbed up the platform to start the seven-mile march to camp in full pack. When we got there, the reception committee of officers, sergeants and corporals stood watching us as we marched in and looked at us as though we were dirt. We were told in no uncertain terms to smarten up.

The Commandant of the camp, Col Charles Vaughan, did however like to welcome the new trainees in style and often sent out a pipe band to lead them in for the last half-mile to camp. Sgt Joe Stringer remembers his arrival as being much less welcoming.

> We had lived on pack food during the long dreary trip up to Scotland and were very tired and fed up. We assembled outside the station expecting some sort of transport to the camp, but our reception committee consisted of a lone bagpiper and we were told to march the seven miles to the training base with our full kit. We marched into the camp with very low spirits and as soon as we passed through the gates a Bren gun opened up, firing on fixed lines. Someone shouted 'Get down you fools' and we all dropped into the dirt. We had arrived in Achnacarry.

Everyone who attended Achnacarry remembers the row of well-kept 'graves' just past the guard room, each with a terrible warning nailed to its stark white cross: 'This man failed to keep his rifle clean,' 'This man looked over cover and not round it,' 'This man stood on the sky line,' and so on. Capt Jimmy Dunning, one of the instructors at Achnacarry, recalls the impact these graves made on the troops as they arrived. 'This unexpected cemetery prompted a dramatic and salutary reaction. Initially it also posed the question, were they real, or were they phoney?' George Hawkins thought some of them were real, for live ammunition was used at Achnacarry and he had heard rumours that several men had got shot during their training.

Each new intake was welcomed by the camp's Commandant, Col Charles Vaughan. His opening address covered the type of training they would undertake and what was to be expected from them. In return he promised that they had the very best instructors in the land to guide them. 'They will not ask you to do anything that they cannot do themselves,' he told them. 'You will receive the best training there is, and, having passed the course, I will give you your green beret and you will then belong to the finest troops in this war – the Commandos.' But, he warned them, not all those present would pass. Some would inevitably fail. They would all be given one chance and one chance only, just as they would in action. If they could not keep up, they would be out. It was not, however, just a question of physical strength and toughness that would bring them through. They also needed a mental inner strength as well. 'It's all in the mind,' he told them.

'Life at the training camp was rough,' Sgt Joe Stringer later recalled. 'The instructors were mainly Lovat Scouts, very tough men. We were two to a bivouac and were permanently cold, wet and tired. We would turn out in the morning on parade smartly dressed, only to return at night covered in mud and soaked to the skin. It was still winter and we were wet all day, going over ground that was just a mudbath. Some of us had seen active service and the instructors rode us hard. We were not forced to complete the course, anyone could ask the CO to be released and return to his unit, but none ever did.' Dougie Gray was one of those who slept in a bell tent. He recalls that it always seemed to be raining: 'Everything was always wet through, the duck-boards on the floor of our tent were almost floating. We had to share a horse trough in a shed to wash and shave in. The water was cold. Nobody was ever idle; we had to double everywhere, but we survived. We were fit and had bags of confidence. We worked in pairs, "my pal and I," helping each other out.'

Even though he was one of the Commando's truck drivers, George Hawkins had to complete the same course as the marines in the fighting troops. 'Once in the camp there was no let up, we dumped our kit and were put straight at it. We did courses on boats and canoes; route marches; speed marches; unarmed combat; knife fighting; landings with machine guns firing on fixed lines over our heads, it was non-stop. If you put your head up too high, or were too slow in taking cover, you had it. It was always very cold and you would often think how bloody stupid you were for doing this, but we stuck with it all the way through. I was determined they would not beat me.' The same was true for others who were not part of the fighting core of the Commando. The Medical Officer, David 'Doc' Winser and the Chaplain, John Armstrong, both won their green berets in the mud of Achnacarry.

One of the Commando who trained at Achnacarry after the main party was Derek Turner. He joined the unit in Holland as a replacement and did the full six-week course.

We were divided into squads of around twenty men and we quickly became an integrated unit, realising that it was the best way to survive. Around forty of us arrived together on the course and the two squads were in competition from the first day. If we were to succeed, then all of the squad members had to finish the course together, so the strong helped the weak. We had a large lad with us called Barrell, which was also his approximate shape. He was full of pluck and determination to succeed. The rest of us helped him along, carried his rifle and equipment and got him through somehow. He was a brilliant stand-up comic and rewarded us each evening with his clowning.

Capt Jimmy Dunning was an instructor at Achnacarry and recalls the training regime the marines were put through.

Trainees were introduced to their first speed march on the first or second day of the course; they didn't have to wait long. It was a relatively gentle five miles around the 'Dark Mile' in under an hour, the aim being to get it down to 50 minutes. This first march was followed by

Commandos from HQ of 4 Special Services Brigade landing on Nan Red Beach on D-Day. Like those in 48 Commando, these marines have been transported over the Channel in LCI(S) craft. (*Imperial War Museum, B5218*)

other weekly jaunts progressing in stages through 7 miles in under 70 minutes followed by digging a defensive position, to 9 miles in under 90 minutes, followed by a firing practice. If 48 Commando had done the full course its men would have had to progress to 15 miles under 170 minutes, followed by assault course and firing!

These times were basic guidelines only. Troop leaders were expected to aim at faster times, according to the fitness of the trainees on arrival. On all speed marches, everyone was expected to help flagging comrades to keep up; support on either side was often sufficient, but carrying the tired man's rifle also helped. Capt Dunning continues, 'Trainee officers, as well as their men, were sometimes glad to take advantage of this "sharing the load" philosophy as they, too, often struggled to keep up on the speed marches.' Even a colonel was expected to help carry a rifle if need be, as Charles Vaughan used to tell senior officers on the courses. Indeed, Col Moulton makes a point of describing his experiences of load sharing in his memoirs.

Percy Bream, a signaller, also had a rough time in Scotland: 'Our training at Achnacarry came as a big shock, it was very tough training indeed. It was winter so it was cold and wet and you were soaked to the skin all of the time. You lived in bare huts with only a small tortoise stove for warmth, which you were not allowed to light until 4 o'clock, so that by the time the place got warmed up enough to dry your things it was morning. Our clothes were never really dry.' Dougie Gray remembers the pipers most of all: 'You heard the pipes all of the time you were training. The pipers always seemed to be practising. By the time we finished our course, we were actually getting used to them, even liking them.'

The commandos were taught self-sufficiency during the training. On overnight exercises they drew from the cookhouse individual rations of raw foods – a few carrots, potatoes and some meat, two slices of bread, some tea, sugar and tinned milk – and were then sent out to fend for themselves. They were not allowed Tommy cookers or blocks of solid fuel. They were told to go out into the countryside with what they had, light their own fires and get on with it, or go without. Harry Timmins remembers this ordeal: 'It rained continuously and we could not get a fire started so we ate our lamb chops raw.' Ron Pugh recalls being out on the mountains for days, always hungry. 'We were taught to live off of the land. I was a fisherman and always carried some gut and a few hooks with me. I was able to supplement our food with fresh trout caught in the Highland streams. After one meal of stew which we enjoyed very much, the sergeant threw down some rat skins and told us that they were the meat in the stew. I have to say it tasted good though. I think by then we would have eaten anything. All we wanted was to get back to camp and those awful metal spring beds to sleep.'

One of the obstacles that everyone hated was the 'death slide', as Derek Turner recalls.

A river ran through the camp and roared over the rocks at great speed. On one bank was a tree about forty feet high and a rope stretched from this tree to a large tree stump on the opposite bank. Men would have to climb the first tree, pass a 'toggle rope' – a length of rope six feet long with a wooden toggle at one end and a loop at the other – over the rope spanning the river and then push away from the tree, sliding down the rope to, hopefully, arrive on the other side of the river. I said hopefully, because when both toggle and rope were soaking wet it took a good push to keep the momentum going to reach the far bank. If you stopped anywhere before this, the only way out of the predicament was down into the tumbling river.

Ted Brooks actually enjoyed his time at Achnacarry so much he went there twice, as he later explained:

I had originally been attached to 46 RM Commando and was ordered down to Deal with six Lance Corporals to assist the formation of 48 RM Commando. We had already been trained as commandos at Achnacarry and were sent to help deal with the 7th Battalion and the MNBDO when they came back from Italy. After a week or two I was asked if I would like to stay with the Commando. They seemed such a nice bunch of lads that I decided I would. This meant I had to go back to Achnacarry with them to do the commando course again. It was a shortened course this time, just eighteen days I think, rather than the six weeks that I had previously done. I was fit in those days; the training did me the world of good. I was from the country and had always worked hard. My father had a smallholding and life was tough. I ran a lot and kept myself fit, not intentionally, it just seemed natural for us to do so. We all were very fit at that time. The worst thing at Achnacarry for me was going up the 'Tiger Crawl'. It meant going over a single rope across a river. You had to go down the rope to the centre, where it drops almost down to the water and then you had to haul yourself up to the other end. By the time you got there your arms were out of their sockets. I didn't mind it at all; I quite enjoyed all of the training. We were always wet and cold; you took your clothes off wet and you put them on wet, and so it went on, but it didn't seem to matter much to us.

Another who enjoyed the rigours of Achnacarry was Tony Pratt: 'There was not much to do in the evening and so a few of us used to go back out on the assault course. I enjoyed the "death slide" over the river; it was great fun. I remember one chap was terrified. I told him to shut his eyes and just jump off. He did, straight into the river and was swept downstream in the fast flowing water. He was saved by a net they had stretched across the river.'

The trainees spent some time in canvas boats out on the large loch close by. They had to paddle across about a half-mile of open water and make an assault against the rocky shore. 'The instructors enjoyed these games more than we did,' recalls Derek Turner. 'They were dispersed among the rocks with rifles and live ammunition and prided themselves on how close they could get a bullet without hitting someone. It was not a good feeling to be paddling madly when a bullet suddenly splintered the paddle you were using. To make things more realistic, explosive charges were buried on the landing area and were detonated as we ran for our lives up the beach.' The trainees did not take all this lying down, however, as Tony Pratt later explained: 'We got our own back on the Army Commando instructors by getting up at three in the morning and running down the outside of their Nissen huts, dragging a stick over the corrugated sides.'

What the commandant Col Charles Vaughan had earlier said, about survival at Achnacarry being all in the mind, was true. It took inner strength and will power to survive, as Dennis Smith remembers: 'I feel that when you really want something, you make every effort possible to do it. I was super fit by the end of the training. Many failed, these were men who wanted to do it, really wanted to get their green berets and tried as hard as they could to pass, but still failed. You felt very sorry for them for they tried but could not grind out that last ounce to achieve their goal.'

Those that did survive the rigours of the training were finally awarded their coveted green berets at the end of the course. Each man had learned a little about himself during the hectic and arduous period that he had endured. He felt that he had become part of an elite group and now belonged to a community of like-minded men. Geoff Linnell later summed it up in the unit's official history: 'The object was to test the physical and moral endurance of each man and make him feel that he had qualified in a hard school. It was noticeable that the 400 men who started the course as 400 individuals owing allegiance to their previous units, emerged 18 days later as 48 Royal Marine Commando with their own tradition founded on common endurance at Achnacarry.'

Percy Bream agrees with this: 'There is no doubt that when you got into a commando unit and got engrained into the routine, the comradeship and the universal sense of purpose, it kept you going and you willingly accepted all sorts of hardships. Once you had your green beret you felt that you were something special. Basically, I rather enjoyed Achnacarry. I was proud that I had done the course and survived.'

On 4 April the complete Commando arrived at Gravesend in Kent. This was to be its base until the time of the invasion. The marines were housed in civilian billets and this arrangement was much to their liking as Ted Brooks explains: 'When we were in digs, we were given a lodging allowance of six shillings and eight pence a day to pay the landlady for our keep.' This was a good sum in those days and the landladies did not always charge this full amount so there was often a little left over at the end of the week. The authorities could, however, be parsimonious with their money when the occasion arose, as Ted Brooks again explains: 'When we were living in tented accommodation, such as in the camps prior to D-Day, we received a Lodging Under Canvas Allowance (LUCA) of just six pence a day. It is interesting to note that the Army stopped this allowance for the night we were in transit across the Channel before D-Day because we were being accommodated on board ships and then restarted it again once we were in action in France.'

With just two months to go before the invasion, training continued at a gathering pace. The first ten days were spent on the firing ranges at Sheerness, with each man attempting to attain marksmanship qualities. Then the training became more specialised as the official history explains: 'The next step was the firing of individual battle practices on Cliffe Cooling Marsh Ranges; then Bren and rifle group, subsection and finally Troop field firing with fire support from the Vickers and 3-inch mortars of the Heavy Weapon Troop were practised. Practically all tactical training was done with ball ammunition, thanks to our enormous field firing-range area. The countryside favoured intensive training. The Cliffe Cooling Marshes were a large uninhabited area, five miles long by one mile deep.'

During this period the men became totally proficient with their weapons, as Dougie Gray recalls: 'We were firing on the naval ranges with Bren and rifle. We all got the sights of our rifles sorted out, giving the armourers a lot of work to do. Quite a few of the lads became marksmen. We had a Bisley instructor with us and that helped a lot.'

Training continued with battle-drill, field firing exercises, speed marches and assault courses. Each troop also spent two days in the bombed-out Limehouse district of London practising the art of street fighting. By this time all the troops had been picked and officered and each man became proficient in his own specialism whether it be in a demolition team, Bren gun group or as one of the Commando's snipers.

The Commando was organised along War Establishment lines, conforming to those Commandos already raised by the Army and Royal Marines. This consisted of the Commando Headquarters, Signal Section, Administrative Section, five fighting troops (A, B, X, Y and Z) – named after the big gun turrets on capital ships – and a Heavy Weapons Troop (S Troop). The nominal strength of a fighting troop was three officers and sixty-five other ranks. Each troop contained two sections, each further divided into two sub-sections. The Heavy Weapon Troop had two officers and forty other ranks, armed with two Vickers machine-guns and two 3-inch mortars. These weapons were doubled in number after the landings in June.

Once the training had produced an efficient and effective Commando, it was time to put the organisation to the test in a number of large-scale exercises which simulated an amphibious landing. Exercise 'Fabius' was the first and took place early in May. It was directed by British I Corps and was arranged to examine the formations and staffs of all the units that would be involved in Operation Overlord. In effect, it tested the loading, marshalling, transport and landing of an invasion force. The Commando was moved to Camp C3 at Botley in Hampshire and the men began practising the loading and unloading of landing craft in order to become familiar with the boats. They finally embarked at Warsash on 3 May. At 2200 hours the force sailed and spent the night in the Channel, landing in the area of Bracklesham Bay early the next morning.

The exercise did throw up one casualty, as Capt Geoff Linnell, commander of the Heavy Weapons Troop, painfully remembers:

The exercise was very difficult and I seemed to spend a great deal of time up to my neck in water and stayed out all night without any cover or blankets. I went down with what I thought was the flu, but had what turned out to be malaria. I knew that if I went sick I would never be allowed to rejoin 48 Commando and take part in the invasion, so the MO agreed to visit me twice a day in my civilian billet at Gravesend. Just before the invasion, the Commando moved to a sealed camp in Southampton. I was still too weak to go down by train so made the journey with the padre in the Colonel's staff car. Even on D-Day itself, I was still weak from the illness, but I was determined to be part of the invasion.

Further exercises followed; two for signallers and one, Exercise 'Tramp,' for the full Commando, in which the whole unit marched 40 miles in

Sgt Percy Bream, who ran the signals section at 48 Commando's HQ. Colonel Moulton called him the 'redoubtable Sergeant Bream'. (*Percy Bream*)

forty-eight hours, slept rough and 'fought' several incidents on the way. Endurance training and bivouacking in the open continued, hardening up the stamina of the marines. 'I don't think that the first few exercises were too brilliant,' recalls Dougie Gray, 'But then again you needed a few attempts to iron out the snags and to get things right. By the time we had practised over and over with the same people, the same troops and the same landing craft, we had improved a great deal.'

Towards the end of May, Lt Col Moulton felt that his Commando had become as ready as it ever would. He was satisfied that his unit could take its place with the other Commandos in 4th Special Service Brigade. Final preparations were made to stores, weapons and equipment, and 48 RM Commando readied itself for the off. The day of the invasion was drawing ever closer.

CHAPTER FOUR

To France

On 20 May, the Commando received the long-awaited orders which were to set in motion a move that would take it to the shores of Normandy. Its initial destination was Southampton, where it would enter one of the sealed marshalling camps to receive its final objectives and be ready for embarkation when the invasion was launched. During the next four days the Commando's transport was pre-loaded with stores, equipment and ammunition and sent ahead to Warsash at the head of the Hamble River overlooking Southampton Water. This transport would travel separately to France, being carried over the Channel in tank landing craft to arrive after the initial waves. The men set out for Southampton on the 25 May, each carrying with him the rifle and pack that he would take to France.

At 0800 hours, the marines of the Commando marched along the near-empty streets of Gravesend to the railway station. To the people of the town going about their business, they were just another party of troops on manoeuvre. For security reasons the move and its destination were secret. Harry Timmins was told that it was just another exercise, 'But the people of Gravesend watched us move away and they, like us, knew that this was no exercise. We understood that we would be coming back to Gravesend in a few days, this idea followed us for the next 17 months.'

The 150-mile journey across southern England took most of the day, for the Commando was not the only unit converging on Southampton. By late May the region around the town had become the main staging area for the invasion and thousands of British and Canadian troops were closing inexorably on the port and the great tented cities on its outskirts.

48 Commando arrived in the early evening at the tiny station of Swaythling in the northern suburbs of Southampton, just south of the airport and close by the Supermarine factory which had seen the birth of the Spitfire just a few years previously. Here the marines stretched their cramped legs and gathered themselves together in marching order ready to trek the two short miles up Burgess Road to the town's common, a large area of woods and parks, completely surrounded on all sides by residential estates. Through the heart of the common ran the main road from Southampton to London, still open to traffic and still served by buses and trams throughout the day. On either side of the road large tented camps had been built, surrounded by triple belts of wire and patrolled by armed American guards. The Commando had arrived in

Marshalling Area C and were about to become residents of Camp C19, one of four camps on the common given over to the Commandos of 1st and 4th Special Service Brigades.

Everything was ready for the men when they arrived in the transit area. The camps on the common had been built by the Americans ready for the post-invasion build-up of troops when Southampton would be given over to the US as their 14th Major Port. Over 2 million American soldiers would pass through the town on their way to the front before VE Day. As the camps were built by the Americans for eventual American use, they had very good facilities. On Southampton Common there was a cinema, large briefing marquees and a NAAFI. 'The food was also good,' recalls Vince Horton, 'but it was difficult to get used to hash being served on the same tin plate as the sweet.' Once the commandos had arrived and settled in, the camps were closed and sealed. No one below the rank of lieutenant colonel could now get out without permission from the Brigadier.

The next day, Brig 'Jumbo' Leicester, commander of 4th Special Services Brigade, called together all the officers of the brigade and briefed them on their role in the invasion. He outlined the objectives of Operation Overlord and described their part in the assault. He told of the massive scale of the landings and the support that would blast them ashore. With the use of scale models, maps and aerial photographs, Brig Leicester concentrated on the sectors to be assaulted by 41, 47 and 48 Commandos. All the real names of places were replaced by code words, enabling the operation to be briefed in detail without identifying the actual location of the landfall. These briefings were then rolled out in a programme which ensured that each man in each troop knew of his role and the task of his immediate group. The identity of the actual landings was still kept secret, but the more knowing among the men soon worked it out. Each man taking part in the Overlord invasion had been given a small booklet about France, together with some French francs. In the book was a map of France and it soon became clear that if you matched the maps of the coastline around the landing places with the map in the book, it could be seen that the destination was to be Normandy.

When the plan was briefed down to the men, they accepted it completely, with little thought that things might go wrong. It was a straightforward plan, well within their capabilities and they had great trust in the support that was promised. Sgt Joe Stringer remembers his detailed instructions. 'Our final briefing included an address by the CO of the Canadian North Shore Regiment whose men were to carry out the initial assault and clear the beach before we landed. He finished with the phrase: "Come Hell or high water, we will get you ashore." We had every confidence that they would.'

The objectives of 48 Commando were now made clear. The previous months of training for the 'event' were to be put into practice. Col Moulton's task was to hold the left flank of Canadian 3rd Infantry Division while its troops concentrated on their advance inland towards the city of Caen. The Commando was to land at the extreme eastern end of Juno

Nan Red Beach today, looking towards the German strongpoint at St-Aubin. The prominent house on the right was one of the landmarks for the landings. The large house surrounded by a sea wall that was in the middle of the landing area has long gone: it would have been positioned in the centre of the picture. The beach exit was located about twenty yards behind the photographer. (*Ken Ford*)

Beach, in the sector code-named Nan Red just to the west of St-Aubin-sur-Mer. It was to follow behind the men of the Canadian North Shore Regiment, coming ashore 35 minutes after their initial assault. The beach should be clear of German resistance by then, enabling the Commando to form up and swing to the left to advance on the seaside town of Langrune 2 miles away, clearing the coast as it went. Once the town was secure, it was to attack the German seafront strongpoint WN 26 from the rear. At the same time it was to send a party further eastwards to the hamlet of Petit Enfer to make contact with 41 RM Commando who were to land over Sword Beach with 3rd British Division, thus linking Juno and Sword. Once the landing beaches and the coastal sector between Juno and Sword were secure, and the battle had rolled on inland, 48 Commanodo's task would be over. In four to seven days, it would be withdrawn back to the UK to train for its next assignment.

As the whole of 48 Commando's objectives would be within just a mile or so of the beaches, it was to be given support as required from warships at sea.

A Forward Observer Bombardment Officer (FOB) from the Royal Artillery, Capt Jim Tyrer, joined the group with a small team of radio operators and signallers to act as liaison between the Commando and the ships at sea. Working with the group was one of 48's signallers, Dennis Smith. His job was to carry a large Aldis lamp on the landings so that if all the radios failed, Tyrer could still get through to the ships by signalling-lamp. Once he was ashore, Tyrer could call down the naval gunfire of warships of various sizes from destroyer to battleship wherever Col Moulton required it. Of course not all of these guns would be anchored offshore waiting for his call, and during the initial stages of the invasion there would be many demands on this support, but it was thought that as the main battle moved inland, more and more supporting gunfire would be available to the Commando. This was welcome news, for the lightly armed marines of 48 Commando would be taking with them just what they were able to carry themselves. It was comforting to know that they had some big guns backing them up.

One of Capt Tyrer's men was Sgt Ralph Dye and he remembers joining 48 Commando in Camp C19.

> We arrived at the concentration area near Southampton where we were briefed and shown pictures of the beach we were to land on, taken by low-flying aircraft. The briefing was very good, for when I arrived on Nan Red Beach, it was startling to find it was just like they had explained. I was then told that my Captain, Jim Tyrer, and the three telegraphist, would go in with the initial waves carrying a backpack set, while I would arrive thirty minutes later in the follow-up waves with the jeep and two long-range sets. This would mean that I left the camp at Southampton and went into a 'lock up' camp at Warsash with the rest of 48 RM Commando's transport. In that camp I met up with some of the transport section, they were big strapping chaps, fit and resplendent in their green berets. I was kind of awe-struck by these guys and proud to be part of them. I remember that I managed to slip out to a pub with two of the chaps, one was called Dick who sang a risqué song about a lady from Paris. He was killed on the landing. I met his mate just as I got ashore. He had tears in his eyes and said that Dick had got killed just as he was leaving the craft.

The Commando would make its journey across the Channel in Landing Craft Infantry (Small) – LCI(S) – from the 202nd Flotilla based at HMS *Tormentor* at Warsash. These large landing craft were 104 feet long and were capable of achieving 11 knots. They carried 96 fully laden troops below decks and 18 bicycles on the upper deck. The size of the craft meant that the marines could be transported all the way to Normandy and be landed directly on the beach, without having to tranship from larger troop-carrying vessels into smaller assault boats. That was about their one advantage, for the vessels were very uncomfortable to take passage in. They were very light and wallowed and rolled incessantly, even in a moderate sea. They were made of wood and incapable of providing shelter from any kind of fire. Troops on board were also exposed and vulnerable during disembarkation, for they had to negotiate their way in single file down steep ramps from the bows of the ship. Below decks the vessels were cramped and stuffy. The momentous sea journey to France was certainly going to be memorable for the commandos, but not in any way pleasurable.

The Commando had only been in camp for a few days when Sgt Colin Travers was called to see Col Moulton, as he later recalled.

The RSM we had at the time did not get on very well with the CO. He was a marine who had spent the most part of his career at sea on capital ships. He was a good man, but Colonel Moulton thought that he would not be suitable for the type of warfare that the Commando would be involved in, so he sent him back to Plymouth. The Colonel then said to me, that we could do without an RSM for a while and told me that I would stay with Z Troop for the landings, wherever they would be, and when we had arrived on the other side he would make me the RSM.

Sgt Percy Bream was kept busy while in the camp as were the other sergeants. 'We had plenty on our minds with briefings and keeping the men in good heart. We tried to keep the men occupied in one way or another, organising sports and such like. The general feeling was that we all wanted to get cracking and get on with it. We were fed up with all of the mucking around and training for so long. We were all glad when the bubble burst and we were off.' Dougie Gray remembers one of the sports events that was organised, a rugby match between the officers and the NCOs: 'It was played at a seriously fierce rate; it was war. There was no way that at that late stage that anyone was going to be turfed out of the unit, so everybody played it hard. There were some good players in the unit, I think one of the NCOs played for Bristol and one of the officers played for United Services. We all got on marvellously well together.'

Sgt Joe Stringer was not so happy; he had promised his fiancée Peggy that they would be married on 3 June. Immediately after arriving at the camp he had asked both the padre and Col Moulton if he could contact Peggy and explain. He was met with a blanket refusal; the camp had been sealed and no communication with the outside world was allowed.

Ted Brooks remembers that his briefing included a sobering message. 'We were given strict instructions not to stop at any time to help anyone who was wounded. We were told that other people would help them, our mission was to press on and complete the job we had to do.'

May passed into June and the big day arrived, or so they thought. D-Day was set to be 5 June and on the 4th everything was made ready. The commandos prepared themselves to be taken to the boats. Just outside the wire endless streams of transport lumbered slowly past on their way to the docks. The weather was fine and sunny, but bad news was on the way in the shape of a depression from the west, which would sweep along the Channel just at the moment the great invasion was planned to hit the beaches. The operation was postponed for one day.

'The day before we left camp several large boxes were placed among us which when opened revealed thousands of packets of cigarettes,' remembers Harry Timmins. 'The padre told us to help ourselves, so we filled any odd pockets with them and tucked them among our grenades and phosphorous bombs. We also had a service that day and the padre in his sermon told us to ignore the bodies that would be dropping around us when we hit the beach.

They meant nothing any longer as their souls had already gone to heaven. This cheered us up no end!'

Sgt Bill Hudson was with A Troop and remembers the night of 4 June:

> At 9.30 p.m. I was called out of my tent by the sergeant of the guard to speak to the adjutant, Captain Dan Flunder. He proceeded to give me a blast for allowing the men to have a singsong before turning in. Looking back, I suppose I deserved it because we had been told in the afternoon to be quiet that night as we would be moving off the next day. Little did I know then that in just thirty-six hours a lot of those men would never sing again. I thought about this for some time and resented it. Not long afterwards, Dan Flunder became our troop commander and proved to be a first-class leader who always put his men first. He led us right through to the end of the war.

Then, on 5 June, the order to go was issued. Transport arrived and the commandos left the camp, passing through the blitzed streets of Southampton, over the Itchen Bridge and out towards the eastern suburbs. On every road other convoys criss-crossed the town, bringing Canadian troops and armoured vehicles to the docks and to the numerous landing yards that had been built along the Itchen and Test rivers. By late morning 48 Commando had arrived at the estuary of the Hamble River and lined up along the quay at Warsash. Double- and treble-banked along the river were the landing craft of Lt Cdr Timmerman's flotilla, ready to take them over the Channel. In the early afternoon the order was given to embark on to the boats and 48 RM Commando went aboard.

There were six LCI(S)s to transport the Commando, one for each fighting troop and one for HQ Troop. The Heavy Weapons Troop (S Troop) was divided among the six craft.

'There were two troop decks on each craft, like large open cabins, one forward and one aft,' remembers Lt John Square. 'Lieutenant Rigby's half troop was in the stern, while mine was in the front. We stood around having cigarettes waiting for the off and I remember seeing three beautiful Wrens pass close by us watching our departure.' Below decks the marines were left to fend for themselves. The low headroom and wooden benches were not made for comfort as Sergeant Percy Bream remembers: 'The boats were a bit cramped with just an open hold below deck. We had to bed down where we could, each man trying to find some place of his own.' Below decks the air was foul, diesel fumes mixed with fresh paint. It was not long before many men were stretched out on the wooden benches, clasping a soggy bag and turning various shades of green. Hyoscine tablets had been issued to everyone to prevent seasickness, but they did little to quell the men's stomachs. At around 1500 hours each craft cast off and nosed its way out into Southampton Water. Ted Brooks recalls the departure: 'For my part I played cards until they were blown away then retired below deck, wedged myself on top of a rolled hammock along the side of the craft and stayed there for the rest of the voyage.'

The sight that greeted those on deck was quite memorable. Long rows of ships and craft stretched all the way down to the Solent and were backed up right to the docks at Southampton itself. In single file the landing craft turned to port and pushed down the waterway to the assembly area off the Isle of Wight. Sgt Joe Stringer was on deck watching as the LCIs made for their 'slot' in the great armada that was assembling: 'We passed down lines of ships all ready for the voyage to France and the CO told us all to get on deck with our green berets on and let them see us for encouragement.' George Hawkins clearly remembers one of the naval vessels at anchor: 'As we passed one of the ships off the Isle of Wight its band was playing "A Life on the Ocean Wave", it was HMS *Hawkins*! I felt that this was a good omen and a great send-off for me.'

The Commando's transport which was at Warsash had moved around to Lee-on-the-Solent to embark on tank landing craft for the journey across to Normandy. With the transport was Ralph Dye, the artillery-man from Capt Tyrer's group. He had a lonely crossing, remote from everyone he knew, as he later explained.

> I embarked in my jeep on to a Landing Craft Tank (LCT) at Lee-on-the-Solent on 4 June. I was entirely on my own; I did not know anybody on the ship. Next to my jeep was a bulldozer and this probably saved my life because it gave me some protection from machine gun fire during the run in to the beach. The rest of the LCT was full of vehicles and equipment belonging to the Canadian North Shore Regiment. Every truck seemed to be full of mortar bombs and ammunition. The LCT went up to Southampton water and joined with a great throng of other ships.

The small craft nosed out into the Channel into the full force of the deteriorating weather. It was not a rough sea particularly, but there was a long swell and the small wooden ships began to pitch and roll. Everyone on board spent a very uncomfortable night. Lt John Square recalls this discomfort. 'We had to sit on wooden slatted benches with no space to lie down. There was just one lavatory between all of us which was soon blocked up. The night was rough and everyone seemed to be sick. Fortunately, I was not. Once one man was sick, the heaving bodies and the acrid smell set off a chain reaction. Soon numbers of men were queuing for the heads or leaning over the boat's rails vomiting into the sea.'

The night passed quietly for the men below decks. Some slept fitfully, some played cards – Dougie Gray won a small fortune in French money, but gave it all back – while others stared aimlessly around the dimly lit craft lost in their own thoughts, unable to sleep. 'We were given some cans of sardines,' recalls Sgt Tom Clark of A Troop, 'One man near me made a hash of opening his can and lost the key. I demonstrated my manliness by using my teeth to open his can.' Few men spoke; each had withdrawn into his own shell trying to put aside the realisation of what tomorrow might bring. To make matters even more dreary, there was a 'no smoking' order in place, which did not help the nerves of those gasping for one last 'fag.' Officially, no one was allowed 'top sides' until general orders, but a few men who were far from sleeping went out on deck during the night and watched the long lines of ships ploughing inexorably towards Normandy.

Dawn comes very early in June. As the first rays of a still-hidden sun began to light up the blustery cloud-strewn sky, those aboard the craft started to stir. On his boat, Lt John Square was summoned up on deck with the other officers of Z Troop:

> The Commando's second-in-command, Maj Sanders, called us up on deck and gave us our real maps, with the correct place names. We were all feeling a bit queasy and it was so windy, so rough and so wet that nobody seemed to be particularly interested in them or what we were supposed to do with them. It amuses me now to think of it. The situation was in stark contrast to what you see in most war films where everyone is fired up to get going and to charge into combat with the enemy. We were feeling slightly sick, detached from our surroundings and just wanted to get it over with.

On A Troop's craft, Sgt Bill Hudson also had his final briefing. 'We were given information about our destination in France, what our job would be and how we would do it. The Canadians would be landing before us with amphibious tanks and the hope was that we would be able to walk ashore with no casualties. Once this information was passed on to the men they seemed to be more relaxed about the situation and started to think that it was more important to try to overcome their seasickness and let events take care of themselves.'

As the day dawned, the line of landing craft continued ploughing its way through the choppy sea, pressing closer and closer to France. All around the light wooden boats, other warships and transports filled the water to the horizon. Much further ahead of the LCIs, already at anchor on their lowering points, were the great infantry landing ships. Each of these pre-war liners was disembarking its assault battalions into smaller landing craft from which they would make the initial landings. Close by them were tank landing craft (LCT) filled with duplex-drive Sherman tanks capable of swimming the last few hundred yards to shore and rising up out of the sea with the initial waves of troops. Supporting these vessels were other landing craft with guns and rockets, ready to support the attacking infantry on their run in to the shore. Keeping the Luftwaffe at bay, should any of Göring's aircraft brave the Allied fighter screen and approach the great armada, were Landing Craft Flak, simply bristling with anti-aircraft guns. Very soon it was time to launch the attack and the bombardment of the enemy coastline began. Great warships opened fire with calibres of guns from 4 to 15 inches, each of them programmed to concentrate on one particular enemy position. Overhead Allied aircraft came in low and fast to strafe and bomb the areas along the beaches. To all of the men of the Commando below decks in their cramped landing craft the volume of noise began to rise louder and louder the closer they came to the shore.

Capt Michael Reynolds, commander of A Troop, left the lower deck and joined a few sailors who were on lookout duties topside: 'I clambered my way to the upper deck and looked around. It was an outstanding sight: warships, vessels, various landing craft and aircraft everywhere, each with their own assigned task and yet it looked chaotic. I knew then beyond doubt that we were all indeed part of an irresistible force.'

Lt John Square was beginning to feel the enormity of the situation that was unfolding, as he later recalled.

After speaking with Major Sanders I then went down below and had another short doze. Then the engines began to slow and I knew that the time had come for me to make a move. I climbed up the ladder and achieved a privileged position on deck near the bows and looked out. There before me was the coast of France. It was a very murky day, overcast and gloomy. I could see gun flashes and smoke along the shore line, but don't remember looking around at the vast array of ships that were in the area. I seemed to enjoy some sort of 'tunnel vision,' just concentrating on the task in hand and what was in front of me, putting everything else out of my mind. I think that this attitude was one of the mechanisms I used to cope with events. In times of action, I just looked ahead and tried to blot out the enormity of events going on around me. In this way I was able to focus on my job rather than worrying about what might be happening to others nearby.

It was now time for the last of the preparations before the final run into shore. Capt Michael Reynolds went back down to ready his men.

I ran through my mind again anything that I had forgotten to do. We had had prayers, I had spoken to the rest of the troop and had reminded them how lucky we all were to have a free trip to France. To the seasick ones, I promised them that they would be all right when we reached terra firma! My radio was netted to my opposite number in the right-hand sector. Everything seemed secure enough, so I moved up towards the bows, waved goodbye to the bridge and waited till we beached.

On his craft Sgt Colin Travers was beginning to get his men ready. 'In the early morning we were told to stand to and make sure that all of our gear was fastened. Our lifebelts were like motor tyres and had to be fastened underneath all our equipment. I went round to check that the men had theirs fastened properly. A lot of men did not have their lifebelts right up under their arms, for they felt awkward and were an encumbrance to easy movement.' The atmosphere below decks was fetid and stale. Few men took advantage of the tea. Biscuits were offered and refused for the stomachs of most of the men were still turning over, a product of seasickness and apprehension. Dennis Smith was just satisfied that it would soon be over, he had had enough of the crossing: 'I was very glad that we would shortly be off, despite the thought of what we would have to face when we landed.' Tony Pratt thought everything looked very quiet: 'On the run in we came out on deck and I could just see a few puffs of smoke and turned to my mate and said, "It's going to be a quiet landing."'

On board the HQ craft, Col Moulton had woken up cold and seasick. He rose on deck to face the grey morning with a cup of tea and some hard ship's biscuit. He found Lt Timmerman on his bridge bright and well, even though he had been up all night bringing his flotilla over the Channel. He reported to Moulton that he was a little worried about the state of the sea for the landings, considering it to be a little rougher than he would have liked it to have been to take his unwieldy craft ashore. The passage had been without incident and his ships were slightly ahead of their allotted timings so Timmermans took the six craft in line ahead in a wide circle to use up time.

In the crowded seas he had to be careful how he completed this manoeuvre. He did it by making a wide circuit around HMS *Hilary*, the headquarters ship for the landings on Juno. On board were the commander of Canadian 3rd Division, Maj Gen Keller, British I Corps Commander Lt Gen Crocker and the Naval Force Commander Force J, Cdre Oliver.

Timmermans regained his position and continued towards the shore. The coastline was now beginning to take shape and trees and individual buildings could be made out through the smoke that marked the line of the beach. Moulton scanned the haze through his binoculars and picked out the shapes of the two distinctive buildings that marked the Commando's landing place on Nan Red Beach. Timmermans had lined up his ships right on target. The Colonel studied the shoreline. There still seemed to be a good deal of firing going on and one or two stranded landing craft littered the beach. He could also see a dark line running along the base of the sea wall and low cliffs which could be men taking shelter. His first thoughts were that the Canadians had been held up, but he was too far out to be certain.

Just then the craft approached the beach control vessel which was responsible for that stretch of the coastline. On board the infantry landing craft, a converted LCI(L), was Lt Cdr Arbuthnot, one of the Deputy Senior Naval Officers Assault Group (D/SOAG) whose task it was to control the landing ships, craft and barges in his allotted area during the assault. Lt Timmermans slowed his craft until it passed slowly alongside the control vessel and hailed her. Two lone seamen were on deck and they viewed Timmermans's boat with a certain detachment, but no one on board responded to the call. The naval commander and Col Moulton watched as the control vessel slipped slowly past, rolling gently in the stiff swell. The two men looked at each other. 'There can't be much wrong, if they are taking it as easy as that,' commented Timmermans. Moulton agreed: 'May as well beach, Timmy,' said the Colonel.

Timmermans responded with a flurry of orders and the six grey craft of the 202nd Flotilla began to pick up speed, instantly changing formation from in-line ahead, into in-line abreast. The final run to touchdown on Nan Red had begun. On board A Troop's craft, Sgt Bill Hudson noticed this increase in speed. 'Suddenly, we changed course heading for the beach. It was at this time that we had our first casualty when Lance Corporal Larkin, who was standing just ahead of me, was hit in the head by a stray bullet, killing him instantly. He was a very old comrade from 7th Battalion and to be killed in this way a mile out to sea had a bitter irony.'

The craft were close enough now to attract the attention of the enemy defenders and they started to come under more and more sporadic fire. Capt Geoff Linnell of S Troop recalls that his craft was shot at the whole length of the run in: 'Most of the heavy stuff passed straight through our wooden sides. When we arrived close to Nan Red we could see that the beach was still under heavy enemy fire and the Canadian North Shore Regiment who had landed before us had not managed to clear the area of Germans.'

This picture gives a good illustration of the difficulties encountered when trying to disembark from an LCI(S). It shows men from 4 Special Service Brigade HQ arriving on Nan Red Beach during the morning of D-Day, well after 48 RM Commando had left the beach and moved on Langrune. (*Imperial War Museum, B5219*)

Sgt Joe Stringer of B Troop had recognised that there was trouble ahead. 'As we came in we could see that the Canadians were in difficulties and the beach was not completely taken. We could see a lot of fire on the shoreline, most of it coming from the left, whipping down the length of the beach. The pre-landing bombing looked as though it had not been successful for there were still many active German pillboxes and other defences. The North Shore Regiment had obviously not cleared the beach. There were lots of casualties lying about.'

Ted Brooks's voyage up until then had been quite uneventful, as he later remembered.

I think that lying on my back prevented seasickness and it wasn't until we stood by to beach that I became very queasy, especially when many around me were suffering. I was, however, very pleased to be getting off the craft. We were all confident in our task; we were well trained and felt that we were going to be OK. This was my first time in action; I was apprehensive, but not afraid. It was obviously very noisy during the approach, but one thing that as always stuck in my mind was the silence on the landing craft just as we went in. I presume each man had his own thoughts on the forthcoming action. This silence was broken only when the craft received a small burst of machine gun fire while still some few hundred yards from the shore and one man shouted with a most indignant tone in his voice, 'Who the fucking hell's firing.' I thought that was so funny at the time and still do today.

CHAPTER FIVE

Nan Red Beach

The two assault companies of the Canadian North Shore (New Brunswick) Regiment landed on Sector 7 of Nan Red Beach at 0805 hours. A Company touched down on the right and swung to the west to clear the easternmost buildings of Bernières and link up with the Queen's Own Rifles of Canada who were landing on the adjacent beach of Nan White. B Company of the North Shores was on the left-hand flank of the Canadian landings and swept ashore alongside A Company with the objective of turning left and attacking the German strongpoint on the seafront of St-Aubin-sur-Mer.

B Company landed on an open stretch of the beach which backed on to sandy cliffs and undulating grassy dunes. In the middle of its planned landfall was a high sea wall that ran around a large house which was built right on the shoreline. To the rear was a lateral road which ran parallel to the sea, linking Bernières with St-Aubin. The company's objective, Strongpoint WN27, lay 400 yards to the east.

The Germans held their fire until the Canadian landing craft were close in and then opened up with a variety of light weapons and mortars. When the troops of B Company struck the shore they came out of the boat fighting, only to be met with a hail of fire from the unseen enemy. The tide was only half in and 100 yards of open sand had to be crossed before any shelter could be had. Many of the men ran directly to the only cover available, the high sea wall. Here they were safe from direct fire, but were still susceptible to crossfire from houses further along the shore. Casualties began to mount alarmingly. Number 4 Platoon alone lost seventeen men dead and wounded from this sniping and mortaring. Here they waited, gathering their thoughts while the next move was organised.

The main volume of fire hazarding the beach was from the enemy in WN 27 strongpoint. As soon as they could, the officers of B Company got the men moving off of the beach, through a minefield and along the lateral road towards St-Aubin, but until the German resistance post could be eliminated, Nan Red Beach remained overwhelmed by enemy fire. A few DD tanks landed in support. Some were knocked out in the surf, while others tried to pick their way inland through the minefields. Thirty minutes after the assault waves had touched down, the beach was still as deadly as it had ever been and the next wave was rapidly approaching to make its landfall.

The six landing craft carrying 48 RM Commando into Nan Red sector of Juno Beach came in at full speed in line abreast. On the bridge of the

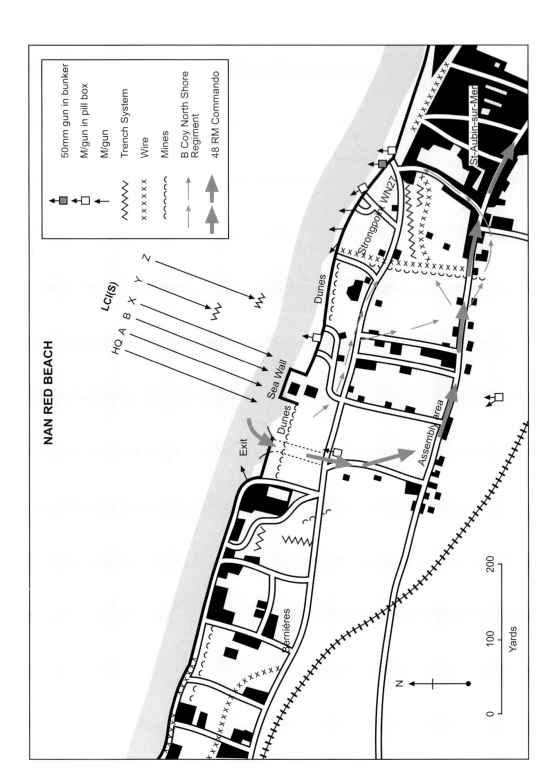

NAN RED BEACH

LCI(S)

HQ A B X Y Z

Exit

Sea Wall

Dunes

Dunes

Bernières

Strongpoint WN27

Dunes

Assembly Area

St-Aubin-sur-Mer

50mm gun in bunker

M/gun in pill box

M/gun

Trench System

Wire

Mines

B Coy North Shore Regiment

48 RM Commando

N

0   100   200

Yards

LCI(S) on the extreme right flank, Lt Timmermans and Col Moulton tried to pick out the signs laid by the beach parties, but all seemed to be smoke and confusion; the beach was a mass of troops, equipment and chaos. From the bridge the two men were able to locate what could be a beach exit to the right, but could not see the large canvas signs which would identify their landing place on Nan Red.

The craft pressed on, Timmermans aiming to bring his flotilla ashore beneath the low sea wall slightly to the right of the tall three-storey house that was so prominent in the briefing photographs. Enemy fire began to increase in intensity the closer the craft approached the beach. Harry Timmins recalls witnessing this German bombardment from on board A Troop's craft.

> As we got nearer the beach the noise was more than you could possibly imagine. There were explosions all around us in the sea and the shells and mortars were kicking up sand all over the beach. A couple of buildings were on fire and, to add to the tumult, the Oerlikons guns on our boat also joined in the barrage and deafened us. As we were getting closer, I was looking at the boat alongside us when a shell hit it, falling among the lads waiting to get off. I saw one fellow completely cut in half, his waist and legs went one way into the sea and the top half followed an instant later.

After some confusion, Moulton got his mortar men in the bows of each craft to begin firing 2-inch smoke bombs on to the beach to help try to shield the landings from this fire.

Beach defences now clearly stood out in the smoke and haze, littering the shore with their angled and pointed barbs. But for all those obstacles that were visible, many more lay hidden just below the surface of the rolling surf, covered by the incoming tide. This should not have been so, for the timings of the landing should have meant that the tide would have been low enough to expose the obstacles, but the high winds and rough seas had driven the tide in much higher than expected, covering the jagged defences and reducing the width of the beach to just a narrow strip. The craft now began to ease back, slowing down their mad dash for the shore, their crews watching for danger in their paths. To add to their troubles, the heavy swell and vicious tidal stream which swept along the shore now made control of the craft very difficult at low speeds.

With so many uncleared obstacles still untouched on Nan Red, it was inevitable that a few craft would strike at least some of them. The flotilla leader's vessel was one of the first to run foul of the beach defences, when its sides snared a jagged steel tetrahedron and slowed to a halt. For a moment the craft was hung up on the metal spikes before an incoming wave caught the stern of the vessel and swung it broadside towards the shore, rolling uncontrollably. On the extreme left of the group, the ships carrying Y and Z Troops fared even worse. They both ploughed headlong into the obstacles and had jagged gashes torn into their wooden hulls, both coming to a

Opposite: 48 RM Commando's Landing on Nan Red Beach

shuddering and untimely halt in deep water close to the guns of German strongpoint WN27 at St-Aubin-sur-Mer.

The craft carrying Z Troop was pinned at the stern just below the waterline on a hedgehog obstruction that had been made up from welded sections of railway line designed to rip the bottom out of any landing craft that was unfortunate enough to strike it. The sudden halting of the small ship was the signal for the two seamen up front to launch the landing ramps ready for the commandos to disembark. The solid wooden walkways were slowly pushed out and their ends crashed down into the heaving sea, even though the boat was still more than fifty yards from the beach.

Capt John Square was on board that craft:

> I remember telling the men that we were approaching the beach and for them to stand by with their kit ready. Very soon the craft hit an underwater obstacle and came to a halt. We had been snared by one of the beach defences and we began taking in water. The ramps went down and we were just getting ready to storm ashore when Major Sanders, the Commando's second-in-command, told us to stop. The boat was sinking by the stern and it was important to get Lieutenant Rigby's section out of the rear of the craft, so Sanders ordered them to disembark first.

The LCI(S) had halted about fifty yards from the shore in fairly deep water. Capt Lennard, commander of Z Troop, Lt Rigby, a half-section commander and Sgt Colin Travers were all well forward ready to disembark, as were some marines from Rigby's section who had been ordered forward. Although the boat was lodged well out from the shore, it was still close enough for a landing to be made, or so their commander thought. It would be a wet landing, and there would be a long struggle to get up to the beach, but Capt Lennard and his troop had arrived in Normandy and they were intent on battle. With a great sweep of his arm, he beckoned his men to follow him as he climbed on to the wildly bucking ramp and began his precarious descent down the near-vertical walkway into the sea. Close behind him came Lt Rigby. Troop Sgt Maj Colin Travers later recalled the scene.

> Captain Lennard was eager to get us off of the ship and signalled us all forward to the ramps. He was first down the ramp, followed by Lieutenant Rigby and then me. I struggled down the ramp and sank immediately into very deep water. The sixty pounds of equipment on my back dragged me right under until I touched bottom. Fortunately, I had my life belt on the right way right up under my armpits and inflated, so I immediately shot back up to the surface. I think I may have been knocked unconscious for a short while by the underwater explosions that we going on all around me, for I then recall being on my back in the water. The weight of my pack had turned me over and I was looking up at the sky. I could see nothing of what was going on around me, nor any sign of Captain Lennard or Lieutenant Rigby. I started to kick for the shore and tried to paddle my way on to the beach, but it turned out that I was actually moving parallel to the shore, being swept eastwards by a swift current.

The two officers in the water, weighed down by their heavy packs, immediately got into trouble. The strong undertow that was sweeping Sgt Travers away was dragging them under. Both drowned as they struggled to get to the shore. Other marines now took to the water. Several suffered the same fate as Lennard and Rigby and perished, but some managed to disengage themselves from their equipment and make for the shore. One of these was Ernie Taylor: 'I lost my balance the moment I left the boat and was thrown into the water. My clothes were heavy and wet and dragged me down, but I made it to the beach.' Lt John Square was at the front of the craft waiting until his section could get ashore and saw the horror unfolding in front of him.

> I was right up in the bows and could see what was happening. All those who had gone over the side were in trouble. One of the men was struggling in the water just below me, shouting for help. There was nothing I could do; I couldn't reach down to him. If we had had a rope to hand we might at least have made an attempt to save him, but no sooner had I spotted him and given him the thumbs up in encouragement, than he was gone. The craft was swinging violently as each incoming wave caught it broadsides on; it was clear that the disembarkation was turning into a disaster. Major Sanders also recognised the plight of those already in the water and immediately stopped any more people going down the ramps.

Below decks, Lt Mike Aldworth and his machine-gun section from the Heavy Weapons Troop were waiting for their moment to disembark. Aldworth went up on deck to see what was happening and noticed men coming from the stern running along the deck. He popped back down below and told his men to hang on as it was not their turn yet. 'Well when will it be our bloody turn then,' someone shouted from the back, 'The ruddy hold's filling up with water.' It was clear that the craft was sinking fast so everyone was sent up on top. There Aldworth was confronted with a sea covered in boats, some of which seemed to be coming to the aid of the stricken landing craft. 'It was rather like hailing a taxi in Bond Street,' Aldworth later recalled.

Fire continued to rake the boat and casualties began to mount. One of them was Cpl Bert Skinner.

> I was struck in the right hand and knee by fragments of bullets that had hit the armour plate round the port Oerlikon anti-aircraft gun situated just abaft the bridge. There was a gun in a pillbox ashore firing at the craft and it killed and wounded many of our men. At this point I decided to man the Oerlikon and I fired best part of a drum of ammunition at our tormentors ashore before I was ordered to cease fire by the Captain who was worried about the safety of his ship. I was then knocked out by an incoming shell which blew me over backwards and I hit the back of my head on the cupola of the gun.

To the right of Z Troop's craft was the one carrying Y Troop. Donald Nicholson was on board. 'Our LCIs approached the beach at speed and at first all seemed well. Enemy activity was only moderate with an absence of any significant fire directed at our incoming craft. As we prepared ourselves for what we expected would shortly be a landing on French soil, our craft struck a submerged obstacle about 150 yds from shore and began to sink.'

The young naval lieutenant in command of the boat now decided that the craft was near enough to shore for the commandos to strike out for the beach and ordered the two narrow ramps at the bow to be launched. Nicholson describes what happened next:

The first of Y Troop started to descend only to find that the water was so deep that they were compelled to swim. Most of these men, heavily encumbered with their equipment, were swept away and drowned. The depth of water and the heavy swell then caused the inshore ends of the ramps to float and the tidal stream swept them backwards towards the stern of the vessel thus making them useless anyway. Although badly holed, the depth of water was insufficient for the vessel to go completely under and the bow was securely anchored on the beach obstacle.

Y Troop's craft was stuck in a very exposed position, harpooned and immobilised on a section of 'Rommel's Asparagus', as the obstacles were wryly named by the troops. The obstacle had achieved its design intentions perfectly, snaring an incoming craft while the troops manning the coast defences raked it with fire. Machine-gun and mortar fire now tore along the length of the vessel. On board the craft, Donald Nicholson and his comrades suffered in consequence, as he later recalled:

By now, all the men had climbed the vertical steel ladders from the troop deck and were out in the open, where they became sitting targets for enemy snipers. The young naval lieutenant supervising the ramps suddenly collapsed, clutching at the rails on the starboard side. I just managed to prevent him from falling through the rails and into the water, and dragged him back to some kind of housing just forward of the bridge. In an almost inaudible whisper he said, 'Morphia.' I called out to the RAMC orderly Lance Corporal Wilkinson who immediately came forward, knelt beside the lieutenant and started to look through his medical haversack. As he did so he silently slumped forward and I realised he was dead. He had obviously been shot by a sniper. The crack of bullets passing through the air was almost continuous. I then rummaged through the haversack and found a small tube of morphia, but was unable to determine how to uncap the short needle. I tried unsuccessfully unscrewing what appeared to be a needle cover. I then tried to break off the tip to allow morphia to flow, but was again unsuccessful. In my frustration and dismay I began to wonder why something as elementary and important as this was not part of our training. I gave up in disgust and had no option but to abandon the lieutenant to his fate.

One man who was determined to get ashore was Y Troop's Commander, Maj de Stacpoole. Although wounded in the leg, he jumped into the sea and proceeded to swim for the beach. Fortunately, he made it to dry land, exhausted and shocked, with blood streaming from his wound. One of his officers, Lt Yates, was not so lucky. He tried to swim for shore with a line and was swept away to his death.

On B Troop's craft, Dougie Gray was up in the bows waiting to help push the ramps out when the boat touched the shore. Alongside him his friend Marine Cusack was hit by a burst of machine-gun fire and fell back through the open hatch into the well below. Further over to the right, the LCI(S) carrying A Troop touched down without any mishap and its commandos began to disembark. Harry Timmins remembers a sudden big roll of the craft, a jerk and a scrape and then someone shouting 'Everyone ashore'. Capt Michael Reynolds was at the head of his troop as his men moved forwards to negotiate the steep ramps. He later recalled his ignominious landing.

When we grounded I shouted some sort of exclamation to the rest of the troop, plunged down the ladder and disappeared from view into the sea. Weighed down by my radio set, I had become completely submerged in deep water. I felt the craft go full ahead again and managed to grab hold of a piece of rope. I remember thinking that as I was born with a caul, I couldn't possibly drown and that I should have to get rid of the wireless set to survive. The rope was attached to the boat and I was dragged ashore. Eventually, my feet touched the bottom as the craft surged forward in the surf. Waterlogged and gasping for breath I emerged from the sea to join my Troop.

Harry Timmins was also on board this craft and remembers the load he was carrying. 'We were in full marching order when we landed which, of course, included our large pack, but we each also had to carry a heavy 3-inch mortar bomb. The idea was to release this large pack immediately we got to the assembly area and give our bomb over to the mortar men when we arrived into a position where they needed them. We had no transport with us when we landed; everything had to be carried by hand. It was a hell of a load.' Sgt Tom Clark remembers coming down the ramps and witnessing a 'complete shambles'. 'We hit the beach and then flopped down into the sand behind a line of wounded and dying men.'

Another marine from A Troop was Sgt Bill Hudson. His landing was wet, as he later explained:

The sea was very rough and caused the bows of our craft to swing about from side to side. Several of the crew and the first few marines down were hanging on to the ramp in an effort

Nan Red Beach looking eastwards towards the St-Aubin strongpoint, late in the morning on D-Day at high tide, showing the sea wall behind which so many men took cover. The commandos have moved inland and left the dead and wounded behind. (*Imperial War Museum, B5225*)

to hold it on the beach. I started to run down the best I could, but halfway down the heavy pack I was carrying swung me over the side and I was tipped head first into the water. As I hit the sea the mortar bomb I was carrying on top of my pack hit me on the back of the head causing me to take a deep breath and I swallowed what seemed like a gallon of water. I struggled to the beach, crawling the last few yards away from the waves then collapsed and was violently sick. A few minutes later I had recovered and looked around to find myself in a living nightmare. A few yards away from me was a Canadian soldier lying on his side grinning at me, so I got to my feet and walked towards him. His legs seemed to be covered in blood and I suddenly realised he was dead. I had a splitting headache. The noise from the bullets, mortar bombs and tanks moving about was deafening. I could see bodies lying around all over the place. Some were wounded, but most were dead.

Dougie Edwards of A Troop never made it to shore; he was hit just after the craft beached and the ramps were dropped.

I had always supposed that I had been hit by sniper fire we were experiencing during the run-in, but I suppose it was more likely that it was shrapnel from shell-fire. I was hit so severely at the top of my right leg that the main muscle was practically severed. My recollection was of falling down and not knowing just why. I remember hearing a matelot close by shouting, 'There's a lad here with his leg off.' The next thing that I recall was being transferred from the landing craft to a large support ship lying offshore. I was strapped to a canvas and bamboo stretcher and hauled by jackstay up the side of the ship. Because of the rough sea that was running, the crew of the landing craft first transferred the body of Lance Corporal Joe Larken, killed during the run in, just to ensure that the transfer would be safe.

Marine Jock Mathieson was one of the Commando's dispatch riders and he also made a dramatic exit from his craft:

I landed with HQ Troop with a small motorbike, the type that was issued to paratroops. I carried it above my head coming down the ramp, determined that it would not get wet. I hadn't gone more than a few steps down the near-vertical walkway when the bike took a hit from a German machine gun. Petrol began running down my face and on to my clothes. For a moment I thought I had been hit and it was blood. Immediately after this the ramp gave way and the bike and I were both flung into the water. It was the last I saw of it.

On board B Troop's craft the run in had been relatively free from enemy attention, with just an occasional burst of machine-gun fire raking its sides. Lt Anthony Rubinstein, one of the half-troop commanders, watched as the landing craft on either side of his were either hit by enemy fire or hung up on obstacles, while his sailed on undamaged. When it plunged through the breakers and shuddered to a halt the seamen up in the fo'c'sle pushed out the ramps and disembarkation began, the marines hurrying down on to a beach lit by flying tracer and gunfire. Rubinstein later recalled seeing the crew members blazing away at some nearby houses with the boat's guns as he waited to descend the ramp. Then his turn came. He climbed up on to the walkway and began his descent just at the moment when the man in front of him was shot straight through the head. The marine fell back dead against Rubinstein and blocked the way. Without a thought, the young lieutenant pushed the body over the side and into the sea, watching as it splashed into the water, wondering if the man had been quite dead. Behind him other men were pressing forward to get off of the boat. Rubinstein was hurried down to the water in a daze and ran for the shelter of the sea wall, revolted by his actions.

Rubinstein looked about him at the dreadful scene. The scattered bodies of the dead and the dying littered the beach, packed together with damaged and burning vehicles. Just offshore the lieutenant watched the frantic efforts of the men from the trapped landing craft. Some were struggling in the water, while others were suffering the effects of the enemy fire which raked the decks of the boats. Those in the water were being swept away to the east by the strong undercurrents. Rubinstein was both sickened and fascinated by the scene. He watched in horror as men struggled for their lives, recognising his old friend Lt Yates among them. He knew at a glance that Yates was going to drown. Instinctively he felt he should throw off his clothes and go to his aid, but orders had been to help nobody; his duty lay with his men. For a moment he hesitated as he struggled with his conscience, but soon the moment had passed and it was too late to act. While he watched, his friend gave up the struggle and sank beneath the sea. He averted his eyes only to find the body of the man he had pushed overboard lying there at his feet, the limp torso washing backwards and forwards in the surf. He knew that the man had been dead when he hit the water, but he still felt as though he had murdered him.

Sgt Joe Stringer, also of B Troop, remembers his landing:

> I was the leading man on the left-hand side of the craft going in on the left-hand ramp. Lieutenant Curtis and Sergeant Bill Blyth were leading No. 1 Section on the right-hand ramp. We were all immediately exposed to the machine-gun nest at the far end of the beach. Our progress down the ramp was very slow, not like the popular image of a landing, where a flat-bottom boat dropped its ramp and the troops came running off and up the beach. Our craft had light wooden ramps which floated about in the heavy surf, lurching with every wave. Some matelots from the boat tried to hold them down in the water, but they were too heavy and difficult to control. As each man stepped from the craft on to the ramp he became very exposed. He then had to struggled down the near-vertical boards that were shaking and tossing about beneath him. Immediately behind me two of my men were hit by machine-gun fire. We lost a lot of men this way. When we came off of the craft it was into at least four feet of water, about chest high. We stormed across the beach to the far side, avoiding the wall where the poor Canadians had bought it, but moved more to the left towards the dunes trying to get away from the worst of the machine-gun fire.

Also on B Troop's craft was Dougie Gray:

> We were heavily laden with gear, I came down the ramp with a full pack on my back, spare bags, ammunition, grenades, a rifle in one hand and a Bangalore Torpedo in the other. We had to carry enough of everything to support ourselves once we were ashore. When I got off of the ramp and into the water, it came almost up to my neck. I was immediately hit by the strong undertow which nearly swept me off of my feet. The Bangalore Torpedo was wrenched from my hand, but I hung on tightly to my rifle. I managed to get a good grip with my feet and struggled up the beach, but many others around me were in real trouble. Once they had gone over in the water, it was a hell of a job for them to get back up on their feet with the heavy packs on their backs.

Once out of the water, Dougie Gray ran up the beach towards the sea wall, picking his way through the bodies of the Canadians who littered the shore. The wall gave protection from machine-gun fire, but not from the mortars.

Dougie Gray continues:

> The Germans in the strongpoint at St-Aubin had our range and bearings and the mortar bombs came over in regular waves. One bomb landed right among us and I was hit by a piece of shrapnel in my back. I found it hard going when I moved down the wall to try to get off of the beach; my wound was slowing me down. At the end of the wall I saw the padre directing some people. He had a cut above his eye and a wound to his leg. I asked him if he was all right, but I was struggling myself. A little further on I made it to what I thought was the beach exit, but had to give up and collapsed in a heap on the sand. A Canadian medic picked me up later and took me further over to the right to their aid post. It was situated beneath the promenade on the edge of Bernières. A large shell dressing was put on my wound and I was laid out on the sand between two Canadians, one from Le Régiment de la Chaudière and the other from the North Shore Regiment. We were left there all day. The French Canadian had a stomach wound and died during the night. I nicked his blanket later to keep warm.

Marine Dennis Smith came in on HQ Troop's landing craft. 'As soon as we landed I lost the two Canadian signallers who landed with me. I got ashore before them and waded through chest-deep water on to the beach, making straight for a group of marines who were sheltering under the sea wall. I looked back to the Canadians behind me and saw them both cut down by a mortar shell. Behind them, our Canadian officer moved away to the right and I never saw him again.'

Enemy fire was sweeping Nan Red from several angles. Most was coming from the area of the German strongpoint on the western edge of St-Aubin, about 400 yards away to the left. By this time B Company of the Canadian North Shore Regiment was off the beach on to the lateral road which ran behind the dunes and was fighting its way towards it, but progress was slow. Closer to hand, enemy infantry were positioned in the houses at the back of the beach and were punishing anyone unfortunate enough to be caught in their cross-wires. Capt Reynolds remembers one of them:

> I never noticed much about the smoke and the gunfire, but was very aware of a sniper being active near the exit through which we were to leave the beach. I was hit in the shoulder and thought that the fire was coming from a particular house which overlooked us. Fortunately, there was a Royal Marine Centaur tank close by and I banged on the side until a head appeared. I pointed out where I thought the sniper fire was coming from and he said 'OK'. The next thing I knew his tank surged forwards and drove straight through the front door of the house.

The severity of the enemy fire and the problems experienced through the underwater obstacles had completely disorganised the Commando's touchdown. Orders for the landing itself had been simple: the men were to arrive over an already captured and cleared beach; turn immediately to the right to make for the beach exit and then advance 200 yards or so inland to the forming-up point in a field where they would regroup ready for the move against their main objective in Langrune. No one had made provision for the immediate loss of control that had resulted from landing on an uncaptured beach swept by heavy enemy fire. Each man confronted with so much death and destruction quite naturally sought cover and safety where he could, which for the most part was to be found in the lee of the low cliffs and sea wall at the top of the beach. Here, the worst of the fire passed aimlessly overhead, or swept the exposed beach behind them, but to seek refuge here did mean that the impetus of the assault had been lost. It would take a great deal of effort from all the officers of the Commando to get it going again.

On Z Troop's craft the disembarkation had stopped. It was clear that no more men could get ashore from the position that the boat was stuck in. It was immobilised just a few hundred yards from the machine guns and mortars of the enemy strongpoint and German fire swept the craft. Signals Sgt Percy Bream was on the upper deck alongside a Canadian Forward Observation Officer's radio operator. 'He was sitting on a bollard, resting his back because of the weight of the set. The Germans started mortaring us and raking the craft with machine-gun fire. The next thing I remember I looked round at the Canadian and he had slumped forward with all of his insides hanging out through his stomach. He had taken a hit from a mortar. This set me back a bit and I quickly moved away.'

John Square was also on board this craft:

> Major Sanders decided that we needed help and hailed an LCT which was near us, asking it to pull alongside to take us off of our sinking craft. The first thing that I notice on going on board the LCT was, why is that soldier covered in red paint? Why and what was he painting at this moment in time? It was of course his own blood for he had been badly wounded. The things that go through your mind at times like that can be quite absurd. The LCT we had boarded was leaving the beaches and there was a strong chance that we were being taken back to England, but we managed to get the assistance of a small LCA to come and take us off and to ferry us to the beach.

Meanwhile, Sgt Colin Travers was still in the sea, being swept eastwards by the current. 'I struggled for what seemed a long time until the pack on my back struck the bottom. I found myself in the surf and, with solid ground beneath me, I was able to turn myself over and get to my feet. I had arrived on a stretch of shore that was completely empty. There was nobody else around.' Travers had escaped from Nan Red Beach, but was now alone on an enemy-held part of the shoreline.

Trying to get ashore from X Troop's craft was Tony Pratt:

> I was coming down the ramp behind someone who was carrying a bicycle and he was moving very slowly. On my back was a little spade and this got caught up in a rope on the gangway. I turned to knock it off and tipped myself over into the sea. Fortunately, it was fairly shallow and all that happened was that I got a soaking. As I struggled out of the water I looked down the beach and saw that it was utter carnage. I joined with others rushing up to the sea wall and we managed to get some shelter between it and a Canadian tank which was stopped there. We were leaning against this tank trying to get out of the fire, when a chap called Ginger McCaine caught a bullet and fell forward just as the tank began to move off. It ran straight over him. At the same time, another chap beside me caught his arm in the tank track and it was pulled right off. I helped to lay him down and told him that help would soon be with him and that we had to move off. I remember thinking he was bound to die through loss of blood before anyone could deal with him.

Landing from the HQ Troop's craft was the Heavy Weapons Troop's Commander, Capt Geoff Linnell. He found that the design of the craft walkways caused a great deal of trouble. He later recalled,

> The ramps were too light for the ends to sink to the sea-bed, they floated about in the surf. As each man tried to come down them, the foot-way beneath him heaved alarmingly with each incoming wave. Many men were thrown completely off the sides and floundered in the water, dragged down by their heavy packs. When I got down the ramp there was a big sea and a great undertow that nearly took my legs away. Some men with inflatable lifebelts up around their chests had been knocked over by the swell and were floating away upside-down with their legs in the air, drowning as we watched. It was most unpleasant. I managed to make it to the beach, wading through chest-deep water, but many of the others were cut down around me by machine-gun fire. One of my mortar crews was almost completely wiped out by an enemy mortar bomb. One marine, Arthur Thompson, a relatively old man of 35, went back into the water four or five times on his own and rescued every piece of the gun and set it up on the beach and said to me, 'Number One mortar ready to fire, sir!' I put him in for a medal.

Another member of the Heavy Weapons Troops was Sgt Ian Mair, in charge of two of the 3-inch mortar teams. There were four men for each mortar and Mair led one of his teams ashore, as he later recalled.

> I was carrying a canister of three 10 lb bombs in each hand, plus rifle, ammunition and other equipment, all of which probably weighed about 80 or 90 lb. We came in right on target and waded ashore through knee-deep water. I was only on the beach for a few minutes before a

Nan Red Beach after the battle, taken from a viewpoint facing away from the St-Aubin strongpoint. In the foreground is a burned-out self-propelled gun and a destroyed assault landing craft. In the background, looking west, is the side of the sea wall around the large house which fronted the beach. To the left are the high dunes behind which so many of the Commando took shelter. (*John Square*)

large shell landed close by and wounded me in the left leg and both arms. I was by the wall and was relatively lucky, the two marines behind me were killed and another badly injured. I was gathered together with some of the others who were wounded when I was hit and left there at the top of the beach for the next twelve hours before anyone could help me. Those stretcher bearers who were still alive had to go ahead with their units and we were left for the follow up troops to attend to.

Also landing from HQ Troop's craft was Ted Brooks. He saw a lot of injured men on the beach as he later recalled: 'When I came out of the water the first man I saw was very badly wounded, I would say he was dying. He lay there just waving his right hand. There was no way I could move him, I tried to make sure he was just out of the water, but he was far too heavy with all his equipment on that we all carried. I just wasn't strong enough; I just had to leave him and the tide was coming in.'

Vince Horton landed straight into the water from HQ's craft and made for the cover of a large shell hole. Inside was a badly injured man. 'I did all I could to help him,' he recalls. 'But I couldn't stop the flow of blood from his wound. Fire seemed to be coming at us from all angles and for a while all I could do was take cover. It soon became clear that the man alongside me was going to die and so would I if I remained there. So I left him and moved up to the top of the beach looking for the exit.'

Sgt Bill Hudson had become confused in the smoke and fire after his wet landing: 'I thought we had landed about halfway along the edge of the beach so I had a choice to bear left or right. As it later transpired, I picked the wrong way and went to the left. A short while later I passed a tank which had exploded after running over a mine. I knew that this must be the edge of the minefield and as the smoke was starting to clear I looked around for cover. I saw several men sheltering near a buttress of a ruined wall so I joined them.'

Under the sea wall was a jumble of men from other units, many dead or wounded. The Royal Marine commandos joined Canadians, naval personnel and beach groups all sheltering from the enemy fire. Among them was Jack Desmond. 'I was with Lance Corporal Appleyard MM sheltering by the sea wall when he suddenly stood up and started firing at a pillbox where he thought there was a sniper. The next second he collapsed beside me dead, shot through the head. The sniper had got him first.' Pinned down and unable to move, Ron Pugh was somewhat cheered by the sound of the crack/thump of each bullet that passed by him, sure in the knowledge that you did not hear the sound of the one that kills you. Further over to the left, Ted Brooks of HQ Troop and a few men were crouching behind a sand dune below the earth cliff, completely immobilised by German fire, unable even to lift their heads. 'The dune afforded some shelter from German fire, but we still took hits,' remembers Brooks. 'Corporal O'Boyle, who I had known since before the Commando was formed, was killed by the side of me.' Ernie Taylor of Z Troop was also sheltering beneath the dunes: 'The whole beach was a German killing ground; we just knew that we had to get off it to survive.'

The men aboard Y Troop's stranded craft were still the target of German fire as they tried to complete their landing. The bows of the craft were hung up on the underwater obstacle and the vessel was rapidly sinking. Nothing could save it now. Those on board felt that they were 'sitting ducks'. Donald Nicholson was one of them. 'Most of us marines were at the stern of the vessel which, being slightly lower in the water than the anchored bow, gave some protection from sniper fire, but many soon become casualties. Quite soon a tank landing craft came alongside as it approached the beach and its commander offered help. A line was thrown and secured to our stern which swung round enabling able-bodied survivors to clamber on to the stern of the LCT,' recalls Nicholson. 'Once on board we were able to get into cavities on the sides of the tank deck away from the tanks themselves, whose engines were running in preparation for landing.' Then the Canadian LCT continued its passage to the beach, as Nicholson later remembered.

> By this time the beach was under sustained mortar and shell fire and the LCT was peppered with small-arms fire. We touched down and the tanks began to leave the craft over the landing ramp. As the last of the tanks was moving forward to cross the ramp, about two or three of my comrades managed to clamber on to its rear and hitch a ride ashore. As soon as this tank left the ramp the rest of us rushed forward to get ashore. To our dismay the ramp suddenly rose up in front of us preventing us from doing so. We were to learn that skipper of this craft considered he had fulfilled his orders by getting the tanks ashore, and his next responsibility seemed to be the safety of the vessel, so he reversed off of the beach and headed for the open sea. Some way offshore we were transferred to a troop ship which had LCAs slung from the davits, the troops having already been landed on the beach. Once on board we learned that our destination was to be Plymouth!

Men from Z Troop were now coming ashore from their stricken craft, ferried to the beach by the determined coxswain of a single assault landing craft. Lt John Square was one of the commandos on board.

> We landed almost opposite the beach exit, just to the right of the big house. The tide was almost right in and all we had to cross was just a very short stretch of sand. I remember being focused on just getting off of the beach. I probably thought it best not to look around at the carnage that was taking place beside me and headed straight for the assembly area. Looking back, I wish I had taken more notice of what was happening, but I just wanted to get inland and away from the melee on the beach as quickly as possible.

There was now complete disorder on the beach. The narrow strip of sand was congested with self-propelled guns, tanks and other vehicles, their numbers growing alarmingly with each new LCT that touched down. The incoming tide had reduced the stretch of dry sand to a band no more than twenty yards wide. The rough surf that raced up the shoreline pushed a jumbled tide of dead bodies, disabled landing craft and floating debris along the beach until it almost lapped at the heels of the men sheltering behind the sea wall. This gruesome flotsam edged and flowed with each incoming wave. Ted Brooks remembers a pervading smell catching his nostrils. 'I don't think I shall ever forget the sweet smell of blood on our beach. While I was growing up in the countryside I used to shoot and during harvest I often bagged countless rabbits. There was always the smell of blood in the harvest field and I experienced that same smell on the beach. Before then I had not realised that human and animal blood give off the same scent.'

Harry Timmins had thrown himself down beside the padre, who was tending to some badly wounded men. The padre looked up and said to him, 'Don't stop here, its dangerous.' 'If I had been in a jovial mood,' recalls Timmins, 'I would have thought that the remark was funny being that it was so obvious, but any sort of thinking was right off course at that moment.' Timmins then raced along the water's edge and took shelter behind a stranded assault craft, but the incoming tide swept another LCA into him, trapping him for a short time. He then tried to get off the beach behind a flail tank that was trying to beat a path up to an exit. 'I looked down the length of the beach; it was pure chaos.'

Sgt Tom Clark of A Troop also saw the padre on the beach that morning while he was sheltering with a group of men. 'He was walking up and down with his five-foot-long shepherd's crook and banging on the turret of a tank demanding that the crew open up to look where they were going. Then the Chaplain saw me and said very softly, "Take them up the beach Sergeant Major." I was terrified and led the remaining men up to the exit at a run, not in a straight line, but by zigzagging over the sand.'

Col Moulton had arrived into this chaos from his craft at the start of the landings. Capt Flunder was at the front of the boat when it touched down and helped the crew push off the ramps at the front of the ship. Once the treaded walkway was down, the Major became the first of the marines to leave the HQ craft, closely followed by some men from the HQ Troop and some signallers. Flunder's progress down the steep walkway was precarious. The wooden ramp beneath him was bucking and swirling with each incoming wave. Then disaster struck. The craft rolled to one side and then swung out from the shore, twisting the ramp from its rollers and flinging Flunder and the men behind him into the sea. The craft then reared up above them on the next wave and came crashing forward on the surf. Fortunately, Flunder suffered no more than a ducking and some slight grazing as the craft rolled him along, but his lanyard and pistol were torn from him while underwater.

Moulton left the craft by the other ramp, following behind some of his heavily-laden men, silently urging them to hurry up, but knowing that the manoeuvre was much more difficult than it had been in practice because of the heavy swell. Then it was down into the water and a quick wade ashore. The colonel could see that things were going very badly, many dead and wounded men littered the water's edge. Ignoring his own instructions, he paused without thinking and helped to pull a wounded man who was lying in the shallow water. He grabbed him by the shoulders and began to heave him a little way up the beach. Moulton then looked around him and saw the enormity of the problems facing the Commando.

To the left, along the sea wall, a line of still figures crouched against the stonework. Among this mass of men some were wounded, some were dead and some were dying, all had been stalled by the ferocity of the enemy fire. Further to the left others lay in the lee of the small sandy cliff which edged the beach. To the right, through the smoke and haze, work looked to be continuing on clearing an exit from the beach. All along the sand small black puffs of smoke marked the fall of mortar bombs and the air was thick with the crack of bullets as they zipped along the beach. Occasionally a larger shell would whine over and explode on some random spot, filling the air with acrid fumes and red-hot splinters of shrapnel. The scene was chaotic and Moulton now set about bringing some order to the beach.

Close by he found Capt Dan Flunder behind the sea wall, wet and exhausted from his ordeal in the sea. Together they walked along to the exit to see the situation for themselves. The mine clearance teams were still working on the breach in the dunes, but a path had been cleared and taped which led off the beach and on to the lateral road at the rear. A little further on was the field that Moulton had selected for his assembly area. This too was clear and it seemed to be much quieter there. The Colonel and the Major returned to the beach, determined to get the marines away from the deadly shoreline and into the safer assembly area as quickly as they could.

CHAPTER SIX

Off the Beach

Twenty minutes after the initial landings made by the Commando, the shoreline was still under extremely accurate enemy fire. The turmoil on Nan Red beach that had begun in the first few minutes after H Hour, when the assault companies of the North Shore Regiment had touched down, continued unabated. The Canadians had made little further progress towards capturing the St-Aubin strongpoint and the German defenders there continued to harass the landings with small arms, mortar and machine-gun fire. Further inland, German field guns brought down occasional salvoes of high-explosive shells on to the exposed Allied troops to add their weight to the interdictory fire which was raking the beach. Along the line of surf, burning and disabled landing craft swung wildly with each incoming wave and presented additional hazards to the vessels waiting to land. Just off the beach, more craft carrying support vehicles and the second wave of Canadian infantry circled looking for openings through the confusion before making a run in to shore.

Lt Harold Smedley, the Commando's Intelligence Officer, was on board Z Troop's craft for the landings. Along with Maj Sanders and some support personnel he made up the standby HQ which would take over if Moulton's main HQ could not land. In the event it was they who had the difficulty in coming ashore after their craft had struck the beach obstacle. By now, however, the marines who were isolated on that craft had all been taken off and most of them had been ferried ashore in an LCA. Harold Smedley recalls his arrival on Nan Red Beach:

> At that point in time I was acting as an individual and there was nothing much I could do for the Commando itself. I came ashore without further incident and left the beach from an exit to the right. I met with some others and we formed up in the assembly area. I had instructions on landing to go liaise with the Canadians to ensure that our efforts were tied up together, but the circumstances of the day were such that it wasn't feasible to do exactly what one wanted. I did eventually make my way to where the North Shore Regiment was and found out the local situation, then set off back to join Colonel Moulton. I was one of just a few British on the Canadian sector of the beach and one of the Canadians I met on the way said, 'Watch out boy, you'll get yourself shot as a deserter!'

At the top of the beach the number of men crouched behind the sea wall was still growing. Among them was Jock Mathieson, one of 48 Commando's dispatch riders:

Nan Red Beach on the morning of D-Day by the exit from the beach used by the commandos. In the foreground is a Centaur tank from the Royal Marine Armoured Support Regiment. On the dunes sappers are still sweeping for mines. In the background is the large house with its sea wall jutting out on to the shore. The LCI(S) carrying HQ Troop touched down along here, with the remainder of the landing craft bringing the rest of the Commando landing at intervals further along the beach near the sea wall. (*Imperial War Museum, B5224*)

I was sheltering beside the sea wall along with others from HQ Troop. Also there were many of the wounded who had crawled up the sand to find protection from the enemy fire. By that time the tide was well in and the beach was very narrow. Then a Canadian tank came forward and began running along by the wall trying to get off of the beach. The driver could not see men on the ground because all of the tank's crew were battened down inside away from German sniper fire. Nothing could stop the great vehicle and it began to run along the base of the wall, over the wounded men stretched out on the sand. Captain Flunder banged on the side but got no response from the tank's crew so he slipped a mine in the path of the tank and blew its track off. It was a terrible sight to see those poor helpless men crushed in this way.

Further along the shoreline to the east, away from all the chaos and dying that was taking place on Nan Red Beach, Sgt Colin Travers was trying to drag himself out of the rolling surf to safety. Unknown to him at that time, he had been swept far to the left by the tidal flow and had landed right under the German strongpoint at St-Aubin, 400 yards adrift from the rest of 48 RM Commando. Soaked to the skin, exhausted and in shock, he struggled to get clear of the sea, as he later explained.

The equipment on my back was saturated with sea water and very heavy, making it difficult to get up, so I unstrapped my backpack and abandoned it in the surf. At the top of the beach there was a sandy cliff and I could make out a German gun emplacement on the top of it. I immediately made my way up the beach to the shelter of the cliff. I took my revolver out, cleaned it and tried to dry it. It was fairly quiet on this stretch of the shore; there was still no one around. A little later, I watched someone from the army come out of the water and I beckoned him to come and join me. He came up and said a few words then set off along the beach. I cleaned and dried a grenade and then began to take a look at the German emplacement behind me. I saw a head pop up with a German helmet on and he got down quick when he saw me. I threw the grenade at him and thought that I had better set off along the beach to find the Commando. After a few hundred yards, one of the first people that I met was a beach controller. I still had my pistol in my hand and the silly man said to me 'Put that pistol away!' I ignored him and went on to discover where the rest of the Commando were and to find Colonel Moulton.

While the Commando was fighting for its life on the shoreline, its transport and support vehicles were beginning their approach to Nan Red. On board one of the tank landing craft was Ralph Dye, a forward observation officer with 3 Bombardment Unit Royal Artillery, who was attached to 48 RM Commando. He later recalled his arrival off Normandy:

We were told that our landing on Juno Beach should be quiet, for the German troops there were all away on a scheme and that it was too rough in the Channel to expect an invasion. When we arrived off the French coast we could see lots of craft heading for the shore, but we were waved off by the landing command ship because there was chaos on the beach and no room for us to land. About twenty minutes later we were told to go in. I recall that during the run in I thought to myself 'This is it!' Up on the bridge a major of the North Shore Regiment, with a face that was absolutely pea green in colour with seasickness, was calling down to a sergeant below, 'Get those men shaved!' The sergeant replied, 'The men are fed up with shaving, Sir.' The major replied, 'Get those men shaved!' So on the run in to the beach, during the greatest invasion in history, the Canadians were having a shave. I was rather impressed with this, for I had always thought that the Canadians had a rather democratic attitude to discipline.

The LCT carrying Dye and his jeep also carried some of the Commando's transport. On board was Cpl Fred Wyatt, a jeep driver with S Troop: 'I remember even before we landed a chap called Simpson was very curious about what was happening on the beach and had his head up looking over the side. He was soon struck by enemy fire and died later.' The LCT pressed on through the melee of circling and damaged assault craft, through the smoke and the shells, heading resolutely into the tightly packed jam of men and machines on the beach. Ralph Dye continues:

As we got closer to the shore I could start picking out the landmarks that we had been briefed on. I could clearly see the tall building on the left that had been imprinted on my mind. Then there was a terrific explosion as the craft hit a mine, but the ship kept on running. It was almost high tide when we arrived and most of the underwater obstacles were covered. The beach was narrow and congested but we surged through the surf and struck bottom. Then the ramp went down and the chaos on the beach became clear. What struck me most of all was that it was all in colour. Everything we had seen of the war up until then had been on black-and-white newsreels. It was as though the war was being fought in black and white, but here I was seeing it in full colour. It was terrifying.

Sgt Bill Hudson was still trying to find the beach exit. The smoke had cleared and enemy rifle fire seemed to him to be increasing, then he spotted the taped exit about 100 yards away to the right.

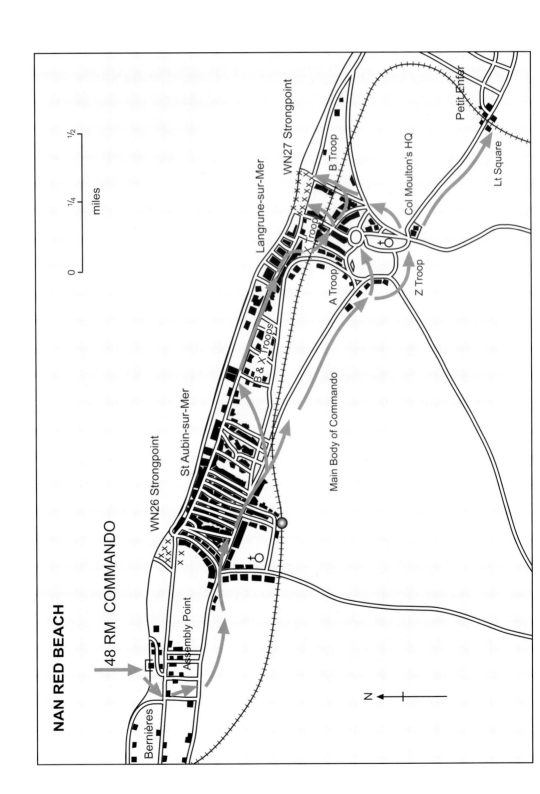

NAN RED BEACH

48 RM COMMANDO

Bernières

Assembly Point

WN26 Strongpoint

St Aubin-sur-Mer

B & X Troops

Langrune-sur-Mer

X Troop

A Troop

Main Body of Commando

Z Troop

B Troop

WN27 Strongpoint

Col Moulton's HQ

Petit Enfer

Lt Square

N

0   ¼   ½

miles

I started towards it looking for cover as I moved. I could see a smouldering tank about halfway to the exit and it looked a bit dangerous. Not far from it I could see an old black tree stump which had been washed up by the sea, so off I went to seek cover behind it, reaching it in record time. It was smaller than I had first thought and then the smell hit me. Within seconds I realised that the 'tree stump' was in fact two bodies welded together and burnt. What I had thought were its branches were in fact what was left of their limbs. The two men had obviously been blown out of the tank.

Sgt Joe Stringer of B Troop was still sheltering behind the sea wall, waiting for some orders. 'There was a lot of chaos on the beach, lots of wounded lying about. The Fort Gary Horse in their Sherman tanks were coming in at this time, landing from LCTs quite close to us. They had the hatches of their tanks battened down and the men lying wounded on the beach were vulnerable to their tracks. It was very chaotic everywhere, order seemed to be lost and this is where Colonel Moulton really shone.'

Col Moulton now made his presence felt on the beach. With an exit open and the assembly area now located, he wanted his men off the beach as quickly as possible. Through the fire and the smoke, he sought out the officers and men of his unit to get things moving. Harry Timmins was there on the beach watching. 'I saw our colonel walking steadily and steadfastly, bolt upright, despite the shells and mortars dropping all around and the ping, ping, ping of the bullets whizzing by. He stopped, looked around and at the top of his voice cried out, "Four-Eight Royal Marine Commando – this way," pointing along the beach. Everyone within earshot got up and followed him.'

The commandos were moving, but there were still more casualties to suffer before they were clear of Nan Red, as Capt Geoff Linnell explained. 'There was a very good German rifleman firing very accurately at a junction of the beach where it was necessary to go around a wall outside a house. He managed to produce a whole heap of bodies at this point. One of my young men, Marine Stanley, who was just 18, was shot and his friend stood aghast looking at him till it was his turn next. This German got, I estimate, 20 bodies at this particular point.'

There were many injured men on the beach who would not give up and were determined to go on. Capt Linnell recalls seeing Capt Michael Reynolds of A Troop, who had been badly wounded in the arm and one shoulder; his chest and his battledress were soaked in blood. 'He insisted that he was mobile and quite able to cope. He was, too, advancing, smoking cigarettes that one of his troop had lit for him.' Col Moulton was another brief casualty. While he was rallying troops on the beach a mortar bomb landed close by him and blew him off of his feet. He felt a sharp pain in his leg and arm. At first he thought that his leg was broken and admits that he was glad of it, thinking that he would now be evacuated from the senseless

Opposite: The Advance to Langrune from Nan Red Beach

48 RM Commando on its advance from Nan Red Beach to Langrune. The commandos are moving along the inland road, with St-Aubin to the right. Smoke from the beach helps shield the area from long-range German artillery. The marine in the rear centre has commandeered a French pram in which to carry his load. (*Imperial War Museum, B5220*)

chaos, but he soon realised that he could walk and had suffered no more than just a spattering of mortar bomb splinters. He was bleeding from the hand and leg, but suffered no serious harm and continued with his walk along the beach.

Sgt Bill Hudson was one of those still on the beach, trying to get to the exit. Away to the right he could see Lt Mackenzie walking upright among the bodies, disregarding the small-arms fire and mortar bombs, giving morphine injections to the wounded. On his way to the exit he found a man crouched by the sea wall, as he later recalled: 'He was a medical orderly and he was in shock. He was gazing at the carnage around him, knowing that he was expected to treat them. So I grabbed his arm, pulled him to his feet and said, "Come on, we're off," and made for the exit.'

On his beached LCT, Ralph Dye was preparing to come down its ramp and enter into the jumble of men and machines which littered the sand.

I remember the machine-gun bullets rattling off of the hull. We had clearly not taken the beach and it dawned on me that I was going to have to drive out of the ship into all that fire. On either side of us, landing craft were landing bringing the follow-up waves of infantry. In front of me a bulldozer set off down the ramp to land. Its blade was up for protection and a spare driver on the top was calling down directions to the driver below. He must have felt expendable. I followed in my jeep, trying to touch down in the shade of the bulldozer. Unfortunately for me, I had a trailer strapped to the bonnet of the jeep and I could not see where I was going, so I had to drive leaning out of the side with my right hand on the steering wheel. Right in front of me was a burning tank. Its ammunition was exploding and I kept saying to myself, 'The killing range of a 25 pounder shell is 35 yards,' and wishing myself to put distance between my jeep and the burning tank. I steered round to the right, but realised I couldn't go on with the trailer on the top obscuring my view. I called out to two men to help me get the trailer off of my bonnet so that I could see where I was going. Two men sprang forward and helped unleash the trailer and just as we were pulling it off, machine-gun bullets started whizzing about our heads. I crawled around the side and decided it would be healthier for me to get off of the beach as soon as I could, so I leapt in and roared forward towards the rendezvous point to meet my captain who had landed earlier. He and his telegraphists had had a shocking time during their landing. I jumped out of the jeep and snapped him a salute and said, 'Good morning.' While I was standing there with him I noticed a clump of wounded marines about fifty yards away, sheltering behind the sea wall. Two mortar bombs then came over and dropped right among them. I remember the terrible groaning that they let out; they must have all been badly hurt. Then another bullet went past my head and we decided to move.

Also landing from the LCT was Fred Wyatt. He was bringing one of S Troop's jeeps ashore loaded with mortar and machine gun ammunition. 'Our task was to get the ammunition up to the guns and mortars as soon as we could. The beach seemed to be completely chaotic when I got ashore. I saw the tapes marking the outline of the swept exit, but found it difficult to get to it through the jam of tanks and vehicles milling about on the sand. Once I got away from the shore I started ripping off the jeep's waterproofing material because it had been drummed in to us that the vehicle would seize up if we didn't and I certainly didn't want to find myself stranded with all of that enemy fire flying all over the place.'

Troop Sgt Maj Colin Travers had found his way to the exit and moved along the white tapes marking the mine-swept path up to the assembly area. He was very glad to rejoin the Commando. 'I found the CO with Captain Grant and when he saw me he said, "Ah Travers, I'm glad to see you. You are now my RSM." I was very cold and wet. I had left my pack on the beach and had no change of clothing or anything. Colonel Moulton asked me if I has seen Lennard or Rigby. I told him that I had not seen anything of either of them once I had gone into the water. I never saw their bodies. Then I had to take over RSM's duties although I was not sure of what they were.'

Jock Mathieson, a dispatch rider with HQ, also made it to the assembly area. 'When I got off of the beach I fell in with B Troop. We assembled in a ditch by the side of the road. Already in the ditch was the body of a young French boy, no more than about eight years old. It looked as though he had been killed by blast, probably during the preliminary bombardment. The sight shook me up considerably.'

When Capt Geoff Linnell had collected together as many of his men as he could, he also left the shore. Linnell had lost the machine-gun section who were travelling in X Troop's craft, when all of the section were taken back to England on an LCT. He also lost a complete mortar crew on the beach to enemy fire and had all of his NCOs on the mortars either killed, wounded or missing. Those that were left joined with him and advanced to the assembly area. 'We went up a re-entry through the twenty-foot-high dunes and moved away from the fire on the beach. When we finally assembled in the field a little way back from the sea, my heavy weapons troop was down to just 40 men. I decided that Lieutenant Mike Aldworth would fire the mortars and I would fire the machine guns, although it was much later before Aldworth could join us, for it took him four tries to get ashore from Z Troop's craft.'

The assembly area itself was not entirely free from enemy interference, as Ted Brooks recalls. 'At the rendezvous point three of us came under fire from a sniper in the tower of St-Aubin Church and after we had loosed off several rounds into his position without results, we solicited the help of a Canadian sergeant in command of a disabled tank. He very obligingly put several rounds into the tower and that silenced the sniper. At a church service there many years later the vicar wanted to know just how the tower was damaged.'

When he had gathered together as many of his men as he thought were able to get off the beach, Moulton had a roll-call to assess the Commando's losses. In the assembly area Lt John Square found that he was the only officer left in Z Troop; Lennard and Rigby were still missing. Both were in fact dead. Maj de Stacpoole of Y Troop had made it ashore but he was wounded. At the rendezvous point, Moulton recognised the seriousness of his injuries and ordered him to the aid post to have his wounds treated. De Stacpoole's second-in-command of the troop, Lt Yates, had been drowned and the other officer, Lt Fouché, was lying badly wounded on the beach. Most of Z Troop's marines and some of Y Troop's had by now been landed, but they were very short of officers with just Lt Square the only survivor of both troops. Moulton reorganised his Commando into four fighting troops, with the men of Y and Z Troops being distributed among the others. Casualties had been heavy; Moulton estimated them at about 30 per cent.

Lt Smedley returned from the North Shore Regiment's HQ with a situation report. After hearing it Col Moulton decided that it was time to begin the advance on Langrune. The Canadians were still trying to take control of St-Aubin and the German strongpoint overlooking Nan Red Beach was still in enemy hands. Canadian infantry from B Company of the North Shore Regiment were fighting towards its seafront bunkers from the south, working their way through the tiny side streets of the town, but progress was slow. Tanks had been sent up to join in the attack and confidence was high that the strongpoint would soon fall. In the meantime, 48 Commando would have to make its advance with its left flank in St-Aubin open to the enemy.

Col Moulton intended to split his force for the move, sending B and X Troops to advance closest to the sea moving along a lateral road which converged on Langrune's seafront, while he took the remainder of the unit, led by A Troop, along an inland route directed towards the church at Langrune, about 600 yards inland. B and X Troops would clear the coastal strip between St-Aubin and Langrune, while Moulton's group consolidated the village against counter-attacks from the south. Once the Commando had established itself in Langrune, it would move in strength against the enemy strongpoint WN26, which dominated the seafront of the village.

Capt Michael Reynolds was happy to be reunited with his men. 'I met up with most of A Troop just off the beach and we organised ourselves to advance, setting off to win the war. By this time I had been hit in the other arm by a piece of shrapnel. One of my boys bound me up and I continued on. Despite all the horror on the beach we were still in high spirits. I thought of the old maxim as we gaily started down the road: "The object of all military training is to so exasperate the soldier in times of peace, that he will regard war in the light of a holiday."'

Harry Timmins was with Capt Reynolds as they set out on the march, but was not happy with his commander as he later explained:

Captain Reynolds came alongside me and said: 'Timmins, put my revolver in my hand.' I looked at him, he had blood running down both arms, leaving a trail along the road. 'You can't possibly hold that sir,' I told him. He said: 'Do as you are told.' So with a struggle I managed to get his fingers wrapped around his revolver and we continued. He was a wonderful leader, I am quite sure he would have won the VC if he had stayed with us, instead of just the French Croix de Guerre that he was awarded.

A Troop's commander did not get very far into the advance before Col Moulton spotted one of Reynolds's men lighting a cigarette for him and placing it in his mouth. It was clear to Moulton that the captain was incapable of any further involvement in the operation. Capt Reynolds recalls what happened to him: 'Eventually we halted and I am afraid that I had to give up. The shrapnel had broken my shoulder and Colonel Moulton ordered me to the aid post. I was very reluctant to leave my Troop and just wanted to get patched up and return to it. I knew the doc, he and I were at Winchester together, so I pleaded with him to let me get back to my men, but he paid no attention to what I said to him. He ordered me to be evacuated and I was dumped on a jeep and taken back to the beach.' It was another blow for Moulton for he had lost now lost three of his six troop leaders.

Sgt Joe Stringer was with B Troop as they started their advance.

As soon as we moved out along the road that ran parallel to the beach we came under fire. Our officer, Lieutenant Jeff Curtis, second-in-command of B Troop, was fatally wounded almost immediately by Oerlikon fire coming from one of the warships off the beach. I think one of their lookouts had seen our advance and had assumed that we were Germans. The bullets had ripped through the lieutenant's stomach leaving him in a bad way. We had to leave him by the side of the road. The gunfire had also killed another marine and wounded a couple of others.

Ralph Dye joined up with the Commando in his jeep and set out for Langrune at the rear of the main group. 'We advanced along the long straight road that was later to be called Route de la Libération. Halfway along the road we were held up by some obstacles up front. There was a group of wounded marines by the side of the road. Their officer, Lieutenant Curtis, had been shot in the gut and badly needed medical help. I got him on to my jeep and took him back down the road to the aid post. He told me it was the third time this had happened to him during the war. He was still articulate although obviously in bad way. He later died.'

Dennis Smith, a signaller with HQ Troop, found he had an encumbrance as he started the advance. 'I was still carrying my Aldis Lamp, but realised that there was no way I could signal to any ship out at sea. I think their lookout had seen the troop movements and assumed they were Germans, so I discarded it and took up the duties of a rifleman.'

By the time Ralph Dye had delivered the wounded Lt Curtis to the aid post near the beach and returned to the outskirts of St-Aubin, the Commando had disappeared.

> I should have been up with the leading files in the attack, ready to call down supporting fire from the naval vessels offshore, so I sped back along the road towards Langrune to join up with the rest of the marines. I came to the edge of the built-up area, with nothing but green fields ahead and nobody in sight, when I saw a marine lying alongside the last house by the side of the road. He turned and waved to me and shouted, 'Sniper!' I got out of my jeep and joined him in the shadow of a house and two rounds went 'crack' right past my ear. Clearly I could not stay there because I was needed up ahead, so I thought that I would chance my luck. I got back into the jeep, revved the engine and shot off just as fast as I could, with sniper fire pinging past my head.

Those that were dead on Nan Red were beyond help, but the wounded on the beach had to endure a great deal more misery before they finally reached proper medical facilities. The fact was that all medical facilities along the landing beaches had been overwhelmed by casualties of their own. Until the enemy could be pushed back inland and his artillery sites overrun, the beach remained a killing ground upon which death and injury were distributed in a perfectly arbitrary way. Stretcher bearers, aid men and medical officers had no magic armour to protect them as they went about their work; bullets and bombs killed and maimed those unfortunate enough to get in the way quite indiscriminately.

The Commando was well served by its own medical team that day. Lt 'Doc' Winser worked tirelessly bringing aid to the wounded throughout the whole of the morning until he had to leave and advance inland with the unit. For his work he was awarded the Military Cross. Others of the Royal Army Medical Corps were also recognised for their work: L/Cpl Tickle was awarded the Military Medal and L/Cpl Ivor Jones was Mentioned in Despatches.

Marine Bert Skinner was on his way back to England. He had been transferred from the landing craft which carried Z Troop out to a warship for treatment to his head wound.

> I did not know it at the time, but I had suffered severe concussion and a hairline fracture of the skull when I was blown over by a shell. I kept passing out and was taken out to a frigate and put into the wardroom. There was a Polish sergeant lying alongside me. He asked for a cigarette and I noticed that when he inhaled, the smoke started coming out through a big

German prisoners being escorted back through St-Aubin by 48 RM Commando.
(*Imperial War Museum, B5229*)

hole in his chest. He did not survive the night. I spent two days on the frigate and was then transported to Gosport, thence to a Canadian General Field Hospital, from there to civilian hospital in North Staffs. Discharged after 3 weeks, the MO assured me the fracture would heal in six weeks. It did and I was then sent back to rejoin 48 Commando.

The assault waves of the invasion had broken through the outer crust of Hitler's Atlantic Wall. There was still a lot of fighting to be done that day before a lodgement could be secured, but at least the Allies were off the beaches and moving inland. The Germans who had surrendered were being rounded up and sent back to England on LCTs. One of the Commando's jeep drivers, Richard Cannock, recalls one of these prisoners: 'I saw this German looking absolutely shattered and dismayed. I felt sorry for him and offered him a cigarette and, as he had one arm in a sling, I put the cigarette to his lips. He spat it out on the ground and then spat at me. I responded by swiping him in the ear with my rifle butt. I still regret this action even though it was spontaneous.'

CHAPTER SEVEN

Langrune

Two hours after the initial assault, the Canadian North Shore Regiment was still having problems capturing WN 27 at St-Aubin-sur-Mer. The support of some tanks had allowed B Company to close on the fortifications, but the process of winkling out the German defenders was a lengthy task. The battalion's other three companies were two miles away, advancing inland on Tailleville, so B Company had to continue to try and solve the problem on its own.

This job of reducing the strongpoint was proving to be much more difficult than had been expected. WN27 not only overlooked the eastern edge of Nan Beach, but was also fully interconnected with the streets and buildings of the town by minefields, wire entanglements, roadblocks and trenches. It had a 50-mm gun as its main offensive weapon, the gun which had done so much damage to Canadian tanks and landing craft on the beach. It was also supported by seven machine guns and numerous mortars. Most of the strongpoint was impervious to fire from the sea as its concrete emplacements were sited to fire along the beach in enfilade, with their thick concrete sides facing outwards towards the Channel. It could not be subdued by shellfire alone, the Canadians had to approach right up to the wire and take the garrison the hard way, hand to hand.

When 48 RM Commando finally set out towards Langrune, it passed through the edge of St-Aubin while Lt Col Buell and his North Shore Regiment were still engaged at the strongpoint. There was a good deal of enemy fire zipping through the air and, as the marines passed by, sniper and mortar fire harried them on their way. The stretch of coastline between St-Aubin and Langrune was only lightly held by the enemy, for the main resistance here relied on the interconnecting fire between the two strongpoints, WN26 at Langrune and WN27 at St-Aubin, spaced about 2,000 yards apart.

With X Troop during this advance was Tony Pratt: 'We were going down a pathway and the bloke in front of me had his foot blown apart by an anti-personnel mine. It was hanging on by just a few strips of skin. The medic with him told him that he had lost his foot and he would have to cut it off. The wounded man was a long-service marine and he turned to me, clapped his hands and said, "Back to Blighty, no more long service for me!" He was happy with his wound.'

On the eastern outskirts of St-Aubin the Commando split, with B and X Troops moving down to the left to join the lateral road behind the beach which linked St-Aubin and Langrune. Moulton took the remainder of his unit along the diagonal inland road which led towards the centre of the village near the church. B and X Troops' route would eventually bring them right into the south-western corner of Langrune's seafront strongpoint, WN26, and the closer they got to this resistance nest, the sharper the exchanges with the enemy became.

The strongpoint itself was still under bombardment from the warships at sea. Capt Tyrer and his observers were seeing to that as Ralph Dye explained. 'After dropping off the fatally wounded Lieutenant Curtis I managed to rejoin the marines. Further down the road I found my Captain with the radios. We began ranging the destroyer offshore that was assigned to support our attack. The strongpoint at Langrune was battered with accurate fire from the destroyer but showed little sign of giving up.' Like all the other German strongpoints sited along the coast, naval gunfire forced the defenders to keep their heads down, but did little damage to the reinforced concrete structures that made up the fortified areas.

Moulton's group advanced without incident and made for the centre of Langrune itself. The long line of commandos, led by A Troop, moved in open order with their heavier pieces of equipment being carried in a collection of 'liberated' transport, such as a pram and an ice cream barrow. Moulton set up his headquarters in a building he had previously identified from an aerial photograph. Joining Moulton was Lt Harold Smedley, the Intelligence Officer, Capt Dan Flunder, the Adjutant, Capt Noel Godkin, the Administration Officer and the new RSM, Colin Travers. The house selected for the HQ was a walled manor house just to the east of the church. Further to the east were open fields which looked across to Petit Enfer and Luc-sur-Mer. Sword Beach, the landing point of 3rd British Division, was just 3 miles away.

Colin Travers now found out what being the regimental sergeant major really entailed. He began by getting things straight in the headquarters and arranging the replenishment of ammunition. Things were different when on active duty as he later explained. 'As RSM it was not the same in the field as in the barracks. At the unit's home depot the duties are more fixed, overseeing the discipline of the NCOs for example, but when in action in the field, things were different altogether. One of my most important tasks was to make sure that sufficient ammunition was available and delivered to the forward troops. I was also responsible for the security of the Headquarters, sorting out sentries and that type of thing. During the night, I would often get up and do a round of the sentries making sure they were awake and everything was all right.'

Opposite: Strongpoint WN26 at Langrune (*Courtesy of Geoff Linnell*)

LANGRUNE-SUR-MER
STRONGPOINT 6–7 JUNE 44

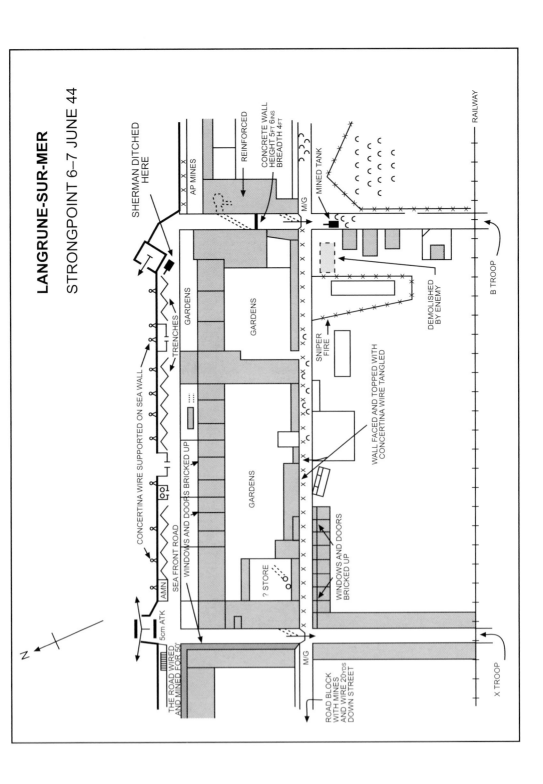

SHERMAN DITCHED HERE

AP MINES

REINFORCED

CONCRETE WALL
HEIGHT 5FT 6INS
BREADTH 4FT

M/G

MINED TANK

RAILWAY

DEMOLISHED BY ENEMY

B TROOP

SNIPER FIRE

WALL FACED AND TOPPED WITH
CONCERTINA WIRE TANGLED

GARDENS

GARDENS

CONCERTINA WIRE SUPPORTED ON SEA WALL

TRENCHES

WINDOWS AND DOORS BRICKED UP

SEA FRONT ROAD

GARDENS

? STORE

WINDOWS AND DOORS BRICKED UP

AMN

5cm ATK

THE ROAD WIRED AND MINED FOR 50'

M/G

ROAD BLOCK WITH MINES AND WIRE 20yds DOWN STREET

X TROOP

N

Dennis Smith also moved into Moulton's HQ at the manor house with the signal section. 'The high wall surrounding the place made it a very confined position. We could not easily see who was approaching, so a few of us occupied two cottages by the courtyard. There was an old man and two women in the cottage I was in. We each took a bedroom window and kept watch for any Germans. The old man gave us some cider and while I was drinking it the thought crossed my mind that within a few hours of landing as part of the greatest invasion in history, I was in a lady's bedroom drinking cider.'

Cpl Fred Wyatt had brought his jeep up to Langrune and was wondering to himself what the hell he was doing there. The landings on the beach and all of the death and destruction had unsettled him. 'Then I saw the local parson come out of the church with a lot of children,' he recalls. 'They had been sheltering in the church from the bombing and shellfire and now thought it was safe enough to come out and meet their liberators. Seeing the faces of those children made me realise what it was all about. It settled me down in my own mind.'

By this time, B and X Troops were closing on the strongpoint, winkling out snipers and chasing away German patrols. B Troop moved directly to the beach defences immediately to the east of St-Aubin, clearing the shoreline as it went. Little resistance was met for most of the enemy withdrew as the commandos approached. Once B Troop's marines had cleared their section, X Troop took over the advance and cleared the next section. The commandos advanced through gardens and over walls along the lateral road until they approached the minefields and wire which marked the outskirts of the fortified area. Here X Troop was halted by enemy fire coming from the houses around WN26 and from a well-entrenched machine gun set in the crossroads in front of the strongpoint. Unable to move any further along this route, X Troop swung to the south and tried to approach the enemy position from inland. Again they were stopped by the troublesome machine gun which was set into a pit with concrete overhead cover.

Marine Jack Desmond was up with the leading men.

We climbed through some back gardens of some houses trying to get nearer to the defences. The Germans saw us approaching and we got mortared. One of my mates was killed instantly and another had his face splattered with shrapnel from a mortar bomb. I had a piece hit my arm causing a great stream of blood to run down my sleeve and drip on the ground. We started walking back to get treatment at the aid post. On the way there I took my arm out of my jacket to have a look at my wound and found that all I had got was a tiny pinprick on my arm, so I had to let my mate go on to the medics on his own and made my way back towards the strongpoint.

The strongpoint on the coast at Langrune was, like that at St-Aubin, a formidable defensive position. A whole block of houses facing the seafront had been reinforced with concrete. They had had their doors and windows blocked up, were lined with barbed wire entanglements and were joined together internally to form a continuous impregnable block. The houses were interconnected by tunnels to outlying trenches and two machine-gun posts. All the approaches were blocked by more wire and minefields. The minefield on the western side was over 50 yards deep. At either end of the block, the roads passing down each side to the sea were closed by obstacles. The eastern one was barred by a four-feet-thick concrete wall. Covering the approaches from the town were two casemated machine guns located in each crossroad at the eastern and western ends of the strongpoint. Mortars located within the compound covered every square yard which surrounded the resistance post. In front of the buildings, along the old peacetime promenade, were more trenches, wire and mines. At the heart of the fortification were the gun emplacements facing the beach. Two large guns, one 75 mm and one 50 mm, each housed in a concrete bunker, formed the strongpoint's main firepower and were sited to counter any seaborne landings against Langrune. The actual approaches to the area were via four small streets: the lateral roads to the east and west and two narrow roads from the village. All of these roads were lined with houses, some of which still contained enemy snipers. From every viewpoint, this German resistance post was a formidable obstacle.

With two of his troops now in contact with the enemy, Moulton began to formulate his next move. Z Troop, strengthened by the marines of Y Troop that had managed to land, was ordered to hold Langrune to cover the HQ and the ground to the south. A Troop, now commanded by Lt Mackenzie, was held in reserve. Part of X Troop was told to keep pressure on the enemy from along the lateral road from St-Aubin while its commander, Capt Hoare, took the remainder of his men up the road from the village which met the strongpoint at its western end. Capt Jim Perry was ordered to take his B Troop towards the fortified position from the south to try to get behind the enemy who were holding up X Troop, using the right-hand road to the strongpoint as his axis. Moulton wanted to bring his men close into the fortified area to engage the strongpoint and test its defences, before he made his final attack.

Now the Colonel turned to his other main objective, making contact with Sword Beach. He selected Z Troop's only surviving officer, Lt John Square, for the task. Square recalls:

Moulton instructed me to take a party eastwards to Petit Enfer to meet up with 41 Commando who were landing on Sword Beach. Our role was to form a link between Sword and Juno Beaches. I took four or five marines with me and we set off eastwards. I remember passing a dead civilian who had been blown into a hedge from his bike. He looked as if he was resting, sleeping peacefully. It is quite extraordinary, but dead bodies don't always look dead. We arrived in the south of Petit Enfer and occupied a big house near a stream. The house was empty and we had a good look around to see if we could find anything interesting. We did find an enormous pile of eggs there and later discovered that the house had previously been a German brothel. Then we settled down for a while and I began to feel rather vulnerable. We were well ahead of anyone else, at least a mile into enemy territory with no immediate support available. I told my sergeant to dig up some sods of turf and lay them out across the road to make the enemy think that we had mined the road. A short while later a farmer came down the road leading a herd of cattle and they started chewing up the grass! There was no sign of 41 RM Commando.

Marine Dougie Gray of B Troop, whose sea-going career began on tugboats in Plymouth Harbour until he signed up for the Royal Marines. He then served with MNBDOII before joining 48 RM Commando. (*Dougie Gray*)

Back along the seafront, both Hoare and Perry's troops were now in contact with the enemy. Sgt Maj Joe Stringer was in the lead of B Troop as it advanced, passing through, or knocking down, gaps in the walls between one garden or yard and the next. 'We cleared houses as we went and arrived in the rear of the village of Langrune. We then turned seawards along two roads running parallel with each other towards the sea. I was on the right-hand road which is now called Rue de Captain Perry, named after B Troop's commander. We moved from house to house as we progressed down the road and got within striking range of the strongpoint along the seafront. X Troop was moving along the left-hand road keeping abreast of us.' Moulton now moved up from his HQ to see the situation first-hand.

The Colonel had to approach Capt Perry's position through back gardens, scrambling over walls and through gates and side doors to get close to the seafront. The direct approach down the road was made impossible by enemy machine gun fire coming from the concrete pit in the middle of the crossroads. Even this oblique approach was fraught with danger as German mortar bombs were falling vertically into the gardens and houses, causing some casualties among the commandos. In reply, Lt Aldworth had set up one of his 3-inch mortars to provide some counter fire. In almost the last house before the strongpoint Moulton found B Troop's commander in the loft, closely watching the enemy. Capt Perry could see right down into the German post and was confident he could attack and capture the position as soon as he had a fire plan arranged. Moulton was pleased with the news and left the Captain to move over to X Troop to coordinate the attack.

Sgt Joe Stringer recalls:

After the colonel had left, Captain Perry called an O Group, attended by Lieutenant Rubinstein and all senior NCOs, giving us plans for attacking the strongpoint. We were in one of the last houses at the end of the street. After briefing us on the situation, he stepped outside to take a last look at the opposition before we put in our attack and he was immediately hit by a sniper's bullet and killed. Our only surviving officer was the very junior Second Lieutenant Rubinstein and he now became the Troop commander. He was new to the Commando and had only joined us just prior to D-Day.

The death of Capt Perry was another blow to Col Moulton, who had now lost his fourth troop commander in a matter of hours.

Rubinstein was shocked to find that all the men were now looking at him for orders as to what to do next. The nineteen-year-old subaltern had been catapulted into the unenviable position of leading a complete troop of commandos on this, his first day in action. He called all of his NCOs to him, badly in need of their advice and support. Joe Stringer remembers what happened next. 'At that same moment the enemy began to mortar us. A bomb crashed into the house and blew Rubinstein down some steps into the cellar. Two of the sergeants with me were injured in the blast. The lieutenant was not badly hurt, but this now left just Sergeant Bill Blythe and myself as the only sergeants in the Troop.'

More bad news followed shortly afterwards when 48 Commando lost its fifth troop commander that day. Capt Hoare was hit by sniper fire and had to be evacuated, leaving another junior officer, Lt Goodlet, in charge of the X Troop. The loss of these two commanders from the battle caused Moulton to rethink his plan of attack. He now told X Troop to keep up the pressure on the western end of the strongpoint while B troop closed right up to the eastern end. A Troop would then follow through the houses until it reached B Troop, then swing to the left and clear the houses fronting the strongpoint. This manoeuvre would completely surround the landward side of the German fortification.

At about this time, two Centaur tanks from the 1st Royal Marine Armoured Support Regiment arrived at Moulton's HQ and offered their help. The Colonel sent them on down the road to join B Troop. The Centaurs were slow, almost obsolete, tanks armed with a 95-mm (3.7-in) gun-howitzer. These armoured vehicles originally had their engines removed and were planned to be used on LCTs during the run in to the beaches as artillery, but Montgomery suggested that the engines should be replaced and the tanks used as self-propelled artillery during the first few days after the invasion to help establish a lodgement. Their presence up with the assault waves would add firepower to the infantry and help support them on their initial advance inland. The tanks were crewed by Royal Marines and fought, not together as a unit, but individually as and when required. Their arrival at Langrune was just what the Commando needed to get the attack going.

The first of the tanks lumbered down the eastern approach to WN26 firing its gun as it went. This enabled B Troop to close on the crossroads immediately in front of the right-hand concrete wall. Progress was good at first, as the shells of the tank's gun blasted the machine gun post on the crossroads and smashed into the reinforced houses marking the edge of the strongpoint. With B Troop now close to the edge of the German fortified position, its marines were well placed to launch an attack on its eastern corner. The main obstacle in their way was the six-foot-high wall blocking the street that led into the resistance post.

Col Moulton now came up to help direct the attack. Marine Jock Mathieson, one of HQ's dispatch riders, accompanied him: 'I was with the Colonel when he went forward to survey the strongpoint. He wanted a tank to blast the concrete wall that spanned the road ahead. He spoke to its commander through the phone on the side, but learned that the tank could not depress its gun sufficiently low enough to hit the base, so Moulton told him to keep pounding the concrete until it broke up.' The tank pounded the wall as instructed and expended all its ammunition trying to complete the destruction of the barrier, but the high-explosive shells it was firing just burst on the face of the wall hardly causing any more damage than just pockmarks. After it had fired its last shell, it reversed down the road and allowed the second Centaur to come forward.

The next tank was advancing along the road to take up its position when it suddenly shuddered to a halt in a sheet of flame and smoke. It had struck a buried anti-tank mine which had blown off its track. The Centaur was completely disabled by the blast and its crew baled out to join B Troop in the houses to the left of the road. The stranded tank was now blocking the main approach to the enemy position, isolated in a hitherto unknown minefield. It was another blow for Moulton.

For a moment the attack stalled, but Lt Rubinstein soon got it going again when B Troop tried once more to get across the road into the houses on the eastern side of the strongpoint. Now that the machine gun at the crossroads had been destroyed, the young officer was able to cross over and get into the right-hand house on the edge of the objective. The Germans did not like this move at all and began pounding the few marines with mortar and machine gun fire. Lt Rubinstein was in the house, but he could go no further, The rooms were sealed off by concrete and all doors led to dead ends; the only way into the strongpoint was through the concrete wall. Frustrated, the young subaltern brought his men back to the houses on the left-hand side of the road.

Col Moulton watches as the Canadian Wolverine self-propelled gun begins to manoeuvre past the knocked-out Centaur tank on its way forward to the strongpoint at Langrune. The house in the background behind the Wolverine marks the right-hand edge of the strongpoint. (*Imperial War Museum, B5148*)

While Rubinstein was isolated in the house on the opposite side of the road, Col Moulton spoke with B Troop's Sgt Maj Joe Stringer. 'By this time, because of the shortage of officers, we had started getting directions from Col Moulton himself. One of these was directed to me and my section. He told me to gather as much explosive together as I could and make a pole charge, then have a go at blowing the concrete wall which barred our way into the strongpoint.' Joe Stringer later described how he attempted to do this.

My section and I retreated to the railway line and scrounged some timber together. This we made into a sort of a builder's hod and put slabs of guncotton in to it. We then made our way down to the wall under some considerable fire, but fortunately not very accurate. We got right up to the wall, placed our charge, withdrew slightly and fired it. There was an almighty bang, but the demolition was unsuccessful. I didn't have much hope that it would be of great use, because we were unable to bring enough pressure on it to make any impact. The wall was very solid. By then my section and I were immediately under the wall and the Jerrys behind the wall were slinging over stick grenades. They were not very effective for they seemed to be made of thin metal more like cocoa tins. They were, however, tying them in bunches to make them more deadly. One bunch landed behind me and one of my section yelled out, 'Look out Joe!' I turned my back to it in a natural reaction and it went off, spattering me and one of my men with shrapnel. The amount of blood on my tunic led me to believe that I had a bad wound. We were by now in serious difficulties. Colonel Moulton saw what had happened and was concerned about us, so he called for us to withdraw. When I got back to our side of the road I called for a medic to have a look at me. He looked very hard to find any wounds and the only major thing he could discover was that the lobe of my ear had been badly serrated and that was where the large amount of blood was coming from. So it wasn't a 'Blighty' wound! A few bits had got into my rear end and thighs, which I carried for a number of years after I had come out of the services. They used to fester up occasionally and cause me some discomfort and would then work themselves out.

Once again an attempt to break into the strongpoint had come to nothing. Moulton felt that his Commando was now almost back where it had started from. His numbers were being whittled away by persistent enemy fire, the Germans holed up inside WN26 seemed as entrenched as ever, armoured support had achieved very little and the afternoon was turning into evening. In a few hours it would be dark.

Six miles away to the south-east something was happening which would divert the Colonel's attention from the strongpoint and give him a more sobering problem to contend with. The enemy were counter-attacking the beachhead with tanks.

In the late afternoon, Lt Harold Smedley received a signal from Brigade: 'Intelligence there had kept me up to date about the enemy situation throughout the day, then they informed me that a possible German armoured attack against our sector might take place that evening. It seemed that 3rd Division was being attacked by tanks and they were coming our way.' Moulton received the news with some dismay for his lightly armed commandos could be no match for tanks.

Brig Leicester, Commander 4th Special Service Brigade, came up to Langrune to speak with Moulton. He told the Colonel to call off any further attempts to capture the strongpoint and to seal off the garrison holed up inside until the next day. Moulton should then prepare Langrune for possible counter-attack against his rear from the south-east. The German 21st Panzer Division was at that moment driving towards the sea from a position just north of Caen at Lebisey. The enemy division had already halted British 185th Brigade's advance on Caen and were swinging to the north-west, heading for Lion-sur-Mer. If it reached the sea there, just two miles away from the Commando, it would have driven a wedge between the landings on Sword and Juno Beaches.

Orders now went out for everyone to assume a defensive mode, with all approaches to the village, especially from the south-east, to be covered. Harry Lane in Z Troop was part of the force holding the southern edge of Langrune. 'Sergeant Joe Telford came over to me and another marine and told us that a panzer division was heading our way. We were to hold the crossroads. We strung a few Teller mines across the road and then settled down in a slit trench to await the enemy. Two marines with two rifles against a German panzer division!'

Dennis Smith in the HQ signal section was also called to play his part in the defence. 'Towards the end of the day, after we had consolidated the position, we were told to expect a German counter-attack by panzer forces. I spent several hours holding the perimeter with Corporal Hilton, who was later killed at Walcheren. Outside the wall of the courtyard was a narrow lane with a German minefield on the other side. I was expected to lay an ambush for any tanks that might come along the road. So for several hours I lay there with a bag of No. 68 Anti-tank Grenades.'

If an attack by the enemy was to develop against the Commando, then the heavy support from the warships at sea would be required to help break it up. It was therefore essential that Capt Tyrer, and his naval bombardment group, were in a good position to call down this supporting fire. Ralph Dye, one of Capt Tyrer's men, remembers the evening of D-Day.

That night we went into a defensive perimeter. We had lost so many men killed that we were fairly well stretched-out. We were told to expect a German counter-attack by a panzer division. We were in a large villa surrounded by a big wall. There were several gaps in the wall and we looked out across a hillside to a line of trees. We were told that that was where the Germans would be massing for their attack, from about 500 yards away. We were asked to carry out a shoot from HMS *Belfast* to break up this assembly point, but we couldn't get through to the cruiser on our radios. We crawled outside the perimeter to try to get a better range on our backpack set. One telegraphist was peering at the dials with the light of a pencil torch. I told him he had better put the light out because there were German patrols about. I was right, for the next thing we knew there were mortar bombs homing in on us. We crept back through the wall and Captain Tyrer told Colonel Moulton that we just couldn't get through to the *Belfast*. He was a bit miffed with the news.

Still out in no-man's-land, isolated from the rest of the Commando and closest to the path that 21st Panzer Division would take if their attack made it to the sea, was Lt John Square and his men. 'As the day wore on nothing happened on our front. We waited for someone from 41 RM Commando to show up from Sword Beach, but they never did. Much later we saw a great fleet of gliders descend away to the east bringing reinforcements to the airborne division, but nothing of our relief. By this time it was beginning to get dark so I sent a runner back to HQ for instructions. I think they had forgotten that we were still out and sent back a message recalling us into the Commando's perimeter.'

Elements from German 21st Panzer Division did actually make it to the sea that evening. Some tracked vehicles from I Battalion, 192nd Grenadier Regiment reached the coast between Lion-sur-Mer and Luc-sur-Mer, just 2 miles away from the Commando. They joined up with some troops from the static 716th Division that were holding the coast and waited for their tanks to join them. It was a wonderful opportunity for *Generalmajor* Edgar Feuchtinger to exploit, but the German commander did not rise to the occasion. The great fleet of gliders that John Square had seen swooping over the beachhead, bringing British 6th Airborne's follow-up brigade, caused Feuchtinger to believe that these airborne landings were being directed at his rear in order to cut him off and called his troops back from the coast into a defensive position north of Caen. This retreat, however, was not appreciated by those in the beachhead and it took a long while for intelligence to pick this up. All units along the coast remained on high alert throughout the night, each nervously awaiting enemy armoured units to suddenly burst through on their front.

During the night, Dennis Smith was called out of his defensive post to complete another mission, as he later explained.

I was ordered to escort the Intelligence Officer, Lieutenant Smedley, to contact the Mayor of the town. It was very quiet with little firing taking place and only just a few distant flashes lighting up the sky. We did not know who was about and crept cautiously through the dark streets. We arrived at the house and the lieutenant went inside the gate. I was told not to let anyone through. Lieutenant Smedley tapped the door and was admitted. Thirty seconds later he came out and told me to come in. 'The Mayor does not want anyone to see you here,' he said. I think that at that time the French were still not sure that this wasn't just a raid and that if we withdrew those who had helped us would be in great danger from the Germans. Lieutenant Smedley made it very clear to the Mayor that the Allies were in France to stay.

At the close of D-Day, Lt Col Jim Moulton took stock of the situation. For the Commando the day had been a disaster. Casualties had been very high, much higher than had been anticipated. None of the Commando's main objectives had been completed and there was still a real danger of an enemy counter-attack. When Moulton counted the human cost, it made grim reading. Apart from Capt Linnell, the Commando had lost all of its troop commanders. There were just five officers left out of fifteen. In addition, the padre, John Armstrong, had been wounded and evacuated. Over forty commandos had been killed and many more wounded. These included some of the best NCOs and experienced marines in the Commando. Moulton still did not know what had happened to the bulk of Y Troop, except that those men were not now with him. Altogether, there were just 223 all ranks present at the end of the day out of the 500 or so that had left Southampton the day before.

Back on Nan Red Beach some of the wounded were still only just being attended to. Ian Mair of the Heavy Weapons Troop had been lying injured by the sea wall for over twelve hours. It had been an eventful time for him, waiting for someone to come to his aid, as he later recalled:

> I lay throughout the day near the high water mark at the top of the beach. After the main body of troops had moved inland we were sniped at by a German in a three-storey house close by. He was eventually eliminated by a Sherman tank. Later, two or three wounded Canadians had crawled under a disabled tank for protection. When the tide came in, the tank settled in the wet sand and trapped them underneath. No one could help them and the tank slowly sank down crushing and suffocating them. It was terrible to hear their screams. At about 7.30 that evening Sergeant Frank Burton came along the beach collecting mortar bombs and abandoned equipment and was calling out, 'Anyone from 48 Commando here?' He found me and took me, and some other wounded, to an Aid Post where I was given some attention. I was then laid in a ditch outside for two days. On Thursday night, 8 June, I was taken in a DUKW down to the beach for embarkation in an LCT. The German Luftwaffe raided the area that night and strafed the beach. Our DUKW driver leapt out of the vehicle and ran away shouting, 'The gas . . . the gas'. We just lay there helpless and cursing.

Further to the west, the wounded Dougie Gray still lay on the beach at the Canadian aid post. 'I was left on the beach for two days and was evacuated on the morning of the third day. We were left in the open while the worst cases were in tents. I was haemorrhaging from the wound in my back and this was affecting my breathing, but the shrapnel hadn't entered my lungs. They kept changing my dressings, but I needed surgery to remove the shrapnel. Eventually they got me back to a Canadian hospital in Basingstoke where they operated on me.'

CHAPTER EIGHT

The Strongpoint

At 0900 hours the next day, 7 June, two M10 armoured tank destroyers arrived in Langrune to help the Commando attack the strongpoint. Brig Leicester had liaised with the Canadians and arranged for these mobile anti-tank weapons to give assistance to Moulton's unit. Also available to the Commando was a troop commander's Sherman tank from the Royal Marine Armoured Support Regiment. These were the only armour available in the area at that time. All the tanks that had landed were employed on the Canadian advance. The M10 Wolverines had a normal Sherman tank chassis armed with a 3-in gun. Unlike a tank, the gun was mounted in a five-sided open-topped turret on an angled hull, which gave the tank destroyer a low silhouette. It was also lightly armoured and capable of good speed and mobility. None of these attributes, however, were needed in the bombardment of the strongpoint. Nonetheless, their presence at Langrune would give valuable support to 48 Commando and allow the marines to close right up to WN26 during the attack. Before that could be mounted, however, there was the problem of the blocked road to contend with.

Moulton considered, for a while, the possibility of switching the attack from the right-hand road over to the left-hand road. There was no concrete wall blocking the end of that road and entrance into the strongpoint might be more easily gained. Two big problems ruled out this approach. First, the machine gun at the left-hand crossroads in its well-protected casemate was still active, and, second, there was a very deep minefield extending over 50 yards blocking the approaches. He therefore decided to make another attempt along the right-hand road and attack the eastern corner once more, after he had found a way around the disabled Centaur.

Brig Leicester also gave Moulton the news that his area was free from the possibility of an enemy counter-attack. The whole of the Allied lodgement was being expanded that morning through the attacks being made by both the Canadians from Juno and the British from Sword. With Caen as their objective, the Germans would be too hard-pressed holding these advances to launch an counter-attack of their own. All of 48 Commando's effort could now be concentrated on reducing strongpoint WN26.

The Royal Marine Centaur in front of the strongpoint was disabled in an awkward position at the edge of the road, completely blocking the main approach to the concrete wall. To its right was a piece of open ground which was also mined. Moulton decided that a detour should be blown through

German dead in the Langrune strongpoint, lying just in front of one of the exits to a bunker. (*Imperial War Museum, B5196*)

this small minefield to enable the Canadian M10 to bypass the knocked-out tank. He gave the job of clearing this gap to Lt Mackenzie of A Troop. Once through the mines, the tank destroyer could bring its fire on to the wall, this time using solid shot rather than high explosive.

At 1130 hours, A Troop moved forward through B Troop's positions towards WN26. The commandos once again slipped back through the last of the houses near the strongpoint and approached the disabled Centaur in the road. While the rest of the troop gave supporting fire and a mortar laid down smoke, Mackenzie and a few of his men rushed across the road to the cover of the tank. They carried with them lengths of 'Bangalore Torpedo' – steel pipes packed with explosives. These weapons were primarily designed to cut gaps through barbed wire, but when laid on the ground they were also useful in exploding any mines beneath them. Mackenzie's men now connected several lengths of pipe together and pushed them out into the minefield to create a path around the tank. They then set the fuses and dashed quickly back across the road to the cover of the houses.

The explosion when it came was enormous. The Bangalore Torpedoes had set off some mines so the men watching were reasonably confident that a path had been cleared. The tank destroyer now crept slowly forward, gently easing itself off the road and round the Centaur, with all those watching expecting at any moment to see a mine go up underneath it. Nothing happened, the diversion was clear. Then the Wolverine edged back on the road and inched forward to a position just short of the crossroads. In the houses close by the commandos watched, ready to counter any anti-tank weapons that the Germans might bring forward. Inside the strongpoint all was quiet as the M10 brought its gun to bear on the wall and then opened fire. Its first shot hit the target with a metallic clang. The heavy anti-tank round that it fired cut its way right through the reinforced concrete, whining far out to sea. The solid shot projectile, fired at a very high velocity, carved its way easily through the wall, but left just a small jagged hole and a few chips of concrete. This round was followed by another and then another. Still the same result, the shot was penetrating the wall leaving small neat holes, but seemed to be doing little to reduce the structure to rubble.

Over the period of the next hour and a half, this M10 and its partner expended all their ammunition on the barrier. Surprisingly, results actually proved to be quite encouraging. The holes made by the solid shot were gradually being grouped together and the concrete between them had started to crumble. It was now time for the Sherman tank from the Royal Marine's Armoured Support Regiment to come forward and join in the attack. When it had got into position, it opened up with its 75-mm gun firing high explosive. This time the high explosive broke up the weakened concrete. The wall was beginning to come down as was the house to its right, for the ricochets from the solid shot and high explosives from the Sherman were gradually reducing the nearby dwelling to rubble.

Moulton was up with B Troop and decided that the time was approaching when his Commando could make a concerted attack on the strongpoint. The wall was still not down, but the top half had been breached, although not low enough to allow passage for tanks. X Troop, now under the command of Maj Sanders, was brought across from the left close to the strongpoint and Moulton formulated a plan. B and X Troops would be armed with picks, shovels and explosives and attack the wall and the approach by hand, while the others kept the German defenders bottled up with small-arms fire. A Troop would then get into the row of houses that made up the southern edge of WN26 and clear the buildings one by one. This movement would divert attention away from those commandos dealing with the wall. When the barrier had been breached, the Sherman would enter the fortification supported by infantry and sweep through to the promenade at the front of the strongpoint, clearing the bunkers and trenches facing out to sea.

At 1330 hours the attack began. Mackenzie took A Troop across the road and got his marines into the part-demolished house close by the wall. His men then began blowing an entrance into the main row of buildings on the left, clearing and blasting their way westwards along the houses which lined the road. They were soon followed across the road by B and X Troops, and while X Troop and some commandos from HQ Troop dealt with the wall, B Troop helped to clear the houses.

Although they had been surrounded and abandoned for over twenty-four hours, the German defenders fought tenaciously in the defence of the strongpoint. Common sense would have told them to give up the struggle the previous day, but the troops inside were fighting in the best traditions of the German Army and defending the post to the last, even though most of the troops inside were anything but German. The garrison here was from II Battalion, 736th Regiment, from *Generalmajor* Richter's 716th Infantry Division. These were second-rate static troops, a mixture of German nationals and eastern Europeans who had been coerced into fighting for the Third Reich. Their resolve and will to fight was bolstered by their dedicated German NCOs, who made it clear that any desertion or dereliction of duty would mean death. There was no alternative for them but to fight on. This they did with great courage, continuing to resist A Troop's progress through the houses. It was another blow for Moulton. The commandos had to fight from one house to the next, or from one garden to the next, against mortar fire, sniping and grenade throwing.

Outside WN26, X troop continued working feverishly in the open, blasting the houses and battering the wall. The barrier had been reduced to just a couple of feet high by the tanks, and this was now further reduced by the marines. Using picks, shovels and explosives, they demolished the wall, blew up a house and used the rubble from this to build a causeway over the remains of the anti-tank barrier. Then the Sherman came forward, rose up the ramp and flopped down into the strongpoint, spraying the compound with its heavy machine gun and blasting away with its 75-mm gun. Closely behind it came the commandos. Once through the wall they spread out and fired along the trenches and lobbed grenades into buildings. The tank went forward to the promenade and on to the seafront. Here it met misfortune when one of its tracks ran into a communications trench and the Sherman slipped sideways immobilising itself at an angle. Fortunately, it was in such a position that it could still use its machine gun and it continued to rake the seafront with fire.

The end of strongpoint WN26 came quickly. Once the tank had entered the inside of the fortification, its defenders realised that further resistance was futile. To carry on with the fight meant a senseless death. They decided to surrender. Jack Desmond was one of the marines who stormed the strongpoint and later recalled the end. 'Once we were inside, many of the enemy quickly gave themselves up. I began searching the prisoners. One of them was well over six feet tall and wore an overcoat that reached down to the

German prisoners from the Langrune strongpoint lined up after their capture. The commandos have obviously been well trained in the rules of containing the enemy: the prisoners are spaced well apart (to stop them conspiring together); they have their backs to a wall (to prevent escape); they have been stripped of their helmets, belts and packs (to stop them concealing any weapons) and they have been made to stand before an armed guard (giving them a sense of dejection and hopelessness). To those of a more sensitive nature, it does look as though they are about to be shot!
(*Imperial War Museum, B5143*)

ground. I put my hand into one of his pockets and pulled out an English grenade. I nearly shit myself with fright, thinking he had primed it to explode.'

Sgt Joe Stringer of B Troop later looked back over the taking of the Langrune strongpoint.

On the second day we got some help from tanks and managed to blow the wall and get into the strongpoint. Once inside the Germans gave up easily, they were not of high calibre. One was a bit slow in putting up his hands and I gave him a jab in the stomach with my Tommy gun. Colonel Moulton didn't like that sort of behaviour and snapped: 'There's no need for that, Sergeant!' Sergeant Bill Blythe had unfortunately stepped on a mine and received bad wounds which had him evacuated back to England. Sergeant Kemp had a very serious wound and lost a lot of blood from his head before we got him to the RAP. He survived and came back to join us later in the campaign. By the end of this second day, B Troop was down from 50 marines, 6 sergeants and 3 officers to just 15 men, myself and Second Lieutenant Rubinstein. Of course not all of the men we lost were killed, a lot were wounded and a lot had been drowned on the beach trying to swim ashore with heavy loads. Altogether it was a very, very sad day for 48 RM Commando for it had been a tragic introduction to the war. I think Colonel Moulton said that that was the day we finished our training. The youngest commando had come of age.

Thirty-one prisoners were taken at the Langrune strongpoint. When the Commando inspected the fortifications they were amazed at the thoroughness with which they had been constructed. The trenches, gun emplacements and mortar pits were lined with concrete. Ranges, bearings and other information about targets were painted on the walls of the bunkers and pits, allowing the German troops in the strongpoint to bring fire down against any point in Langrune or along the seafront without having to expose themselves. The machine guns in the crossroads were connected to the main position by underground passages. The capture of the 'fortress' owed a lot to the training in the techniques of street fighting that the Commando learned in the bombed-out areas of London.

The reduction of the Langrune fortifications tied up the whole of the Commando for most of the day. In consequence, the task of joining up with 41 RM Commando and Sword Beach was given over to 46 RM Commando, who had landed at St-Aubin at 0900 hours that morning. Originally this Commando had been destined to attack the German batteries at Houlgate and Beneville on the eastern side of the River Orne, but this operation was cancelled almost at the last moment. Therefore 46 RM Commando passed through 48 Commando in Langrune and made for Petit Enfer where its men attacked and cleared a German strongpoint along the seafront. Later that afternoon Sword and Juno Beaches were joined at last when 46 met up with 41 RM Commando at Luc-sur-Mer.

Back in Langrune, the tasks allocated to Col Moulton and his men had been completed. For the next two days their responsibilities were to police and tidy up Langrune and St-Aubin. One of the most immediate duties given to the commandos by their colonel was to attend to their fallen comrades. Lt John Square was the first to receive these orders, as he later recalled.

For some reason I was given the job of being Town Marshal for St-Aubin. I had no idea what my duties were, but I was given two Frenchmen to help me who sat on the floor waiting for instructions. I was then told by Moulton to arrange to bury the bodies of our dead who were still left on the beach. We got a group of our men together and buried mainly men from our Commando, but a few others who happened to be about, including Canadians who were still lying in the garden of the large house fronting the beach. The garden was supposed to be mined, but I don't think it was. We set up a small cemetery in the garden of another house close by. We wrapped up the bodies in their gas capes and conducted a moving burial service.

Moulton later remarked: 'The beach at St-Aubin was a shocking sight.' It was true, for the debris left by the assault still littered the shore. Damaged and burnt-out landing craft, tanks and transport were scattered among the

Graves of members 48 RM Commando, who were killed on D-Day, in the garden of a house behind Nan Red Beach. The bodies were later reinterred in the Commonwealth War Cemetery at Bayeux. (*Imperial War Museum, B5265*)

rolling surf, intertwined with the bodies of those killed in the fighting. Stores and equipment lay smashed and broken on the sand, being picked over by a few French civilians looking for canned food. The Colonel was saddened that nobody was dealing with the dead. All efforts still seemed to be focused on getting men and *matériel* ashore and moving inland.

One of the men delegated to deal with the corpses was Harry Timmins. He later recollected his thoughts and feelings:

About fifteen of us were told to go back to the beach. The Colonel had said that he was not having any of his lads lying there for anyone to stare at, so we had to dig four big graves each large enough to hold twelve to fourteen bodies. In all of the war, this was the most terrible job I had to do and it will live in my memory for ever. When the graves were dug, we then had to collect the lads and lay them in the graves, head to toe. The lad that had been chopped in half, I picked his waist and legs up and then had to collect the other half and fit him together, his blood was running down my tunic. I then found a nice corner for old 'Happy' Appleyard. He couldn't now go home and be admired for winning the MM in Sicily.

Eventually they were all lying in graves, including some sailors and Canadians. As I looked down at them, they were all staring up at me. I had a very strange feeling come over me, I kept thinking 'Why am I here, why aren't I lying there with them? I must be in the wrong place.' I honestly couldn't understand anything for a while. We then had to fill the graves in. We were throwing dirt and stones on their faces. This couldn't be right, I could feel the dirt and stones on their faces and I kept flinching. Finally we put some crosses on the top with a helmet or green beret to mark their resting place.

Another problem facing the Commando was that incoming infantry were experiencing difficulties because of small-arms fire caused by snipers. These newly landed troops would hear the crack of a bullet and start blazing away trying to root out the hidden enemy. This led to more firing and so on. Moulton called upon all British and Canadian units to leave the rounding-up of all snipers to the Commando. He ordered his men to use only bayonet, revolver and Thompson sub-machine guns in the process, thus eliminating rifle fire in the beachhead. Once this had stopped then all the sniper fire stopped also. Of course, there were no snipers.

The role of establishing order in the seaside villages gave the Commando time to reflect on its initiation into battle. The previous two days of fighting had been traumatic and costly to the unit. It now looked for a period of respite, as the Intelligence Officer Harold Smedley later explained. 'After completing our objectives, we looked hopefully at our packs believing that at any time we would be withdrawn. We had always been informed that the Commando would only be in action during the first few days of the invasion and then returned to England to prepare for the next mission.'

Nothing could be further from the truth. Now landed and established, the great Allied war machine needed all the men it could get and 48 RM Commando was seen as infantry to be committed wherever it was required. On 9 June, the Commando received its first batch of reinforcements, with new commanders arriving to take over B and A Troops and thirty other men to spread out among the other troops. The Commando then joined with 46 RM Commando to invest the German radar station at Douvres la-Délivrande.

The radar station was located about three miles due south of St-Aubin. It was another huge defended site full of underground bunkers and gun emplacements containing the principal radar installation for the Luftwaffe in Calvados. All of its weapons were, however, sited to defend the *Wassermann, Freya* and *Würzburg* radar equipment, not to counter any invasion over the beaches. Although heavily fortified and protected by wire, minefields and machine gun posts, it did little to interfere with the passage inland of the Canadians, who had bypassed it. Their role was to press on to Caen and to leave the capture of the station to those who landed later, but they also pressed on leaving the site for someone else. Those 'someone else' were the now resting marines of 46 and 48 Commandos, who were told to surround the site and keep the German defenders bottled up inside.

It was very clear to all who had surveyed the installation that even these two lightly armed Commandos together could not capture the place. The site covered ten acres and was criss-crossed with trenches, weapons pits, bunkers, mortars, machine guns, anti-aircraft and anti-tank guns. The wire surrounding the fortifications was twenty feet deep and the minefields extended fifty yards out from the wire. Beneath the ground there were hundreds of yards of tunnels and trenches linking together giant bunkers. The radar station was garrisoned by 8th Company of Luftwaffe 53rd Line Regiment under the command of *Oberleutnant* Kurt Egle. These men had been reinforced by panzer grenadiers from 21st Panzer Division, whose charge towards the sea on D-Day had petered out close by. Unable to retreat, some troops sought refuge in the radar station. The task of capturing this enormous strongpoint would have to be made through some careful preparation. It would take a huge bombardment and a set-piece attack by a sufficiently large number of troops backed by tanks to reduce it. For the moment 48 Commando's role was one of simple containment.

The Commando held the eastern side of the German complex, nearest to the small town of Douvres, while 46 Commando held the western approaches. Night patrols and daytime observation kept the enemy inside. Lt John Square later remembered one of these night-time sorties into no-man's-land.

> I was told to take a patrol and look around the perimeter of the German strongpoint. I took four men with me and placed a 'getaway' man at the rear. The 'getaway' man usually follows the main patrol about fifty to a hundred yards behind, so that if anything goes wrong with the patrol, he can report back to HQ and tell them what has happened. It was a lovely night with a bright moon clearly illuminating the strongpoint, and us as well no doubt. We moved closer to the German encampment along the hedgerows of the adjoining fields. The trouble was there were cows in one field and they came over and started following us. Very soon the patrol had the whole herd shuffling along behind. We were trying to make a silent approach, but the jostling, mooing gathering around us rather gave the game away. It was clear that we would soon be noticed so I decided to abandon the patrol and started back to our lines. There was no sign of our 'getaway' man; we looked for him but he had gone. He had obviously felt lonely and vulnerable on this his first patrol and had given up. I later found him back with the troop.

Harry Lane recalls holding part of the perimeter on the edge of Douvres:

> A few houses had to be checked out and I was ordered to make sure one of them, a small cottage, was clear of the enemy. Sergeant Joe Telford told me not to go in through the front door in case it was booby trapped, but to try to get in through a back window. I approached the house and forced my way through a downstairs window and found myself inside a bedroom. The bed still had a duvet on it, half thrown back as though it had just been vacated. Above the bed was a crucifix and next to it a bedside table. On the table was a photograph of a wedding scene, with a man and his wife smiling at the cameraman. I felt like an intruder. I had entered someone's inner sanctum, their personal and private place. It was all very strange to me; I was just nineteen years old at the time and it affected me considerably. I was a well-trained, tough commando; I had killed two Germans and yet here in that room I felt I was doing something very wrong. I still think of that bedroom. I can close my eyes and picture every detail.

After a few days at Douvres, the Commando was on the move again. 4th Special Service Brigade had been ordered across the River Orne to join

Veterans from 48 RM Commando pay homage to their fallen comrades by their memorial on the site of the strongpoint at Langrune, 6 June 2002. (*Ken Ford*)

British 6th Airborne Division's lodgement holding the eastern flank of the invasion. Lord Lovat's 1st Special Service Brigade, consisting of 3, 4 and 6 Commandos plus 45 RM Commando, was already in the area and had been since its arrival over Sword Beach on 6 June. It was the force that joined up the invasion beaches with the airborne landings. Brig Leicester's brigade was now to hold the northern part of the Airborne Division's line as infantry.

Across the Channel, those who had been wounded during the invasion were being treated. All of them had been evacuated from the beachhead and sent back across the water to the many hospitals, civilian, military and temporary, that were organised to receive them. Because no one knew what the scale of casualties would be during the invasion, most medical facilities in southern England were requisitioned for military use. Dougie Edwards came back via Southampton. He was one of the first D-Day casualties to return:

> I recall arriving at a small jetty where a fleet of ambulances were waiting to evacuate the wounded to local hospitals. I was operated on and generally tidied up and a few days later taken by hospital train to Bradford Royal Infirmary. Prior to the landing I had been given a yellow aircraft identification panel. This was wrapped around my body to be laid out on the ground as required to advise Allied aircraft of the forward position occupied by Allied forces. The idea was that anything ahead of the panels was the enemy and was 'fair game'. The doctor on board the support vessel who first treated me sent it to my mother with a note saying that as it was attached to me so firmly, it obviously was important to me and therefore he'd like her to have it and to pass it on to me when I was fit.

CHAPTER NINE

Sallenelles

At 1630 hours on 11 June, the Commando moved out of Douvres and headed east, crossing the River Orne and its canal by the now famous 'Pegasus Bridge' which had been taken by Maj John Howard's company of the Ox and Bucks Light Infantry during the first few minutes of D-Day. The marines were put into the line holding the village of Hauger, relieving the 12th Parachute Battalion, who had been in contact with the enemy since their landings. The paras had had a rough time in the line, repulsing numerous German attacks, and they were now exhausted. The Commando took over the positions in and around the village with the grim news that 4 Commando had been attacked the previous day near these positions.

Ralph Dye remembers joining the airborne lodgement.

We marched past fields of gliders and over Pegasus Bridge. I remember seeing the corpse of an Ox and Bucks man who was still unburied. We arrived near the village of Hauger and became front-line troops guarding the extreme north-east corner of the whole Allied landings. We arrived at dusk. I was in my jeep in low gear and you could hear the noise of the engine for miles. We went through the village to the crossroads and woods, turned left and continued up a lane. The Germans laid down a barrage into the area for they had registered their guns previous to our arrival and knew where we were. Everybody was as tense as hell. Halfway along the track we passed a burning truck with a little matchstick figure of a man sitting stiffly inside, burned to death at the wheel. I was in my jeep thinking I bet these guys are cursing me because of the engine noise.

Lt John Square also recalls his arrival in the line. 'It was a wet summer's evening, sunny and sultry. We waited in the orchard before we got to Hauger and eventually took over the village when the paras pulled out. There was a lot of rubbish left strewn about, filing cabinets, papers, furniture and such like, all left by the Germans who had left the place in a hurry.'

Not all the commandos were kept together for this move; some were sent a little further south to help hold the edge of the village of Amfreville while the airborne put in an attack. Ted Brooks was one of them.

I was with a group of about eighteen that reached the outskirts of Amfreville during the early evening. It was decided that we would stay there for the night without digging in. Most of us got under some sort of cover, but never dug in. At 8 p.m. the Airborne Division laid down a barrage of mortars, artillery and machine guns, much of which seemed to land in our area. We didn't know it at the time but the German position was only two to three hundred yards away from us. A three-ton lorry some twenty yards away was set on fire which may have contributed to the intense fire directed at us. At 10 p.m. the barrage was lifted and the airborne attacked, only to be driven back immediately. They ran into the village and within minutes seemed to be running back out again. Then the Germans replied with a similar barrage for the next two hours before the airborne men once more advanced and captured their target. This was an unforgettable experience and my first taste of real fright, no doubt aggravated by the fact that we were not engaged in the battle but just vulnerable spectators.

Hauger was situated on the top of a hill, with a good view northwards to the village of Sallenelles and the German gun positions in the marshes near Franceville Plage. Civilians from Sallenelles reported that the place was free of Germans, but they were holding, in some force, a fortified strongpoint located about a half-mile to the north-east at the Moulin du Buisson. On hearing this news, Brig Leicester decided to move his line 1,000 yards further to the north to the outskirts of Sallenelles and establish new positions on the high ground looking down on the village. Sallenelles itself would be held by patrols. 48 RM Commando would take up this new position, with the line adjusted on either side to accommodate the move; 47 RM Commando would secure the ground on its left, while 3 Commando was established on its right. At 1300 hours the next day, the Commando moved down the hill and dug itself into these new positions.

X Troop, under the command of Capt Linnell, led the commandos into the area and found Sallenelles, as expected, unoccupied by the enemy. Linnell and his men then moved on a scouting patrol through the village and bumped into a few Germans making their own patrol. They took flight immediately when they saw the commandos sweeping towards them. In his official history of the Commando, Linnell described how the sector was defended:

> On our first arrival in the Sallenelles position on 12 June slit trenches were dug and that for the moment was our defensive line. Gradually positions were strengthened. Wire and mines were disgorged reluctantly by ordnance dumps – defence stores were a very low priority in the landing of supplies. Slit trenches were deepened, head cover was put on – an important precaution in orchard country where shells frequently detonated in the trees – and eventually a linked-up series of Troop positions was constructed. Our front was protected by both anti-tank and anti-personnel mines which, while they gave protection, also caused casualties among incautious personnel, especially signallers who once followed cable into a minefield. Houses which we occupied were strengthened by shoring and sand bags, and camouflage netting was erected to lessen the direct observation of our positions from Franceville Plage, of which fortunately the enemy availed himself little.

The Commando was now being used as infantry in a manner for which it had not been prepared, as Lt Harold Smedley recalled: 'We were untrained in defensive tactics, the whole emphasis in our training had been on the attack. Nor were we prepared for this type of service, we had few support weapons of our own.' The training the Commando had received at Achnacarry had been on fieldcraft and commando techniques, while that carried out at Gravesend and in London was on the use of weapons and street fighting. The exercises and manoeuvres which took place in Sussex were amphibious. All of these were focused on the attack. As Capt Linnell later wrote: 'We had to learn the technique of defence and fight as we went along. In the eighty days available to train and equip the Commando before the invasion, only desultory attention could be given to defensive fighting and patrolling against static positions; there was barely time to teach the essentials of battle training and the use of weapons. As Maj Sanders, the Commando's second-in-command said, 'We have only reached page 34 of the training manual.'

Once it had established itself in the line, the Commando set about stamping its authority on the area. The enemy had to be shown who was in charge and just who had the initiative. The unit might be in a defensive position, but its aggressive spirit was not to be dampened by static warfare. Moulton insisted that the enemy must be harassed at every opportunity.

Ralph Dye and the Bombardment Observers from the Royal Artillery remained with the Commando for some time as the warships at sea were still available to support ground troops for the first few weeks after the invasion. Dye remembers looking for advantageous positions from which to observe the enemy, as he explained later. 'Captain Tyrer and I went well forward looking down the lane for a suitable site for our observation post. The battlefield was so silent; you could almost hear the silence. It was a menacing sort of silence as though nothing is happening. You were aware of every twig snapping and every leaf rustling. We drove down the road and I looked across to the captain and he looked back at me. We mutually agreed that we were probably heading for the German lines. I quickly did a three-point turn and raced back to the safety of our lines.'

The actual forward line was a ragged affair which ran along certain lanes and across certain fields. It was by experience that the marines knew where they could show themselves and where they could not. Both sides patrolled by day and night so it was always possible that you could run into the enemy at virtually every bend in the road. It was said that the local *estaminet* in the village was frequented by both sides and more than one commando has admitted to hearing that German troops were going out the back door as they came in the front.

Capt Geoff Linnell recalls this close association with the enemy.

Our lines were just a few hundred yards apart and we shared a house in the middle of no-mans-land with the Germans. It overlooked a concrete strongpoint of theirs. They might use it one day and we would try to use it the next. From the windows we could direct mortar fire on to their strongpoint when we saw any movement. We used it as a forward observation post and were always sending patrols up to it. The Germans were not very aggressive; they preferred to just sit it out. They were not exactly passive for they were very active with their mortaring, but not very active with patrolling. Our morale in the unit was very high and we actively patrolled to deny the area to the enemy.

The RSM, Colin Travers, also remembers the type of warfare he experienced in Sallenelles. 'It was a period of night patrols and observing the enemy. I did not go on any patrols but had the responsibility of controlling our snipers. We had two snipers and I would go out and place them in spots I had selected beforehand. The HQ occupied a farmhouse and its outbuildings. Our medical station was in one of the barns. Moulton

Gen Montgomery pins the Military Medal on 48 Commando's L/Cpl Tickle (RAMC) for his brave work tending to the wounded on Nan Red Beach on D-Day. The commando in the foreground is Marine Vardy from 46 RM Commando, who also won the MM. (*Imperial War Museum, 7391*)

had a large dugout built in the yard away from the house and the signallers and other personnel all had their own dugouts. Most of the day was spent in these, protected from enemy shelling, and at night we came into the house and barns.'

Capt Tyrer's artillery spotters knew that they would soon be leaving the Commando when the warships left the area, but for the time being they needed somewhere to set up their equipment. Ralph Dye's last days with the Commando ended sooner that he was expecting, as he later recalled.

We took over a small villa for our radio post and my three chaps wanted to sleep upstairs. I said to hell with that, we are now in the front line and we are digging slit trenches outside in the garden. So all of us began digging for cover. It was back-breaking work, but we persevered. No sooner had we finished digging than we were shelled by German 88-mm guns. Unfortunately, I was caught in the open and got hit by a piece of shrapnel in the left lung. The piece of metal hit me just by my left aorta valve and I was in a bad way. It was touch and go with me. I was carried down into the basement of the villa where the MO, 'Doc' Winser, saved my life.

Next day at dawn, I was loaded on to a jeep ambulance and taken back to the coast. I remember there was a lot of fighting going on as we left, machine gun fire and mortars everywhere. I was taken to a great medical tent outside Ouistreham ready to be evacuated to England, but the weather was so bad, with great storms in the Channel, that the wounded could not be got out to the ships. After I was unloaded from the jeep I was laid side by side with rows and rows of other wounded men. Above us a Mitchell bomber was circling round and its crew were bailing out. Just as I was being moved into the tent, the bomber tipped over and plunged down into the next field, exploding with great force. I later learned that my brother, serving with the 1st Norfolks, was also close by with his unit and was watching the incident.

I lay on a stretcher for three days. I was in a bad state with my lungs gradually filling with blood. There were hundreds of us there lying on stretchers; we got little individual attention for there were too many wounded and too few medical staff. By the time I was taken off the stretcher and transferred to the hospital ship *Duke of Argyll*, I was pretty near dead. I remember being hauled roughly up the side of the ship and the stretcher catching on every obstacle that it could. We landed at Southampton just as the town was experiencing the arrival of German V1 pilotless bombs. I was moved to the General Hospital and it became a medical test of endurance whether or not I survived.

The airborne lodgement east of the River Orne was vital to 21st Army Group's future plans. Montgomery had been denied Caen by the 21st Panzer Division on the first day of the invasion and was unable to capture the city for the next seven weeks. The area carved out by the paras, and now held by them and the commandos, was surrounded on three sides by the enemy. Its only links with the beaches were across the River Orne and its canal. After Montgomery had failed to capture Caen by a frontal assault, he tried again by attempting to outflank the city from the west. When this operation broke down he devised another plan, which involved an attack round the eastern side of Caen through the airborne lodgement. To do this he needed all the troops and armour he could muster. This meant leaving the 6th Airborne Division and the 1st and 4th Special Service Brigades in the line as infantry to hold on to the lodgement while the attack took place. It was a poor way of using these assault troops, but Montgomery seemed to have no other choice.

Opposing the Allied troops in the Orne lodgement were the German 346th and 711th Infantry Divisions. When the invasion came, British 6th Airborne Division had descended on two battalions of German 716th Division. Both of these units, 1st Battalion 736th Regiment and the 642nd 'Ost' Battalion, virtually disintegrated under the weight of the determined paratroopers that fell among them. During 6 June the 711th Division, based a few miles to the north-east at Deauville, moved into the area to counter the landings, quickly followed by 346th Division from Le Havre. These two divisions now held the airborne perimeter, with two regiments of the 346th Division, 857th and 858th Regiments, opposite the northern sector in front of the commandos. Also in the northern line were the remnants of 642nd 'Ost' Battalion. This unit was made up from 'volunteers' from eastern countries occupied by the Nazis, mainly Poles and Russians. They endured

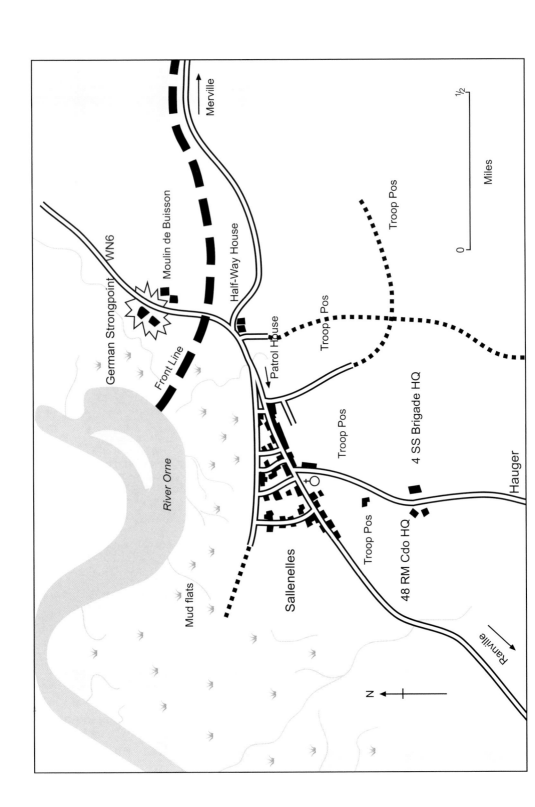

Merville

Moulin de Buisson

German Strongpoint WN6

Half-Way House

Patrol House

Front Line

Troop Pos

Troop Pos

River Orne

Troop Pos

4 SS Brigade HQ

Hauger

Mud flats

Sallenelles

Troop Pos

48 RM Cdo HQ

Ranville

N

Miles

0   ½

a strange war far from their homeland, fighting for the Germans in France against the British. It was not surprising that they had little stomach for it and would often desert at the earliest opportunity.

The northern sector of the airborne salient, from Breville to the Orne estuary, was held by the two Special Service Brigades. This put eight Commandos, albeit each well below strength, into a fairly small stretch of front line. Between them and the sea were probably an equal number of Germans. Maj Gen Gale had considered extending the front northwards to the sea and pushing the Germans eastwards away from this part of the coast, but the gains made would not be worth the inevitable losses incurred. He therefore decided that this front would remain static until the Allies broke out of their beachhead and outflanked these Germans in the north. In the meantime the Commandos would hold the line, restrict German counter moves by constant patrolling and gain intelligence about enemy dispositions. No major German attack was expected from this sector as there was little to be gained there except the ground itself. Both sides knew that the future of the defence of Normandy lay to the south of Caen where armour could come to battle on the plains in front of Falaise.

With so many Commandos occupying a limited front, the areas available for patrolling were strictly controlled. For 48 RM Commando, it was confined to the ground to the north of Sallenelles which consisted of marshland, open fields and a concrete enemy strongpoint. The Commando's official history described the type of patrols that were carried out.

> We sent out various forms of fighting-cum-recce patrols; for example, a listening patrol would lie-up for several hours by a possible enemy patrol route and report movements; an ambush patrol of greater strength would engage the enemy if he approached their position; a fire-drawing party would fire into the known enemy positions and pinpoint his machine guns when he fired back in return. From these and similar operations we discovered that the enemy rarely, if ever, ventured forward of his lines, but that he reacted strongly if we went too near his. Few nights or days passed without someone being forward of our lines.

The defence of the sector was based on troop localities and a Commando reserve. Sallenelles itself was held by a standing patrol of troop or half-troop strength, whose task was to observe the German strongpoint at the Moulin du Buissons and give notice of any enemy approach. The troop positions were set out in an arc across the hills to the south of the village. Moulton's HQ was located in a farmhouse along the road to Hauger at la Perruque, about 400 yards south of Sallenelles. Opposite in a much larger house was the HQ of Brig Leicester's 4th Special Service Brigade. The first few days at Sallenelles were relatively quiet as Capt Flunder's batman, Vince Horton, recalls: 'We were able to get the plates and cutlery out in the officers' mess and actually set the table with a cloth on it, but this soon changed as the enemy sent over more and more shells.'

Opposite: 48 RM Commando's Positions at Sallenelles

Sgt Percy Bream was one of the signallers based at Moulton's HQ and remembers that it was important for them to all be underground during the day because of enemy shelling: 'A Troop was given the job of digging an underground bunker for Moulton and his HQ to use. I had another bunker dug some way away. We used these underground positions during the day, but moved into the farmhouse at night.' In an outhouse, the officers set up their mess and 'Doc' Winser had his aid post in the remainder of the building. He was soon in business dealing with casualties, some of whom were from the headquarters group themselves when the buildings were hit by six shells and closely missed by six others. Marine Gosling, Lt Grant's batman, was hit during the barrage and died in the aid post as the MO was tending to him.

Lt John Square recalls his position overlooking the road from Ranville and the Orne river: 'Z Troop was situated just short of the village. My section held the left-hand side including the road. We had inherited a great hole in the road to house a machine gun and slit trenches were dug for the rest of us. A busy period of patrolling then followed. I seemed always to be hearing the cry "Send John Square out." No sooner had one patrol been completed than plans for the next were being considered.'

CHAPTER TEN

Life in the Line

One of the strangest things about Sallenelles was that the French civilians continued to live in the village. They suffered considerably during this period, but stubbornly refused to leave their homes. They were all most helpful to the Commando, especially the Mayor. He in particular was taking a great risk, for if the Germans should ever take back the village his fate would have been certain death. Capt Linnell thought that there could have been few inhabited villages in the whole of the war that remained so long in no-man's-land. In the surrounding fields the farmers also went about their daily life, herding their cows and trying to bring in a harvest, risking death in the minefields and injury during the shelling. It was a strange contrast for the Commandos to see such normality right there among them while they fought a brutal war.

Fred Wyatt recalls his first meeting with one particular local Frenchman:

We had just arrived in the village and it had been drummed into us to be wary of any locals who might be fifth columnists. I was at the crossroads outside the village when a Frenchman came up to me with a bottle. He seemed very glad to see me and offered me the bottle. I took a large swig and then almost collapsed. The drink seemed to burn a path down into my stomach. I was sure that the Frenchman had poisoned me and grabbed him by the throat, trying to throttle him. Just then Captain Godkin intervened and asked me what was the matter. I told him that the civilian had tried to poison me. The captain took a small sip and said, 'Don't worry, it's only Calvados'.

Sgt Percy Bream recalls his time in the line:

Our lines overlooked the village and we held the built-up area with one troop and kept the Germans out by vigorous patrolling. Our HQ was on a hill looking down on the village alongside the road. Down the road, at the bottom of the hill was a café. My senior corporal, McElhone, and I used to skive down there from time to time. We used to walk down the hill and ask at the café if there had been any Germans there and were often told they had just gone. We would then stay and have a drink. The only thing that they had was absinthe. The Germans used to do the same. Both sides used the café.

At the north-eastern edge of the village, on the road that led out towards the German strongpoint, was a large house called 'Les Aigles' with a walled garden. This was the last house in the village and it overlooked the fields toward the Moulin de Buisson. To the Commando it was known as the 'Patrol House'. Each troop in turn spent some time in the house, watching for the enemy and guarding the approach to the village. Most patrols that went out towards the German lines started from here. It was also a spot frequented by visitors who wanted to see the front line, as Geoff Linnell explains: 'The Patrol House was a favourite viewpoint for "trippers," who could then go back to England and say that they had gone into no-man's-land and observed the enemy. The *Daily Telegraph* correspondent, visiting one day, described his trip to "General Eisenhower's Left-Hand Man" and his glass of cider taken in a café in no-man's-land.'

Lt John Square recalls his time at the Patrol House: 'The house was held at various times by various troops. It had been occupied by the enemy before we came and I think that A Troop found a dead German in the attic there. Whenever any German patrols tried to come close to the house they were shot at and this seemed to keep them away.'

Patrols became the natural order of things. Moulton insisted that they be carried out by day and by night, never allowing the enemy to feel that he could move around in the area between the two lines. They might not be actually occupying this land, but the marines of 48 Commando still regarded everything to the north of Sallenelles as being their territory. With so few men in the Commando – it was still only at about 60 per cent of its nominal strength – everyone had to take their turn out in no-man's-land. Lt Harold Smedley, the Intelligence Officer, besides organising and setting objectives for the patrols was also included in the programme as he later recalled: 'We had an active system of patrolling organised by the Commanding Officer with two main objectives, one was to find out who the enemy was in this area, and, two, to keep the enemy stirred up so that he didn't have a chance to relax. Because of the shortage of available officers – we had lost so many on D-Day – everyone was required to take patrols out at night, including me.'

Vince Horton, Capt Flunder's batman, was on one of the first daylight patrols and he clearly remembers what happened: 'We had only just started out and I was moving along the road close by a hedge with the others when I was temporarily blinded and knocked unconscious by a loud explosion.' Horton had stepped on an anti-personnel mine and his lower right leg below the knee had been shattered. 'The remnants of my leg were just held on by a few strips of skin,' he recalls. 'My left arm was also badly damaged and the blast had peppered my left leg with shrapnel. I was taken to a field hospital near the beaches at Ouistreham, but spent some time in a tent there unable to be evacuated to England because of the violent storms in the Channel. By the time I arrived back in Southampton, medics had managed to save my right leg above the knee, but I lost the whole of my other leg through gangrene from the shrapnel wounds which had became infected.'

Other headquarters troops were also involved in these patrols. One of them was Signaller Ted Brooks:

When we had established ourselves near Sallenelles, we began a period of some normal duty, but with the added detail of several patrols. If things had been normal we wouldn't have gone on patrol, but the Commando was so short of men we had to play our part. Patrols are not pleasant but were made bearable by the fact that those with you were in the main

Marines from the Commando dig slit trenches beside a stone wall near Langrune.
(*Imperial War Museum, B5223*)

experienced and very reliable. Patrolling from Sallenelles was mainly at night. We were always looking for prisoners to take to gather information. We were out for about three hours at a time. There were usually about five or seven men in the patrol, all of whom you could trust. We had great confidence in each other and weren't all that worried at the time. We were usually led by a troop sergeant, sometimes an officer. During our time at Sallenelles the Commando's numbers were increased, but all troops remained well under strength and our overall personal position, lack of sleep, etc., never really improved all the time we were there.

Some patrols were uneventful and some were full of incident. Most men had heart-stopping moments when the enemy was alerted to their presence, or the Germans suddenly decided to rake the area with fire. Occasionally a patrol might stumble into an enemy patrol, or come across a few Germans holed up themselves watching the Commando's line. Each time a patrol went out, it never knew what to expect, as John Square recalls: 'I was taking a night patrol of myself and two others . . . when, just after we had left the base, the enemy guns opened up. The shells were coming in our direction so we threw ourselves down on the road. There was a little bank on either side, no more than three feet high. The shells landed quite near, but we were protected by the bank. I remember seeing the flash of red-hot splinters of shrapnel streaking over our heads in the dark.'

Sometimes it was something quite innocuous that struck fear into a patrol, as it once did to Lt Harold Smedley: 'I remember one patrol in which we wanted to know how far the enemy troops were from us. I was leading the patrol and suddenly the chap alongside me stopped and pointed to a light shining through the bushes. We all froze until we discovered it was a glow worm.'

Lt Col Moulton himself would sometimes take out a patrol, usually when some specific piece of information was required. On one occasion, Moulton was asked by Brig Leicester to see if 48 Commando could mount a small operation against the enemy. 47 RM Commando on the left had successfully made a raid on the German lines, supported with a great deal of fire from the rear. Moulton was now asked to do likewise. In order to find a suitable objective and to plan a different type of raid, he needed to have a closer look at the terrain. He took two of his troop leaders with him, Mackenzie and de Stacpoole, and a small escort. They blackened their faces, gathered their weapons and set out in the afternoon sunshine.

The patrol moved out to the left, avoiding the strongpoint at the Moulin de Buisson and approached the German line. Almost immediately they were spotted by a German sentry, who opened fire. Moulton felt he should have abandoned the patrol then and there, but under his insistence the group pressed on. A short time later, while moving along the line of a hedge, they were pulled up by a burst of machine-gun fire. They stopped and began to go back when another burst of fire raked the hedge, hitting two of the escorting marines. The Colonel thought that the fire was coming from the enemy lines, but there was a German standing at the end of the hedge with a *Schmeisser* sub-machine gun looking for the commandos. The patrol had the sun behind them and, with their dark clothes and blackened faces, were difficult for the German to see. In contrast, the enemy soldier was in the sun with his pink face showing brilliantly above his grey uniform. Moulton took a rifle and shot him dead. The rest of the patrol grabbed the two wounded men and began to make their escape as more German fire ripped through the hedgerow, closely followed by stick grenades. The patrol had met a German patrol coming down the other side of the hedge. Other enemy guns now opened up firing on fixed lines, crossing the area through which Moulton and his men were trying to escape. Both of the wounded men were in a bad way and died while they were being carried back. They were left along the way to be recovered later that night. Without further incident the patrol made it back to the village.

Moulton, however, was soon out on another patrol as Lt John Square remembers:

One night I was told to take a patrol up to the German strongpoint. While I was up at the Patrol House waiting to go out, the Colonel came in. It was not long after Moulton had come back from a patrol that had been shot up. He turned to me and asked me where I was going. I told him and he replied that he would come with me. Moulton, myself and two others left the house and crept out towards the strongpoint. We went through one lot of wire towards another very close to the Germans, creeping along silently, when suddenly a bird right in front of us took flight, screaming loudly into the night. Although this startled us, it startled the Germans even more and they began firing. Fortunately, we knew that we would be safer remaining flat until it was all over. It took some nerve to lay there with all the firing going on, but we were not spotted and eventually returned to base.

Patrols could often improve their striking power by the addition of extra weapons, as Jack Desmond explains: 'We sometimes took with us a PIAT gun and used it as a mortar. I remember once being on the right-hand side of the PIAT when it was being fired. The next thing something hit me in the shoulder. I thought it was a stone, but it turned out to be the tail end of one of the PIAT bombs. Luckily, I had a new type of vest on which had a pack on the back and pouches in the front, I was trying it out to see what it was like. The bomb was cushioned by the vest and just gave me a sore shoulder rather than a wound.'

Whatever the objectives or the role, nobody liked taking out a patrol. Everyone had to do their share of them, from the Colonel right down to the transport section, for even the drivers and the dispatch riders all had to take their turn out in no-man's-land. If picked, it was a question of steeling the nerves and getting on with the job. The thing that bothered most people was the unpredictability of a patrol. You could take all the precautions necessary, listen carefully to the briefings from the Intelligence Officer, camouflage yourself to perfection and proceed with the utmost caution and stealth, and still things beyond your control could interfere. The enemy might be waiting for you, ready to ambush you when you reached a certain point. Perhaps you might suffer from the effects of a 'funny five minutes' when, for no apparent reason, all of his guns would open up firing on fixed lines or known assembly points. The moon might suddenly pass from behind a cloud and illuminate you in full sight of an enemy sentry. Each time an individual was told he was out on patrol that night, his heart sank into his boots.

Between the Patrol House and the German strongpoint was the Halfway House. This formed the base from which the Commando's snipers operated, often in daylight. RSM Colin Travers was responsible for organising and placing the snipers and often accompanied them to their lairs as he later recalled: 'I often took the snipers out and stayed with them for a while. On one occasion they did a shoot, but I couldn't see if they had had a hit or not. Then things suddenly became rather nasty. We had been spotted by the enemy and he had located our position. He started to fire at us, completely pinning us down. We had to crawl all the way back, we couldn't stand up because they knew exactly where we were. We had a very close escape that time.' During their spell at Sallenelles, the snipers had some considerable success claiming twelve of the enemy killed. The disruption they caused to the smooth running of the enemy front line was immeasurable.

Those killed by snipers were very unfortunate, for most deaths in Normandy and elsewhere during the war were not as a result of some enemy soldier getting a bead on him with a rifle. To be killed by a small-arms bullet was the exception, as John Square explains: 'Most men in war were killed by artillery or mortar fire. It is extraordinary, but it was not often that you ever fired your gun at an actual German. I don't know if I ever killed any. I may have done from a distance, but I never saw any individuals that I had killed.'

Life in the line at Sallenelles was not all patrols, for most of the days and the nights were static, boring and endless. Someone was always on guard, posts were always manned and life went on mainly under ground or out of sight of the enemy. Without warning any part of the area might be shelled, mortared or subjected to machine-gun fire. It was not trench warfare as in the First World War, but it was a case of getting below ground as much as possible for safety's sake. As we have seen, Moulton and his team had big dugouts prepared near his headquarters for use during the daylights hours, then withdrew into their farmhouse at night. The commandos in their individual troop positions also dug deeper and deeper trenches for cover, adding little luxuries to them to make themselves more comfortable. Ted Brooks remembers his home from home in the line: 'Gilbert Risden and I had a very good trench. We had dug a wonderful deep trench and had boarded it right over for overhead protection. It had a staggered L-shaped entrance to prevent enemy fire from coming in the sides, quite comfortable really. We were quite safe from enemy shelling.'

Unfortunately, not everyone could be free from the shelling. Work had to go on all the time to keep the Commando operating in the line. Signallers had to go out to fix lines, food and ammunition had to be brought forward to replenish the troops in their positions, and orders had to implemented and carried out. Certain people in the Commando had to be out and about through most of the day. One of them was a dispatch rider Jock Mathieson: 'In the area of Sallenelles we took all messages between HQ and the troops on foot. In quiet areas such as this, once you started up your bike you became a target for German mortars.'

Each side had good observation of the other's lines. The Commando probably had the best, because it had the advantage of height, but the Germans could also get a good view of any movement along certain lanes and across the fields which skirted the village. Sgt Percy Bream recalls this constant feeling of being watched: 'If you went out of your bunker down by the headquarters and looked around, you would almost always get a mortar come over. We could see them and they could see us. I remember that we could see them leaving their main positions to go to their latrines. Few snipers were about; the opposition mainly came from long-range mortars.'

The signallers always seemed to be out, fixing broken lines and setting up new communication paths to various outposts and headquarters. Sgt Percy Bream remembers one particular occasion when he was out with his men: 'We used to have cables down the road that went up to a place called the "Patrol House" on the edge of the village. I was down there one day when Corporal Grayson and Marine Roberts were mending the line where it went through the "gully". The area was often mortared and RSM Travers came down to have look around.'

The Germans had spotted the movement from their vantage point and decided to mortar the signallers. A cluster of bombs came over and caught the group in the open. Bream's men all escaped the explosions, but Travers was wounded, as he later explained: 'I had been hit near my kidneys and the shrapnel had punctured my lungs. Blood was coming out of my mouth. The other three managed to get me back up the lane to the HQ buildings and into the aid post.'

The MO, Lt Winser, got to work on Travers immediately. When Moulton heard the bad news he went to the cottage alongside his HQ where the MO had his aid post and asked Doc Winser if the RSM would live. He was told that the Travers was in a very bad way and it would be doubtful that he could survive. Lt Winser did all he could for him and arranged his immediate evacuation from the area. 'I was sent back to the beachhead into a hospital tent,' recalls Travers, 'where I was stripped and put to bed. Shortly afterwards I was taken by aircraft back to the UK. I thought I was in a bad way and felt very dazed the whole time. In England I was put aboard an ambulance train and sent to Wales where I made a good recovery.'

Whenever the Germans did shell or mortar the Commando, they received a larger dose of hatred back in return. The bombardment of their lines was taken as an affront by the marines and their guns were arranged for them to reply in kind plus a good deal extra, as Capt Geoff Linnell explained in his history of the Commando:

> To counter the enemy's mortars and short range artillery, the mortars of all the Commandos in our sector, that is 41, 46, 47 and 48 RM Commandos, were brigaded and their Observation Posts established along the entire front in contact with a central plotting centre at Brigade. The mortars of two of these units were on duty one day and those of the other two units the next. Each pair was so sited that together the whole front could be covered. By this means enemy guns could be engaged within three minutes of their opening fire at any time of the day or night. Eventually no enemy gun or mortar was allowed to fire without ten shots for his one being returned.

To keep the enemy unsettled, Linnell's heavy Vickers machine guns would also harass the Germans. They brought 'the crack of bullets to the rear areas,' as Moulton put it. Making good use of the exceptionally long range of the weapon, his men would open up with long bursts of fire, aimed at the supposedly safe ground to the rear of the German lines. The introduction of a new boat-tailed bullet in 1943 had extended the useful effective range of this gun to a staggering 4,500 yards. It must have come as a great shock to the enemy to suddenly be ripped by machine gun fire so far back in their rear.

The Commando was under the command of 6th Airborne Division, which meant that its artillery was also available to carry out a heavier shoot if one was required. Signaller Dennis Smith recalls one particular time when he was involved in laying down this type of bombardment against the enemy:

> The Germans seemed to have a good idea of all our movements and it was suspected that they had a good observation point somewhere from which they watched us. Any major movements in our line were often greeted by gunfire and mortars. One day an airborne artillery officer came up with a view that the German OP should be wiped out if it could be found. I was asked to go with him in the early hours of the morning before light to search for it. In the semi-darkness just before dawn, the officer, a corporal and myself, crept out across no-man's-land through the German lines. We managed to get behind their positions and saw their OP in the trees. It was so well camouflaged that it could not be seen from the front. The officer instructed me to radio back and call for gunfire from the airborne artillery on a set of co-ordinates he had given me. The first two or three shells that came over were a little wide of the mark, so the officer changed the range and I radioed back the corrections. The next salvo landed right on target and blew the OP apart and blasted down all the trees. I turned to the officer and said, 'Now what do we do?' 'Get out of here like the hell!' he replied. And we did!

The enemy troops overlooking their lines were not the only worry that the commandos had to face. Closer at hand was an irritant that also caused discomfort and often pain every night. Being located so close to the estuary and mudflats of the River Orne, the area was plagued by mosquitoes. 'The problems with mosquitoes were diabolical. They came into our trenches at

The Patrol House at Sallenelles before the war. (*Ted Brooks*)

night and made life hell,' recalls Ted Brooks. Percy Bream had to go into hospital for about three days from mosquito bites on the leg that went wrong. Although unconnected, during the period in Sallenelles, many men from the old 7th Battalion went down with a recurrence of malaria picked up during their service in the Middle East.

Even while the men were seemingly safe in and around their trenches there was still danger to be faced. Ted Brooks recalls one instance of being on the receiving end of some friendly fire: 'We were dug in close by an artillery anti-aircraft unit. One day when an enemy plane came over, one of the Bofors guns opened fire before it had been elevated and sent a stream of 40-mm shells straight along the floor of the orchard right over the top of our trenches. One poor sergeant was wounded with a piece of shrapnel which severed his spine.'

Percy Bream remembers his life in the line that summer as being quite varied:

> Our stay in Sallenelles was one of holding the line and surviving the daily shelling and mortaring. We lost a couple of signallers to mines when they stumbled into a newly placed enemy minefield while looking for breaks in the lines. In the orchard near the farmhouse there were some German graves. The bodies had been sprinkled with lime, but had not been buried too deep. They attracted flies in great quantities and proved to be another nuisance to us in our dugout. But all in all I think we lived very well considering the difficulties. By that time realisation that we were not going home had set in. One day we were moved into a quarry for a rest out of the line and thought that this was it and we had finished our time and were on our way home, but this proved to be false. A few days later we were back in the line.

Lt John Square did not mind being on this particular front line. For most of the time it was quiet and quite bearable, as he later recalled: 'I found it quite a pleasant place to be, the Germans never seemed to want to come out of their positions and show themselves, or attack us.' During the quiet periods all sorts of things became more noticeable to him, his senses seemed to be more perceptive to the environment about him. 'One's sense of smell was terrific at that time,' he recalls. 'For instance, I still remember the smell of the polish that the Germans used on their belts. Also the honeysuckle, it was so strong when you were out on patrol in the evening. I think that all of your senses were sharpened when in the line, especially smell and hearing.'

The Commando spent sixty days in the line at Sallenelles, holding the northern flank of the airborne lodgement: sixty days of patrols, monotony and minor skirmishes. Elsewhere in Normandy the fighting continued on a grand scale and with a ferocity that matched the worst days of the First World War. From the moment of the landings, Montgomery's 21st Army Group was engaged in a war of attrition with the enemy that stretched into the summer, each side giving and receiving a great deal of punishment. The greater resources available to the Allies eventually began to tell, wearing down the enemy to a point where he faced total collapse. More and more troops, equipment and armour were being funnelled into Normandy across the beaches and through the great artificial Mulberry harbour, building strength ready for the long-awaited break-out. By the end of July, the Supreme Commander Gen Eisenhower was able to introduce a new army into the battle when Gen Patton's Third US Army became active and joined Gen Hodges's US First Army, forming the US 12th Army Group under Gen Bradley. This reduced Montgomery's command to just the British and Commonwealth troops in British Second Army and Canadian Second Army, but paved the way for the great advance across northern France. While Monty held the left wing of the lodgement and contained the bulk of the German armour in Normandy, the Americans broke out of the province. In early August things were on the move everywhere, and this included 48 RM Commando.

Lt John Square recalls the end of the Commando's stay in Sallenelles: 'I remember the last night before we left the area. We were having a meal when a little lad was collecting his cows from a field nearby. Suddenly there was a bloody great explosion. One of the animals had stepped on a mine and bits of cows and everything started dropping on us while we were eating. The boy of course was also killed.'

CHAPTER ELEVEN

Troarn

Maj Gen Gale, commander 6th Airborne Division, received instructions on 7 August to prepare plans to exploit a likely enemy withdrawal on his front. Word was out that the Germans might be retreating. The break-out on the right-hand side of the battlefield by the Americans was threatening to blow the whole German line apart. All enemy troops in the north were in danger of being outflanked by the Allied movement in the south. If the line broke, then the Germans in front of Gale's division would have to fall back on the River Seine or be surrounded. If this happened, General Gale would need to be in a position to capitalise on this turn of events.

Gale was fortunate in that he had just received two new brigades to swell his forces for the move. The Belgian and the Royal Netherlands Brigades had arrived in Normandy and were looking to join the war. Gale placed these brigades in the north, hoping to give them a gentle introduction to the battlefield. If and when the break-out happened, then these two brigades would join with the 6th Airlanding Brigade to clear the northern coastal strip while the bulk of the Airborne Division and the two Special Service Brigades took the direct route to the Seine in pursuit of the enemy.

With the Belgian and Royal Netherlands Brigades coming into the northern sector of the line, the Commandos holding the area could be pulled out. In consequence 48 RM Commando was relieved of its duties at Sallenelles and withdrew, not into reserve, nor into a rest camp, but into another, and much worse, part of the line near the village of Troarn.

The southern part of the airborne bridgehead had been an area of dispute with the enemy since the early hours of D-Day. It was a region of small fields, high hedges and scattered woods and copses; very difficult country in which to fight a war. The flat farmland allowed little visibility of more than a few yards. Sunken lanes and tall trees were perfect for ambush, stealth and surprise. It had been an area loathed by the paras who had spent more than two months there in very close proximity to the enemy.

The 4th Special Service Brigade was to take over the line held by 5th Parachute Brigade so that it might be withdrawn into reserve ready for the coming pursuit. The part of the line allocated to 48 RM Commando was close to the Forest of Bures, just to the north-west of Troarn. Lt John Square remembers arriving in the area: 'We were told by the people we took over from that it was a horrible place, that the Germans came over every night, that they never stopped mortaring and the shelling was accurate and frequent. It was always the same, whatever outfit you relieved, wherever you were in the line, they delighted in telling you how awful it was there and you would be lucky to survive more than a few days, only this time it was true!'

Harry Timmins recalls the new positions in Troarn:

> As we approached the trenches that we were to take over, there were big notices all along the road reading: 'DUST BRINGS DEATH.' All the vehicles travelled at no more than walking pace. During darkness we crept silently into the slit trenches left for us, for the enemy was only a few yards away and could hear any movement. They were so close that we could only stand up in our trenches while it was dark and were forced to keep our heads down in daylight. Our section cook – Marine Burgess – had to prepare the meals and then stealthily crawl forward and drop them quietly into each slit trench in turn.

Ron Pugh of A Troop put his mess tin on the edge of his slit trench and then bent over to pick up his cup and the tin was shot away by an enemy sniper. When he tried to replace it, he showed the bullet hole in the side, but still had to pay for a new one.

Signals Sergeant Percy Bream remembers those signs warning about dust and death everywhere: 'They made us a bit nervous. Every time a vehicle moved down the road, up went a cloud of dust and we waited expectantly for enemy shells to come whining over. The front lines at Troarn were so close together you could hear the enemy talking. There was a lot of mortaring, but HQ was in the brick works and we were able to shelter in the kilns. This gave us a good deal of protection.'

These positions were unlike those in Sallenelles. The tight nature of the battlefield and the narrowness of no-man's-land left the two sides very close together. Capt Geoff Linnell and his Heavy Weapons Troop thought that there was some merit in the place: 'It was not very pleasant to have the enemy so close, but it was great for mortar shoots!' Indeed it was, and both sides shelled and mortared each other at the slightest provocation.

When he saw the positions his unit was taking over, Lt Col Moulton was not very pleased. In his view the trenches were very badly sited to fire from; those who dug them were more concerned about concealment and protection than repulsing an enemy attack. The previous incumbents had also left the ground littered with debris and their sanitation left much to be desired. In mitigation, it was explained to Moulton that the close proximity of the Germans meant that it was very dangerous to realign and dig new positions, because noise or movement always brought down retaliatory fire from the enemy. It was also true that the positions were mortared and shelled every day, but an enemy attack was an extremely rare occurrence. None the less, Moulton was unhappy about the state of the line and insisted on some changes.

The Colonel knew that the work might bring down some mortar fire so arranged for 4th Special Service Brigade's counter-mortar officer to be briefed. If the enemy decided to interfere with the work, he could reply with all the heavy weapons of the brigade. The colonel then set his troops a series of tasks that were to be completed that night: trenches were to be repositioned, wire was to be put out in certain vulnerable spots and the routes of known enemy patrols were to be attacked. Orders went out and after darkness had fallen the work commenced. All through the night Moulton expected the telephones to start ringing calling for counter-fire against the enemy, but none came. The work was completed and the Germans remained quiet. Either they had not heard the work, for the marines toiled as quietly as possible, or the enemy had decided to let things pass.

Lt John Square was in the sector held by Z Troop and recalls what life was like in these confined positions:

> We had a few slit trenches right by a hedge line in a field. As soon as we got into our positions I had a good look around to see just where we could move to without being seen. We could get into the woods a little bit, but no further than a dead German who had been propped up against a tree. I don't know if he was left by them to deter us, just like a dead crow hanging on a line to ward off others, but it did put us off a bit. We could hear their horse-drawn transport coming and going. They used horses a lot, rather than vehicles. The enemy use to fire a good few shells at us, which so often hit the trees so that shrapnel splinters would spray us from above. Sergeant Silk was killed by this type of shellfire. He had dug his trench with good head cover over it, but a shell hit a tree above him and a piece of shrapnel went through the roof of his slit trench and hit him in the stomach. It was a bit hairy in the Troarn area, with the distance between our trenches and the enemy being so close, rather like the First War. Like in the Great War, we often went out at night to put out barbed wire. I remember at the time thinking, which side of the wire do I stand when it is being laid out. Their side, or ours?

The area was a perfect hunting ground for snipers: hedges, woods and tree-lined lanes, all rich in verdant vegetation, provided ample cover for these stalkers of men. One particular enemy sniper caused A Troop a great deal of discomfort and grief, so a plot was hatched to eliminate him. Late one evening his lair had been spotted and the tree he was hiding in pinpointed. Two Bren guns were then set up after dark to concentrate their fire on that particular tree. The next day the sniper duly occupied his hideout and took his aim at a target. No sooner had his weapon fired than the two Bren guns riddled the tree with bullets, sending the German's body crashing to the ground.

For the first few days in the line, the Commando was shelled and mortared like its predecessor. But the new occupants insisted on sending back ten times the number of shells and bombs that they received. Gradually the enemy got the message and accepted that the marines were now masters of the line and he tailed off the amount of hate that he sent over. Soon the line reverted to a state of relative calm. Provided no one did anything untoward or unguarded, the area became no worse than any other stretch of the front.

Jock Mathieson was a dispatch rider with Moulton's HQ, which was located in the brick works at Troarn, and remembers the close-knit nature of the battlefield:

> We were often mortared. I was slightly wounded on one occasion by shrapnel. It was a very difficult area with the enemy sometimes just a few yards away. The school at Troarn was right on the front line and was often used by both sides. I remember our marines were in one end, with the enemy in the other. We were told not to attack or fire on the school because there were wounded British troops kept in some of the rooms. One day after the Germans had pulled out, I entered a room at the end of a corridor and saw that there were a list of names scratched on the wall by the men who had been held there. One of these names was a chap

RSM Colin Travers, who had previously served with the 7th Royal Marine Battalion in Egypt, Sicily and Italy before joining 48 RM Commando when it was formed in March 1944. (*Colin Travers*)

from the Black Watch that I had gone to school with. His family were well known to me. I sent a letter home to my dad telling him to tell Mr Nichol that their son Jimmy was now a POW.

During this period, many of the men who had been wounded earlier were making their way back to the Commando. RSM Colin Travers was one of them:

> After a while in hospital I was moved to a rehabilitation centre. I think that I could have stayed in that place until the end of the war if I chose, but I was anxious to get away. I persuaded them to release me to the nursing home that my mother ran. I talked my way out of the hospital by saying that she could change my dressings and look after me. They let me go, but I went straight home to my wife and had my dressings changed at the local hospital. I wrote to the adjutant of 48 Commando, Captain Grant, telling him that I was now OK and was ready to get back to the unit. After a while, I went to a holding camp in Wales and then eventually caught a landing craft back across to Normandy. I rejoined the Commando at Troarn and Sergeant Hayes, who had taken over from me as RSM, had to revert back to his previous job.

By the middle of August, it was clear that the enemy was pulling out of Normandy. The collapse of German Seventh Army at Falaise had sent those units that had escaped from the debacle hurtling pell-mell for the River Seine and the safety of the far side of the river. Opposite 48 RM Commando, the situation remained unclear. Had the enemy pulled out or was he still there? An officer-led patrol was dispatched to find out. The unfortunate Capt Mackenzie of Y Troop was given the unenviable task. If the enemy was still there, the Captain would be walking into an area full of alert Germans. In the event he found their lines empty; the Germans had gone. The Commando was now looking out on to peaceful fields. For the first time in eighty-four days, its marines were out of earshot of gunfire. As Geoff Linnell noted: 'At last we could stretch our legs and enjoy the sun, and moreover talk aloud and sing once more.'

CHAPTER TWELVE

The Break-out and Pursuit

When Maj Gen Gale planned the route for his pursuit of the enemy, he had only one practical road to take. Between his lodgement and the River Seine were three other sizeable rivers: the Dives, the Touques and the Risle. His advance would have to be relatively close to the sea, clear of the British 49th Division on his right, and yet far enough inland to avoid the tidal reaches of these rivers. This would force him to move along a line with the towns of Troarn, Dozulé, Pont l'Evêque, Beuzeville and Pont-Audemer as his main axis. The spearhead of his advance would take this route, while the Belgian, Royal Netherlands and 6th Airlanding Brigades cleared the area between it and the coast, including the coastal towns of Cabourg, Deauville and Trouville.

Once word reached Gale from various patrols that the enemy had started to withdraw, he moved swiftly. In the early hours of 17 August the 6th Airborne brigade started the pursuit. The 1st Special Service Brigade and the 6th Airlanding Brigade crossed the River Dives, the Commandos heading for Robehomme and the glider-borne troops making for Cabourg. Neither group made much initial headway as progress was slow owing to the heavy cratering of the roads; the retreating Germans were demolishing and mining them as they went. Further to the north, the Belgian Brigade broke through the line near Sallenelles and pushed up the coast road towards Cabourg. By the end of the day the leading elements were fighting on the outskirts of the town against increasing enemy resistance.

In the south, the main drive by 3rd Parachute Brigade moved through Troarn, picked their way across the Dives to Goustranville, stopping just short of the canal that barred the way to Dozulé. In front of the paras fire from the enemy-held heights on each side of the town forced them to a halt. Further progress was impossible without artillery support and they had advanced over 9,000 yards that day, beyond the effective range of the field guns on the other side of the Dives. There would have to be a pause until the guns caught up. This would take some time as suitable bridges over the Dives at Troarn were still demolished, the handiwork of the assault troops on the night of D-Day, and they had to be rebuilt by Bailey-bridging teams from the Royal Engineers.

It has to be remembered that both the Airborne Division and the Commandos of the Special Service Brigades were all light units having little transport of their own. They had been used as infantry of the line since

June, but had never been provided with the normal infrastructure necessary to fight any sort of mobile war. In the main, the men were forced to march into battle and carry with them all that they required to fight it. They were pursuing a retreating enemy and doing so the old fashioned way, on foot.

The enemy position at Dozulé was formidable. Gale later found out that it had been prepared prior to the break-out. It utilised the two areas of high ground either side of the town which looked down on the road up which the paras were advancing. The General knew that this was probably a holding position in order to gain time, but to attack the location head-on could be costly. He quickly ruled out a daylight attack over the open ground on either side of the road and decided on an outflanking movement using the cover of darkness. The hills to the north of the town would be unsuitable ground over which to deploy as their slopes were almost precipitous. Gale therefore chose to make his move in the south.

In front of Dozulé were two major obstructions, a canal and a railway line. There were four bridges over the canal, but all were thought to be blown. Gale decided to launch a two-brigade night attack: 3rd Brigade would start the operation at 2200 hours, advancing to the canal to establish which bridge, if any, was available for the crossing, then would cross the waterway and advance as far as the railway line to establish a start line by 0200 hours; and 5th Brigade would launch an attack from this line to seize the village of Putot-en-Auge and the high ground to the south of Dozulé.

The operation got off to a slow start when three of the four bridges across the canal were found to be blown. The most southerly was still intact and 3rd Brigade managed to get to the railway line after some very fierce fighting. The lead battalion of 5th Brigade then crossed the canal and started its attack on Putot, three hours behind schedule. Strong enemy resistance was met and the area was found to be more heavily defended than was expected. The paras were counter-attacked in some force, but the enemy were beaten off, leaving many of their men killed or captured. By now it was light, and Gale's paratroopers came under artillery fire from the German position on the high ground to the north of Dozulé. By mid-morning Putot had been captured and the brigade moved out to seize the high ground to the south. When the 13th Parachute Battalion attempted to cross on to its objective it received the full force of the enemy's artillery. This was dealt with by a counter-battery bombardment by the field guns which had moved up near the canal. Heavier German guns at Houlgate in the north also joined in the battle. The 5th Brigade got on to the crest of the high ground at Point 134 but was unable to hold it because of enemy fire from the reverse slopes. Flanking movements to the right to get behind this resistance also failed.

Opposite: The Break-out and Pursuit

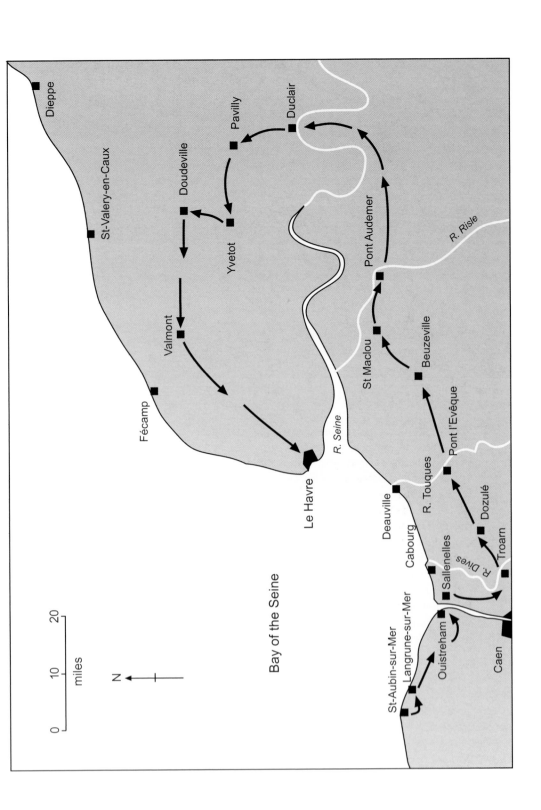

Dieppe

St-Valery-en-Caux

Doudeville

Pavilly

Duclair

Yvetot

Valmont

Pont Audemer

Fécamp

R. Risle

St Maclou

Beuzeville

Le Havre

R. Seine

Pont l'Evêque

Deauville

R. Touques

Cabourg

Dozulé

Sallenelles

R. Dives

Troarn

St-Aubin-sur-Mer

Langrune-sur-Mer

Ouistreham

Caen

Bay of the Seine

N

0   10   20

miles

The Brigade Commander, Brig Poett, decided that the operation could not continue in daylight and ordered his men to dig in and hold. Gale's two brigades had suffered 29 dead and 85 wounded in the attack; the Dozulé position was proving to be a tough nut to crack.

Gale now decided to bring all his resources together and overwhelm Dozulé by wide flanking movements. He ordered Brig Mills-Roberts to bring 1st Special Service Brigade across to attack Brucourt and the high ground to the north of Dozulé and Brig Flavell to take his 6th Airlanding Brigade round from Cabourg to pass behind this high ground further to the north. He also ordered Brig Leicester to take 4th Special Services Brigade around 5th Parachute Brigade further to the south and advance eastwards. These simultaneous manoeuvres to the north and south of Dozulé would completely surround and outflank the town, hopefully trapping the German garrison. When all of these units came at the enemy at the same time, he would be sure to be caught off balance and left with just two options, fight or flee.

When Moulton received word that his Commando would be going forward to join in the pursuit, he was 'stretching his legs and watching the advance go by.' He and his men were enjoying the enforced idleness created by the enemy having melted away before them. The marines walked across the now safe no-man's-land and had a look at the German positions around Troarn. They were impressed with the depth of fortifications and the thoroughness with which they had been constructed.

Early on 18 August the Commando was placed on one hour's notice to move. In the evening, 48 moved out on foot marching in the wake of the paratroopers across the swampy flood plain of the River Dives. By nightfall the unit had reached a small hamlet called Montgassard. Here the marines bedded down for the night, seeking shelter where they could. The next morning Moulton went with Brig Leicester to Gen Gale's HQ and received the news that the Commando had been given a special task in the operation to capture Dozulé. Moulton was told that the high ground to the east of the village was the key to the battle and that its summit, Point 120, looked down on both Dozulé and the road leading out of it to the north-east. This road, passing beneath the hill, would be the Germans' only effective escape route towards the Seine. It was important that this feature be taken before the town was captured. 48 RM Commando was now given the task of seizing Point 120.

The operation by Brig Leicester's brigade would start with 46 RM Commando taking the high ground above 5th Parachute Brigade at Putot-en-Auge. Then 48 Commando would swing further to the right, pass over Point 134 and make across country for Point 120. On the right, 41 RM Commando would provide flank guard. The brigade's reserve was 47 RM Commando.

The Commando began preparations for the attack during the evening of 19 August. At 2300 hours, Maj de Stacpoole took Y Troop forward to provide left-flank guard for 46 Commando's move against the hill below Point 134 and to cover the assembly area of the remainder of 48 RM Commando once they were over the canal. The move to Putot was strictly timed and the marines of 48 had to be over the bridge before 0530 hours so that 41 Commando could cross behind them and get into its initial positions before first light at 0600 hours. The official history describes the move: 'Owing to the bad interior economy and lack of practice in movements, the Commando set off late and without a hot meal. The second-in-command who was in command of F group (fighting group, i.e. the main body) gave the order to speed march and by this means reached the bridge at 0455 hours. The bridge was crossed and the Commando moved into its assembly area in the orchards to the south-east of Putot-en-Auge. This area was found to be under mortar fire. By good fortune only three or four men were hit.'

Ahead of them 46 Commando was putting in a night attack against the hill above Putot. After some fierce fighting, some of which was at very close quarters, 46 got to the top of the hill and sent a message back to brigade. Moulton now sent Capt Flunder with A Troop up to take Point 134. When he got to his objective he found the enemy had abandoned the area just before he arrived. He sent a patrol forward and it brushed up against the enemy rearguard and shots were exchanged with an armoured car which withdrew down a track to the right towards the small village of Clermont-en-Auge. The rest of the Commando came up on to Point 134, but the close nature of the surroundings meant that the jeeps carrying the anti-tank PIATS, reserve ammunition and tools could not join them.

Moulton now sent X Troop and Capt Mackenzie down the track towards Clermont with orders to clear up the situation in the village and find a new route for the jeeps to move along. Lt Hedley Phillips was in X Troop and he later recalled this his first action with the enemy:

The area was covered with small fields and orchards, sunken roads between high banks and tiny hamlets and villages. It was very close country with little or no visibility. It was Sunday, and a beautiful summer's morning, as we approached the village in advance to contact formation. The church bells were ringing and the villagers were all walking down the main street on their way to church. The reception we received was very enthusiastic. Once we had secured a defensive perimeter around the main crossroads, Mac [Captain Mackenzie] told me to take a section – a sergeant, a corporal, ten marines and a Bren team of three men – as a fighting patrol to clear the area around the village. We moved off out through the orchards in a circular route and after crossing several fields we came to a sunken road. Here we saw, and ambushed, a German officer and an other rank who were trying to start a motorcycle. Moving on, two fields later, we reached another sunken lane leading back down into the village. Here we saw a dozen or so Germans approaching. They were all wearing black uniforms and were probably SS troops of one sort or another. I set up another successful ambush and killed or captured all of them. We then carried on along our circular route and came under some long-range *Spandau* fire making us go to ground for a while. A little later we continued with the patrol and rejoined our troop in Clermont. Here we found that they had captured three Germans and a jeep which originally belonged to the Airborne Division. In the early afternoon, elements of 41 RM Commando entered Clermont and relieved us so that we could rejoin our main force. All the while we were in the village, we were out of radio contact with the Commando.

This first action taught Hedley Phillips one very important lesson: always check everything you receive. He explains why: 'On joining X Troop I had only my personal weapon, a Colt .45 automatic pistol. The troop Quartermaster Sergeant issued me with a standard .303 Mark IV Lee Enfield Rifle which I accepted without question. In the first ambush at Clermont the extractor jammed after firing the first round and thereafter I had to fall back on my trusty Colt. It was just as well that we had not been on the receiving end of the ambush! I later exchanged, as soon as I could, the rifle for a Thompson machine carbine which served me well for the rest of the war.'

As X Troop were clearing the area of Clermont, the rest of the Commando were advancing towards Point 120. 41 RM Commando moved in behind them to hold their gains, establishing themselves on the vitally important position of Point 134 ready for the main attack against Dozulé itself, which was to be made by the paras attacking from the west and 46 and 47 RM Commandos attacking from the south. This assault was set to commence at 2000 hours, by which time 48 would have to be in control of the high ground at Point 120.

In the meantime, in the north, 1st Special Service Brigade and the 6th Airlanding Brigade were fighting their battles to take the high ground on that side of the town. The enemy was gradually being squeezed out of his positions and in imminent danger of encirclement.

Z Troop led the advance across the hills and fields above the town, initially making for the hamlet of Panniers. Behind came the remainder of the unit, carrying what weapons and equipment they could manhandle across the open countryside. A jeep route through Clermont was possible, but the ground north-east of the village was still open to the enemy. The advance was particularly difficult as Geoff Linnell's history explains: 'On the way the Commando had to pass through a recently evacuated German gun position in the woods. There was plenty of abandoned equipment lying around including a very well-kept MG34 machine-gun. The difficulty in map reading was due to the fact that neither the contours nor the detail on the 1/25,000 map were very accurate, and the country was very close with thick hedges and small steep features, rather reminiscent of Cornwall.'

The advance continued in fits and starts, each field, hedgerow and sunken lane holding a possible German defender. Once each troop or section passed from one hedgerow to another they disappeared from view. The Commando was moving virtually blindly through the Normandy *bocage*, directions were difficult and bearings easily lost. It was a confusing advance for the Commando and a difficult retreat for the enemy. Through the day, both sides were often surprised by sudden face-to-face confrontations, or in one particular occasion a face-to-rear confrontation, as Lt John Square recalls: 'I remember during this period that Capt McKenzie came round a corner and saw four feet sticking out from under a hedge belonging to two Germans who were keeping watch, fortunately for him looking the other way. He shot them both.'

The Patrol House at Sallenelles at the bottom of the lane on the outskirts of the village. On the left, the walled garden contained slit trenches for the patrol that was holding the village. To the right, the fields lead out into no-man's-land. The German strongpoint is about a half mile ahead and to the right. (*Ken Ford*)

Local civilians reported that there were parties of Germans in the two villages of St-Jouin and St Leger Dubosq ahead of them, but these reports had to be ignored if Moulton and his men were to get on to their objective that evening. Brig Leicester came forward to confirm that the attack on Dozulé would go in at 2000 hours and both he and General Gale considered it to be most important that the Commando capture Point 120 by that time. It was agreed that 41 Commando would clear St-Jouin and St Leger Dubosq leaving 48 to concentrate on its main objective.

At 1630 hours, A Troop, led by Capt Dan Flunder, advanced along the line of a hedge running north-east, making for the cluster of houses known as Banquelion. When they arrived at the hamlet a small patrol entered and found out from the local inhabitants that Point 120 was almost clear of the enemy, there being just a few artillery personnel operating an observation post there. Flunder sent a patrol of sub-section strength further on to the lane which ran up to the objective from the south while he waited for the rest of the Commando to catch up. The patrol was fired on by some of the enemy and just missed capturing a German staff car which came hurtling along the road.

When Moulton joined Capt Flunder he decided to press on immediately with the attack. By this time the sub-section at the lane were experiencing heavy machine gun fire, coming from Point 120. Surprise had now been lost and de Stacpoole and his Y Troop were ordered to make straight for the summit of the hill. This troop came under fire after its commandos had advanced across just two fields. The closely knit countryside made it very difficult to locate the opposition. It now appeared that the hill was being held in some strength by the enemy and the attack would have to be widened in scope. Moulton told Maj de Stacpoole to leave his attack on the summit and make a wide movement around the base of the hill to get on the rear slopes facing Dozulé, while Z and B Troops moved round to the right, sweeping clear of the fire from the enemy machine gun firing down the road.

Almost immediately Z Troop came under heavy enemy fire. The troop had passed across the front of a post of about eighteen Germans clustered around an MG34 machine gun. Capt Nuttall decided to put in a troop attack on the gun and eliminate this opposition. While a sub-section kept the Germans pinned down with concentrated fire and smoke grenades, the rest of Z Troop put in a right flanking movement and began to attack the enemy post from the side. The German MG34 began firing wildly, its gunners seemingly in a state of panic. The commandos closed on their objective, spraying the area with concentrated bursts of machine pistol and rifle fire. It was too much for the enemy; they did not wait for the final assault but fled through the hedges and bushes back up the hill.

While this was going on, A Troop crossed the road and got into the fields on the far side of the hill. X troop closed on the road to occupy the ground on the near side. They now began their attack along either side of the road, up the hill towards Point 120. As they closed on the objective they could hear German horse-drawn transport galloping away to their rear. It was becoming clear that the hill was being abandoned and Moulton ordered all his troops to press home the attack. Bounding through one hedgerow after another the commandos pushed forwards through sporadic light machine gun and rifle fire, closing inexorably on their objective. Point 120 was reached without any physical contact with the enemy. For one short moment a figure appeared with a white flag only to disappear just as suddenly under a hail of fire. Enemy troops were pulling back off the hill, firing through the hedges as they went.

In the meantime, Y Troop had reached the back of the hill and advanced to a position about 700 yards beyond Point 120. Maj de Stacpoole sent a patrol down to the road leading out from the rear of Dozulé and discovered a farm which seemed to have been a German HQ. By this time it was 2130 hours and if the attack had gone in on Dozulé at 2000 hours as planned then the enemy would probably have escaped by now. Moulton's orders had been to seize and hold Point 120 so he told Y Troop to hold its position just short of the main road and then consolidated the remainder of his Commando on their objective. The importance of the position to the enemy meant that there was every likelihood that he would counter-attack to take the feature back again.

During the attack Tony Pratt had had a narrow escape, as he later explained:

On the advance a small group of us got separated from the rest of the troop by enemy fire. We had gone to ground near a farmhouse and we could see German trenches in front of it. After a good while there was no more firing so I went forward to see if the trenches were occupied. I crept round to the right and got close enough to see that they were deserted, so I went back to the others and suggested that we move into the farmhouse for the night. As we approached the house a Frenchman came out and quickly called us inside. He told us that the Germans had moved into a field behind the position we had just left and were now between us and our line. It seemed that we were trapped, so he sent us up into his loft out of sight. I had a look from an upstairs window and could see the Germans not too far away. We spent a quiet night and were woken in the early morning by movement outside. Looking out from our hiding place I could see a party of the enemy withdrawing by the house, passing just underneath the window. We stayed quiet and they moved off. After a while we returned to X Troop's positions. They were glad to see us; they thought we had all been killed or captured.

At about 2200 hours the jeeps arrived on the hill with the long-range radio sets which enabled contact to be made with Brigade HQ. It was then that Moulton learned that the attack on Dozulé had been postponed until first light the next day. In the event this attack never had to be made, for the arrival of 48 RM Commando in the rear of the enemy's main position meant that the town was almost surrounded. Nothing could be gained by holding out any longer so the German garrison set fire to the buildings and left.

The Commando's action at Dozulé was a good example of sound infantry tactics. In the words of Brig Leicester, it had been 'a clever outflanking battle in very close country'. Moulton's commandos had been trained as assault troops: fast in, hit hard and fast out. But in the Normandy *bocage*, through fields and hedges so confined that visibility more than a few tens of yards was rare, without heavy support and with just the weapons they could carry, the marines had fought a battle that any infantry battalion of the line would be proud of. Casualties were light and punishment inflicted great. It was a remarkable achievement.

With Dozulé taken the pursuit continued. Maj Gen Gale's division kept up the pressure on the enemy, snapping at his heels before he could regroup to fight any delaying battles. With the Airlanding Brigade and the 1st Special Service Brigade now moving along roads in the north, Gale could add another effective route eastwards to his main thrust. These two brigades now continued along in the direction Cour Rouge–Touques–Honfleur, while the Belgian and Dutch Brigades cleared the coastal towns and the main part of 6th Airborne Division and Brig Leicester's commando brigade moved along the original main axis.

There now passed a period when 48 RM Commando seemed to be continually on the move. Some transport was occasionally available to whisk them forwards for a few miles, but most of the pursuit was carried out on foot. It was very hard going, for over two months of static life in the trenches at Sallenelles and Troarn had taken its toll on the fitness of the marines and this lack of condition soon began to tell. Sgt Percy Bream still remembers this period:

> We had to march everywhere and everything had to be carried. After two months of holding the line we were suddenly on the move. At that stage we were still wary of what might be found ahead, we had no idea that the enemy would be pulling out so fast and thought that he would fight a rearguard action for every place. The first good march that we had to do we all felt very tired the next morning. We were rather out of condition. We did not have much fighting to do as the enemy seemed to slip away just as we arrived. Often we found food on the table where they had been disturbed at their meals. At one place we found barrels of booze just left there. We were told by Lt Aldworth, one of the mortar officers, that we must not touch the drink because it might have been doped by the retreating Germans. Corporal McElhone had a tin mug and drew some drink out of the barrel and said, 'It looks all right,' and tried a drop. 'It tastes all right. If I drop dead in three minutes, don't drink it.' Lt Mike Aldridge stood aghast and looked at me as much to say, give me some support. But in those days I was just as wicked as anybody.

Between Dozulé and the Seine several spoiling actions were fought by the enemy. The first encountered by the paras was on the line Branville–Annebault–Valseme, but this was taken without too much trouble. The next encounter was at Pont l'Evêque on the River Touques. Here enemy resistance was much stiffer and the Airborne Division lost thirty-four men killed and sixty-one wounded trying to force a crossing through the town. Fighting was fierce and the town was set on fire during the battle. Gale changed his tactics and decided to outflank the enemy resistance in Pont l'Evêque by putting the Special Service Brigades across the Touques downriver of the town and get behind the enemy from the north, but the attack was never put into effect, as the Commando's official history explains:

> On 23 August we received orders to force a crossing of the Touques in conjunction with 1st SS Brigade, to relieve the pressure on 3 Parachute Brigade, who were unable to force their way through Pont l'Evêque. The ground was reconnoitred, approach routes were marked, the Commando formed up in inky darkness, but then the operation was cancelled. Enemy ammunition dumps across the river in the Forêt de St Gatien were being destroyed and the air was filled with the whooping detonations of *Nebelwefers*; it was appreciated that the enemy was withdrawing. So he was. The next morning 3 Parachute Brigade found the town empty and set off hotfoot towards the next river.

The next hold-up was at Beuzeville and 4th Special Service Brigade was again called forward to outflank the enemy. 48 RM Commando attempted to advance on the right flank of the paratroopers but was held up by close-range heavy machine gun and mortar fire near its start line. The

An NCO briefs a group of marines from **48 RM Commando**. (*Imperial War Museum, A28413*)

Commando withdrew and tried an even wider circling movement before coming in against the enemy line. This time it was successful but found that the Germans had in the meantime withdrawn. Scarcely had the Commando got into position than the brigade was off again.

The chase now began to be quite stimulating for the marines. There was a general feeling that the enemy were beaten. Every time he tried to stop and contain the Allied advance by some rearguard action, the Commandos and the paratroopers were among him before he could get organised. Quite often he would pause only to set fire to buildings and destroy bridges and roads, sometimes in a random and vindictive manner as if trying to punish the French people for the position he found himself in.

The Commando moved forwards as liberators, receiving enthusiastic welcomes from the towns and villages along the way. The Intelligence Officer, Lt Harold Smedley, later recalled the advance: 'We had very few vehicles of our own and so whenever the opportunity arose to capture any from the enemy we took advantage of it. In each place we liberated I was called on to act as interpreter with the local mayor and these occasions usually resulted in bottles of armagnac and calvados being produced and handed round. I was always surprised to find how welcoming these people were, even though the towns and villages of Normandy had been often quite badly damaged by the Allies prior to our arrival.'

With opposition melting before them, it was often unnecessary to have to attack to gain an objective, as Lt John Square recalls:

> It was virtually non-stop and all of us were extremely tired. I remember one night advance was so bad that every time we stopped the men, including myself, would just collapse on the road asleep. Every time we planned to attack a town, we found that by the morning the Germans had left. At one particular place we planned an attack to take place at about seven in the morning. We arrived in the area at about six. We waited in some captured German dugouts for the start time. Moulton was like this, he sensibly waited and waited until the last minute to see if the Germans were gone. In the event they had and we did not have to put in the attack.

The enemy's ability to withdraw in an orderly manner was often hampered by Allied air activity. The closer he got to the River Seine the more concentrated this aerial bombardment became. This forced small groups of isolated individuals and their horse-drawn transport to use the winding lanes and dirt tracks that crisscrossed the *bocage*. Sometimes the Commando got ahead of these groups and they would both find themselves travelling down the same roads, or trying to rest in the same farmhouses. Jock Mathieson, a dispatch rider with HQ Troop, recalls how one night he had managed to get ahead of the enemy: 'We holed up for some time in a cottage with orders to observe the retreating Germans and give information on numbers, directions, etc. They were fleeing in horse-drawn trailers and our job was to count the trailers as they came up the road. During the night we heard noises in the outhouse and thought they were coming in after us, but it was only some hens having a row. The Germans seemed more intent in putting as much distance between us and them as they could, rather than stopping to fight.'

Horse-drawn transport was not limited just to the enemy. Signaller Tom Clarke also took advantage of this form of mobility as he explains:

> I found a large carthorse wandering around and decided that I would ride it. I remember one day taking a message up to one outlying troop position which had no radio. I was enjoying the

ride when I suddenly found that a German tank was coming down the road towards me with only a hedge between us. I froze and thought to myself, 'This is it, I've had it now,' but the enemy officer standing up in the turret stared in disbelief at me on the horse and I stared back in horror. Then, in a moment, they were gone. I lost my mount later when we came across the carcass of a dead horse on the road and my horse reared up, threw me off and took flight.

Marine Jock Mathieson recalls the effort required during the pursuit: 'During the break-out we marched fifteen miles in darkness to get behind the Germans as they retreated. We advanced in single file, each man holding on to the toggle rope of the man in front of him. The night was pitch black; we were unable to see anything. Every time someone stopped, those behind would pile into him. The language was shocking!' A more detailed description of this famous night march was given by Capt Linnell in his official history of the campaign.

> We were ordered by the Brigadier to move by night across country to St Maclou. 48 Commando led the march and few who took part in it will ever forget it. The night was inky black. Each troop commander was given a stretch of country to memorise from the map. The march in single file was started by Y Troop which, when it reached the end of its stretch, handed over the pilotage to Z Troop and so on. The march was rather like shunting in a goods yard. When the head of the column halted there was a series of minor collisions all down the line. If the column stopped for more than a few minutes, many men fell asleep on their feet as no one had had a proper sleep for ninety-six hours. When finally we reached St Maclou at 0700 hours, after an eight-hour march, we found the last enemy had left an hour before.

Pont-Audemer on the Risle was the next important goal, but it looked as though this was to be denied to Gale's Division. British 49th Division was advancing on the right and the town had been placed within its zone. Gale thought otherwise and was convinced that as his men were nearer to the town he could get there before the 49th Division. He reinforced his 5th Parachute Brigade with the Royal Netherlands Brigade and mounted the advance guard on the tanks of his Armoured Reconnaissance Regiment and made a dash for Pont-Audemer, hoping to capture the bridge intact. His men missed carrying out their objective by just fifteen minutes, arriving in the town soon after the bridge was blown. It was here that the great pursuit stopped and the baton was handed over to 49th Division. The enemy were streaming back to the Seine just eight miles away, intent on escaping rather than fighting. There were to be no more rearguard actions this side of the river. For the first time since the early hours of D-Day, 6th Airborne Division came out of the front line and made preparations for its return home to England.

Dennis Smith was not happy when he heard the news that the paras were being pulled out of the campaign, as he recalls: 'Both the 1st Special Service Brigade and 6th Airborne Division were taken out of the line and returned home. We had to stay and fight, even though we had initially been told that our operation for D-Day would only be for four to seven days. There were some grumbles at the way we were being treated. A Royal Marine band was sent to the village we were in to cheer us up, but it didn't!'

CHAPTER THIRTEEN

The Pursuit Continues

The Commando spent four days at St Maclou resting. It was here that the Revd Maurice Wood joined the unit and held its first Sunday service since arriving in France. It was a good service and Moulton admitted that all of his Commando felt better for it. Revd Wood had landed on D-Day with the beach parties supporting 3rd Division and his good work on that day had won him the Distinguished Service Cross. 'I had to wade ashore with my valise as the landing craft's skipper would not come close in enough to beach the craft, so I had a very wet landing,' he later recalled. Revd Wood arrived on a sector of Sword Beach that was under continual enemy fire which continued well after the leading troops had moved inland.

> We suffered a lot from enemy shelling and bombing. It seemed a terrible place to be. I wrote in my notebook 'The presence of Christ is so real to me that I am not afraid to die'. The next day things were still bad and I read it again. On the third day while reading it I thought that some time in the future when all this was over I would read this again, so I added – 'But I'm scared stiff of getting wounded!' I was assigned to 48 Commando from the Naval Beach Commandos after our work on Sword Beach was completed and because of this I never had to undergo the rigorous commando training in Scotland. From time to time, when I irritated Col Moulton or any of the other officers, they used to say: 'Padre, if you don't shut up we will send you to Achnacarry!

Maurice Wood brought much-needed spiritual comfort to the marines. They had had a long and very rough time of it since they had arrived in Normandy and the original promise that they would spend no more than one week in France before they were withdrawn for the next operation was beginning to sound rather hollow, especially as other Commandos and elite units were being sent back to England. It seemed unfair, but the war had to go on and the Commando was soon on the move again, this time on TCVs (Troop Carrying Vehicles) rather than on foot. Destination: the River Seine at Duclair.

As they approached the river, each man could see the absolute devastation the enemy had suffered from the RAF fighter-bombers that had strafed columns of German vehicles as they waited for their turn to cross the Seine. The retreating enemy had been forced back by the advancing Allies and were trapped against the river, only able to escape across on the few ferries that remained serviceable. All bridges between Paris and the sea were blown. Most of their equipment and transport had to be abandoned. The roads all around were blocked by tanks, guns, trucks, horse-drawn carts, personnel carriers and men, all easy targets for long-range artillery and low-flying Typhoon aircraft. The destruction was almost indescribable.

Harry Lane witnessed the devastation: 'The bend at Duclair on the Seine was a ghastly place. Everywhere was complete carnage. The planes and artillery had caught the fleeing Germans on the river bank as they waited to cross over to the other side. There were burning tanks, lorries and carts all around. The place was strung out with dead men. I can still smell the roasted bodies of the tank crews even now.' Lt John Square also witnessed the horror: 'We found the river was running with bloated bodies of men and horses. Long lines of vehicles had been bombed and strafed and pushed to the side of the road. All of them were burned to a cinder along with their drivers and passengers. I remember seeing all of these burnt black corpses with white bands around their wrists where their watches had been stolen from their bodies.'

48 RM Commando crossed the river in paddle boats, formed up on the other side and moved on with the chase, except by now the enemy had completely disappeared and the chase was more of a procession along the route Pavilly–Yerville–Yvetot–Doudeville. The unit marched through areas untouched by the war, to be greeted by deliriously happy civilians who fêted them at every opportunity. 'People ran alongside the marching troops, pressing drinks and food on them,' recalls Lt Hedley Phillips. 'Each day, half-troop patrols went on ahead of the marching commandos. The men were carried on three or four jeeps and disembarked from them when they approached any sign of habitation. They then moved forward in an "advance to contact" formation. I was involved on these patrols on several occasions and in the celebrations of the small towns and villages which were liberated ahead of the marching troops. Most of the time the only work entailed picking up enemy wounded and collecting together German deserters.'

Little was seen of the enemy during the advance; he was retreating at speed in front of the Commando, often pulling out of a village just before the marines arrived. Dougie Gray remembers talking to the baker in one particular village: 'He told me that the Germans were quite proper and paid for their ration of daily bread, except on this particular day the Germans had entered as usual early in the morning, collected their bread and then walked out. When the baker asked for his money, the Germans replied, "Oh Tommy will pay for it, he will be here in an hour!"'

On and on the Commando marched until it came to Doudeville. Here it was halted and the patrol from X Troop that had gone ahead on jeeps was told to return and settle down for the night. Lt Hedley Phillips was part of that jeep patrol: 'I learned that we had been stopped to allow the 51st Highland Division to pass through and liberate the small port of St-Valery-en-Caux, the scene of its ignominious surrender to the enemy in June 1940.' Everybody on the road was stopped to allow the Highlanders the privilege of being the first troops into the town. Unfortunately, what they did not know was that Phillips and three jeep loads of X Troop had already been there before them and had been regaled by the French civilians with glasses of benedictine and cognac.

The advance continued to Valmont, where there was a pause while the next move was decided. It was here that the Commando enjoyed a well-earned spell of rest and recreation, spending nine days of idleness enjoying the hospitality of the French townspeople. B and X Troops were actually put in civilian billets, while HQ, A, S and Y Troops, along with Commando HQ itself, were all housed in various magnificent chateaux in the town and in the area nearby. There was one casualty, however, during this period of blissful calm. The MO, Lt 'Doc' Winser was badly burned by a smoke grenade. He and his driver had been trying to smoke out some bees from a beehive to get at the honey and Winser had suffered phosphorus burns to his hands and body. Lt Winser was evacuated and replaced by Lt James Dick RAMC.

After this period of grace, the Commando was sent to Le Havre on 13 September. The great French port had been liberated by 49th and 51st Divisions a few days earlier and 48 RM Commando was required there to help garrison the city and prevent the breakdown of law and order. Lt Col Moulton was made Deputy Military Commander of Le Havre. Capt Linnell later explained their duties: 'We carried out policing duties in the town, mainly guarding German stores chock full of alcohol and other good things. The townspeople were quite hostile to us for they had lost hundreds during the bombing of the port by the RAF. The centre was completely destroyed.' The occupation and liberation of Le Havre had inflicted a great deal of punishment on the local civilians.

Lt Harold Smedley, the Intelligence Officer, recalls the main problems in the town: 'In Le Havre our main work was trying to keep the French civilians and British and Canadian troops out of the captured German stores which were full of all manner of wonderful things, most especially spirits. I remember looking out from the battlements at one particular soldier, staggering around absolutely drunk out of his mind.'

With the Commando policing other troops, who was to police the Commando? No one, apparently, as Sgt Percy Bream later confessed: ' Our job was to keep everyone away from the German booze, fags and cigars that were piled up in the warehouses. I know that some of our officers filled a lorry with the stuff and we also, of course, helped ourselves. I was smoking cigars for months afterwards. There was so much of it that you could see chaps lighting up a cigar and saying, "I don't like that," throwing it away and lighting up another. Sergeant Jimmy Black still had bottles and bottles of booze with him when we were in Holland. He probably left some troops' stores behind to get all that drink away.'

Although these duties had some redeeming factors, the marines were glad to get away from Le Havre. The French people were sullen and reproachful, with good reason, for the devastation of the town and plight of the civilians made Le Havre an inhospitable place to garrison. Food was very scarce and all supplies required careful guarding. For these elite troops it was a shameful waste of their talents to be forced to perform the role of policemen to boisterous Allied troops and dour French civilians. Fortunately, good sense prevailed and the Commando was soon on the move again, this time across northern France to lay siege to the port of Dunkirk.

The Commando's official history explains why the siege was laid:

> With the rout of the German armies in France, their policy of holding the Channel ports and thus depriving us of supply bases became clear. Calais, Boulogne and Dunkirk were all strongly garrisoned. The first two named were reduced by 2nd Canadian Division, but Dunkirk, almost entirely surrounded by water, was a more difficult proposition, and the recent capture of Antwerp intact made the clearing of the German pocket south of the River Scheldt a more important task. Consequently, it was decided to contain Dunkirk with minimum forces, and 4th Special Services Brigade was detailed to take over this task from 2nd Canadian Division.

The front held by the Commando along this perimeter extended for about 10,000 yards, located either side of the walled town of Bergues, 10 miles inland from the port. It was a long front and understandably could only be lightly held by the depleted Commando. Lt Col Moulton brought his unit into these positions on 18 September, taking over from the 8th Canadian Reconnaissance Regiment. To help deceive the enemy into thinking that the line was still held by armoured cars, all marines in the forward areas wore their green berets inside out with their black lining uppermost.

The Intelligence Officer, Lt Harold Smedley, explains his biggest problem guarding the perimeter: 'We were very stretched with our numbers and it was important to get the opposition to believe that we had larger forces than we actually did have.' Capt Geoff Linnell recalls his troop's part in the deception: 'We were fairly few on the ground and wanted the enemy to think we were much stronger than we were. We removed the silencer from one of our lorries and drove it around at night; it sounded like a tank. On other occasions we fixed a Bofors gun on a jeep and sprayed the German lines with small shells then drove off to a safe distance and watched the enemy shelling the empty area with his artillery. I instigated a programme of conducting mortar shoots and machine gun fire from different spots each day, giving the enemy the impression that there were more of us than there really were.'

As at Sallenelles, active patrolling kept the enemy occupied. His main defence line was along the canal two miles in front of Dunkirk and he held outpost positions well forward of it, supported by mortars and 88-mm guns. As the Commando grew more active, the Germans became less so. The enemy was content to stay low and conserve ammunition, only responding if the Commando approached too near his positions. The ground in front of the town was waterlogged and no defensive works could be dug. Most of the positions of both sides were based on farm buildings. Patrols found these easier to attack and used the PIAT anti-tank 'bazooka' to blast the houses, killing the enemy if he came out.

On 26 September the Commando was given the news that it was to be withdrawn, not for the overdue return to England, but to take part in another amphibious assault landing, this time by the whole of 4th Special Service Brigade against the enemy-held island of Walcheren at the mouth of the River Scheldt, although this target was not made known to the commandos until just before they left on the operation. The need to remove the Germans from the island was part of the plan to clear the whole of the estuary of the Scheldt from Antwerp to the sea. The southern side of the river was held by the Canadians, while the enemy still held the northern side in some force. The city of Antwerp had been captured on 5 September with most of its docks and equipment still intact, but the great port would have to stay closed to Allied ships until both the banks of the River Scheldt and the coastal guns on the island of Walcheren had been cleared of the enemy to allow access to the sea. At a time when most supplies to front-line troops were still arriving over the beaches in Normandy, the opening up of Antwerp docks soon became the Allies' number one priority.

The Commando moved to the seaside resort of De Hann in Belgium to prepare for the amphibious assault on Walcheren on 27 September. The area near Westkapelle, where the landing was to take place, was known to be very heavily defended as its strategic importance had been recognised by the enemy. Most of its fortifications were positioned to prevent an assault from the sea. This meant that, to get ashore, 4 Special Service Brigade would have to carry out another full-scale amphibious landing against a heavily defended beach. This would be its second in five months. The vanguard would once again be 48 RM Commando, attacking abreast of 41 RM Commando astride the town of Westkapelle.

De Hann was the perfect place to train for the operation. All along the shoreline were captured German gun emplacements, fortifications and blockhouses. Techniques to be used during the landings on Walcheren were examined, trialled and implemented among these enemy positions on the sand dunes. Unlike the landings in Normandy, this operation was to be more mechanised. For a start, LCI(S)s would not be used. Moulton refused to have anything to do with these flimsy craft and insisted that his Commando be landed from tank landing craft. The marines were to be carried ashore in tracked amphibious vehicles. There were two types available to the unit, the larger Landing Vehicle Tracked IV – LTV(IV) – more commonly known as the Buffalo, and the smaller LTV(II) known as the Weasel. For this invasion, the tank landing craft would bring the Commando to the shore, the ramps would drop and the marines would come roaring out of the ships and up the beach, safe inside the steel-sided Buffaloes and Weasels. At least, that was the plan.

It was fortunate that just before the operation, the Commando received a new draft of 85 reinforcements from England. These brought its total strength up to around 350. This was still short of its nominal strength of about 500, but at least it topped the 300 mark for the first time since D-Day.

Breach made in the dyke at Westkapelle by the RAF. 48 RM Commando landed on White Beach, which is to the left of the gap – 41 RM Commando landed on Red Beach, to the right of the opening. The radar station can been seen on the upper left, just below the groyne that juts out into the sea. (*Imperial War Museum, C4668*)

Also returning were many of the men wounded in earlier fighting. Bert Skinner was one of them:

When I rejoined Z Troop I was put to work teaching others in the use of captured enemy weapons, including the MG34 and MG42 – these machine guns were standard issue to the Wehrmacht and we called them *Spandaus*. Many of us had the famous *Luger* pistols and *Schmeisser* machine pistols which we had picked up. Also among these weapons were German stick grenades or 'potato mashers' as we used to call them. We had a number of French Army weapons with us and, of course, the German *Mauser* rifle, *Gewehr* 98, which was carried by most German troops. At the same time a demolition course was laid on, where we blew up part of Hitler's 'Atlantic Wall'. Blowing the top off pillboxes with plastic explosive was great fun! On the beach at De Haan were some beach defences known to us as

'Rommel's Asparagus' on which were lashed German Teller mines. We shot at them for fun and they blew up with an almighty bang. We were like a lot of small boys at a coconut shy. The spirits of our Commando couldn't have been higher – we were the best! – and our Colonel Moulton was revered by all of us.

Just before the operation began, 'Doc' Winser returned to the unit. His burns had healed and he once again became the Commando's MO. Lt James Dick was now surplus to requirements and prepared to return to his old unit. He was rather sorry to be going, as he later explained: 'I had been looking forward to the thrill of a seaborne attack, but I was not sure that I wanted to be one of two medical officers in the unit. What if my presence meant that Winser would be somewhere else and got himself killed in the process, or vice versa? In fact, Winser was killed, and my return to my old unit stopped. I got to Walcheren towards the end of the battle.'

CHAPTER FOURTEEN

The Landings on Walcheren

The island of Walcheren lies on the northern side of the estuary of the River Scheldt. It dominates the entrance to the river and the passage up to the great port of Antwerp. Under German occupation it had become a fortified bastion covered in concrete defences and heavy coastal batteries, all guarding the seaward approaches to Antwerp. Its only access from the mainland was across a narrow causeway which linked the island to South Beveland on the northern bank of the River Scheldt.

The coastline of Belgium and Holland marked the left flank of Montgomery's 21st Army Group's advance and was in the sector allocated to Canadian Second Army. Command of 4 Special Service Brigade came under II Canadian Corps for the operation. The plan was for the island to be attacked from two directions simultaneously: a seaborne landing by the commandos, while 52nd Lowland Division and 2nd Canadian Division attacked along the north bank of the river and tried to gain access across the causeway. For the operation to be a success, the timing of the attack on the causeway and the seaborne assaults against Westkapelle and Flushing had to be closely linked. The operation was given the code-name 'Fortitude'. Brig Leicester was nominated as Military Force Commander for the seaborne landings.

The amphibious assaults by the commandos were to be made at two points. First, 4 Commando would land, attacking Flushing on the south of the island, followed a little later by the landings of 41 and 48 Commandos near Westkapelle on the western coast. These landings would clear the gun batteries and defences along the coast, while elements of 52nd Lowland Division landed behind 4 Commando at Flushing and attacked the enemy side of the causeway. Behind 48 Commando, 47 RM Commando would land and move southwards through its bridgehead, then clear the village of Zoutelande to link up with 4 Commando.

Most of Walcheren lies below sea level and is protected by a rim of high sand dunes and massive dykes. The operation called for these dykes to be breached before the assault so as to flood the inland areas and confine the enemy to the top of the dykes and higher coastal strips of sand dunes. This task was given to the RAF and on 3 October 252 Lancasters and 7 Mosquitoes of Bomber Command attacked the sea wall and dykes at Westkapelle, Flushing and Veere, breaching the sea defences in four places. Through these gaps the waters of the North Sea swept in and flooded the centre of the island, confining the German

One of the captured guns in strongpoint W13 which wreaked such havoc with the naval craft that supported the landings on Walcheren. (*Imperial War Museum, BU1274*)

garrison and local population to just those areas that remained above water level. This limited the enemy's ability to manoeuvre, but also confined all Allied attacks to these coastal strips, which meant that none of the German positions could be outflanked, each had to be attacked along a defined route, forcing them to be captured one after another, with the commandos leapfrogging from one resistance point to the next.

The landing points of 41 and 48 RM Commandos were to be astride the breach in the dyke made at Westkapelle; 41 Commando on Red Beach on the northern side of the gap, 48 Commando on White Beach on the southern side. The town of Westkapelle itself would be attacked by 41 Commando, which would then clear the enemy from the northern coast of Walcheren. Lt Col Moulton's Commando had been instructed to seize a beachhead and then advance southwards along the narrow strip of dry land

Opposite: The Attack on Walcheren

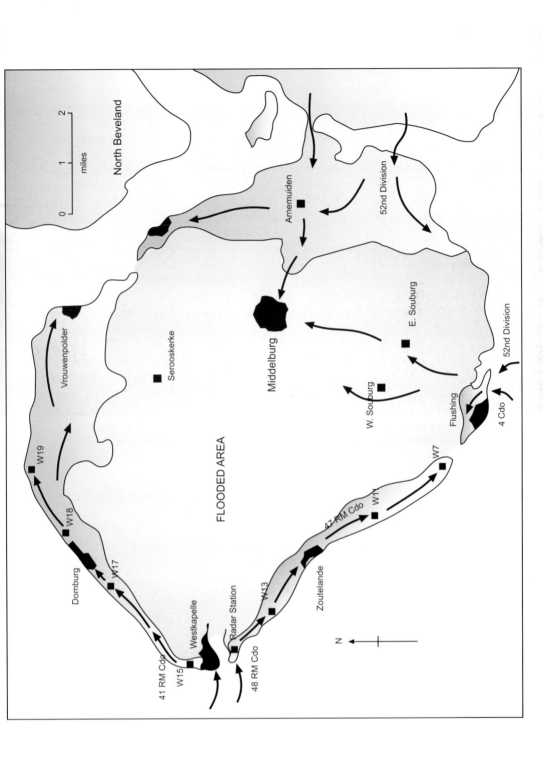

clearing the successive enemy fortified positions that were established among the sixty-feet-high dunes. The axis of this advance was only 150 yards wide, with the flooded land to the left and the sea to the right. There were eight resistance nests along this strip, with the major ones being located around the radar station at W154 and the large coastal gun battery located in strongpoint W13 about 2,500 yards from the gap. Battery W13 housed four 6-inch coastal guns, all in fortified concrete casemates, surrounded by bunkers, wire entanglements and minefields.

The Commando would embark from Ostend in LCTs and make a night approach to the island with H Hour being timed at 0945 hours. B Troop would lead the assault, landing in Buffaloes, followed by X and Y Troops and then HQ. B Troop's initial task was to capture and hold the landing beach and the two casemates overlooking the gap, while X Troop passed through and attacked the radar station. Y Troop would then carry the momentum on towards strongpoint W13. A and Z Troops would land in the second wave and move forward to attack the coastal batteries and to lead the push towards Zoutelande.

The landings were to be supported on a massive scale. Naval Force T, guarding the assault, was commanded by Capt Pugsley and comprised a range of ships and craft. In addition to the LCTs carrying the commandos ashore, a support squadron of craft under the command of Cdr Sellar consisted of Landing Craft Gun, Landing Craft Support, Landing Craft Flak and Landing Craft Rocket. All of these ships would be deployed off the coast to carry out pre-landing bombardment of enemy positions and then give supporting fire to the commandos ashore. Added to this direct firepower were the massive 15-inch guns of the battleship *Warspite* and the monitor *Roberts*. These great leviathans would attack the enemy gun batteries in advance of the landings and remain to support the troops as and when required.

The Germans had garrisoned the island with about 10,000 men, most of whom were low-category troops from the static 70th Infantry Division. The division was commanded by Lt Gen Daser. The unit was known as the 'White Bread Division' because most of its 7,500 soldiers had stomach problems and required special diets. The division had been raised on the island earlier in the year from cadres of 165th Reserve Division and remained there until it was destroyed in the action that followed. The fortifications on the island offered good protection to these static troops and they fought surprisingly well during the battle. The German 70th Division was strengthened by good-quality naval coast gunners from two Kriegsmarine Artillery Regiments and the Luftwaffe anti-aircraft detachments who were based on Walcheren. The flooding of the central areas had waterlogged many of the field gun sites and rendered them useless, so the main opposition to the landings would come from the fortified positions along the thin coastal strips and in the towns. It was hoped that bombardment of these positions by naval warships and the bombers of the RAF would neutralise their effectiveness. None the less, the assault landings by the commandos on Walcheren were expected to experience a high number of casualties.

On the evening of 31 October, 48 RM Commando boarded their LCTs in Ostend, to make ready for the sea passage to White Beach at Westkapelle. Embarkation was completed by 2000 hours and Naval Force T set sail at 0015 the next day. With four weeks to plan the operation, every eventuality had been covered. The assault troops inside the ships were well prepared and equipped, for their training had been specific and relevant to the tasks they were about to undertake. They faced their immediate future with equanimity, but there had been a few problems during the embarkation, as signaller Sgt Percy Bream recalls: 'Our departure was a little bit chaotic because we were to use Type 46 radio sets with crystals, and the crystals hadn't arrived until just before we were due to leave. We had to finish off our work on the sets while the Commando was assembling to leave. I was supposed to go with A Troop, but in the confusion my Weasel was loaded on the wrong craft. I landed with B Troop which was the assaulting troop leading the landings.'

Capt Geoff Linnell later recalled his thoughts on the coming invasion:

> On October 31st, we marched to Ostend and boarded landing craft for the assault. I was in the second wave and was to land in Buffaloes with my heavy weapons troop. Our job was to go over the beach to the inland side of the dunes and give supporting fire from the left. This was the very exposed landward side of the dunes alongside the inner flood waters. I was then supposed to float my way across the gap into Westkapelle and do a ninety degree shoot. This sounded quite risky and I felt that the Colonel might be sacrificing me and my machine gunners. The Buffaloes were large tracked vehicles, with a big rear door in which you could get a jeep, the machine guns and 40,000 rounds of ammunition inside. They were carried over to Walcheren in LCTs, craft that were much more suited to the task than the fragile LCI(S)s that we landed from on D-Day. The second wave of an assault is often not the best place to be, for by then the enemy's defences are well and truly awake.

For some the embarkation brought good news such as that received by Joe Stringer: 'As we were marching along Captain Teddy Dunn came up to me and gave me the crown as troop sergeant major, with Colonel Moulton's congratulations. He also said I was probably the youngest company sergeant major serving in the Royal Marines. I was still only twenty-one. We boarded the craft as the light was fading and knew that the landings on the island would be in broad daylight.'

The sea was calm during the crossing and the convoys experienced no difficulties. The landings at H Hour were timed for 0945 hours and the straight distance from Ostend to Walcheren was only 35 miles, so Force T took a great sweeping voyage out into the North Sea to be ready to land as scheduled. For 4 Commando there was a much shorter crossing over the Scheldt from Breskens directly to its beach at Flushing, for its landings were to be made at the much earlier time of 0545. This would divert German attention to the south of the island, while the remainder of 4th Special Service Brigade landed further to the north four hours later.

Dawn broke at 0715 hours on 1 November and by then the battle was well under way. On schedule, 4 Commando had landed and taken its

A Landing Craft Gun (LCG) which has been hit by German shellfire from one of the coastal batteries. Shortly after this picture was taken, the ship sank, but all of its crew were rescued. (*Imperial War Museum, A26233*)

objectives to allow the first battalion of 52nd Division, 4th King's Own Scottish Borderers, to land behind them at 0730 hours. Out at sea, Force T had turned eastwards for Walcheren and had begun making its run to shore. Well ahead of it was Cdr Sellar's Support Squadron with the *Warspite* and *Roberts* ready to open up with the preliminary bombardment on the German shore batteries.

One extremely important piece of bad news, however, had just been received by Capt Pugsley and Brig Leicester which would mar the operation. There would be no close air support or spotting for the assault guns during the initial attack, because the weather in England had closed in, making flying impossible. The Royal Navy alone would now have to provide the necessary direct supporting fire for the landings and the subsequent fighting. Some help would be on hand from Canadian artillery on the other side of the Scheldt, but for this to be effective good communications with forward observers were essential.

At 0735 hours the *Warspite* and *Roberts* opened fire, concentrating on German coastal batteries. The first to be attacked was W17 on the northern side of the island, which was firing its large 220-mm guns at the landings in the south at Flushing. This was silenced and the ships next turned to the problems of W15 and W13, which were situated either side of the Westkapelle gap, flanking the path of the assault force which at that moment was heading straight for them. Eight rounds of 15-inch shells silenced W15 at 0830 hours, but W13 proved to be a little more resilient. This battery continued firing for some hours and only stopped its 6-inch guns when it finally ran out of ammunition shortly before 48 Commando stormed the position.

The naval Support Squadron deployed its vessels 5 miles off Red and White Beaches at 0848 hours and began its bombardment of the shore with an array of offensive craft. Guns, rockets and anti-aircraft weapons all concentrated on the German positions and known resistance points. For the next three and a half hours the ships of the squadron cruised up and down at very close range, running the gauntlet of German fire to provide support to the troops ashore. It was an epic fight and one which proved very costly for the lightly armoured craft, but the support provided by Cdr Sellar's squadron made the assault in the Westkapelle area possible.

As the naval craft versus shore defences battle raged, the landing craft carrying the Commandos ploughed inexorably towards the landing beaches coming under German fire while still 5 miles out. For the next hour they had to endure this enemy attention until they hit the beach. Donald Nicholson was in the craft carrying Capt Linnell's machine gunners:

> None of us were under any illusions as to the difficulty of the task which lay ahead; we were to make an assault on an island heavily defended by 6-inch gun batteries encased in massive concrete bunkers. As we sailed we rarely spoke. We kept our thoughts to ourselves. At some stage someone produced a small flask of brandy which was passed from man to man, but as I was a teetotaller I declined. Shortly after first sighting the outline of our low-lying objective the sea in front of us suddenly erupted with a curtain of massive waterspouts. The enemy was putting down a barrage of fire through which we had to pass. At that moment I became rather fearful. Unless the enemy was silenced it seemed impossible for us to get through such a barrage of fire without considerable loss. Nobody said anything, and I resigned myself to whatever lay ahead. However, as we proceeded I was not aware of a similar barrage being repeated. Shellfire was evident, but I was also aware of LCGs manned by Royal Marines putting up a spirited response to the enemy.

Lt John Square arrived amid 'great fountains of water from the shellfire from enemy guns'. Percy Bream looked out on a sea wild with enemy fire:

> On the run in to our landing beach we could see the terrific bombardment that was being laid down on the German defences from naval ships and aircraft of all types. The Germans responded in kind and I remember thinking that the beach to our left where 41 RM commando was landing was taking a bit of a pasting. It was the landing craft that seemed to be suffering most. All of the time the landings were under way, you could see boats going down. They had to come close in to the shore and the Germans were blasting them at short range.

The first LCT to arrive on White Beach carried the Commando's assault wave which hit the shore at 1010 hours. On board this leading LCT was Lt Evan Thomas, who later recalled the landing:

> We touched down just a few minutes behind schedule. I felt curiously detached, almost as if I was watching a Hollywood film. With a crunch, the bows of the landing craft hit the bottom, the ramp went down, the Buffalo drivers gunned their engines and we were off into the water and trundling up the wide beach, with me and my men leading the whole Commando. A hundred yards from the top of the beach we jumped out of our Buffalo, spread out and charged the two pillboxes that were our specific target.

Among these leading marines was Sgt Joe Stringer:

> B Troop was given the first job on landing, being carried in the first two Buffaloes. I had made it my intention, as I had done on D-Day, of being the first man in my section ashore. I thought it was a good omen for me. I wanted be the first out of the Buffalo before any German could get a good aim on me, and I was. I was the first over the side of the Buffalo once it had left the LCT. Our task was to clear the two pillboxes alongside the beach where we landed. When we got to them we found they had been smashed by the bombing and were unoccupied. So we had an easy walk in. We were very fortunate with our first objective. Other troops then had to pass through us and head for their jobs along the dunes.

As Col Moulton closed on the shore he watched the Oerlikon guns on his craft sweep the radar station and other fortifications with small-calibre shells. This fire was taken up by the Polsen guns on the Buffaloes manned by the men of 79th Armoured Division who operated the amphibious vehicles. He felt some satisfaction as the area over which his men would soon be attacking was sprayed with a deluge of fire. Then the LCT scrapped against the bottom and the ramp was dropped. Out stormed the first Buffaloes with their contingent of marines, followed by the smaller Weasels, including Moulton's command vehicle. Down into the shallow water, a small swim to the beach and then the tracks gripped the sand and the Weasels shot forward towards the dunes. 'This was the way to land,' thought Moulton, 'Dry shod, plenty of firepower, very few casualties, and my wireless set with me.' This was such a contrast to the shambles on Nan Red Beach just five months previously.

There was little small-arms fire to greet the leading marines as they touched down. What opposition there was came from heavy shelling and a few mortars, but most of this was still being aimed at the landing craft out to sea. Ten minutes later Capt Mackenzie and X Troop were ashore and moving through B troop towards the radar station. Leading one of Mackenzie's half-troops was Lt Hedley Phillips. He later recalled the first moments of the assault:

> We made an accurate landing on the south side of the gap in the dyke. By then the beach had begun to come under mortar fire. We lost no time in disembarking from our Buffaloes, stacking our packs at the bottom of the dunes as planned and scrambling up the loose sand towards our first objective, the radar station. It was Mac's plan that we should each take a half-troop, with him keeping as far as possible to the seaward side of the dunes to keep station on the right flank, and I would do the same on the landward side on the left flank. In the event, although the German station was under small-arms fire, it had been bombed to destruction and was deserted.

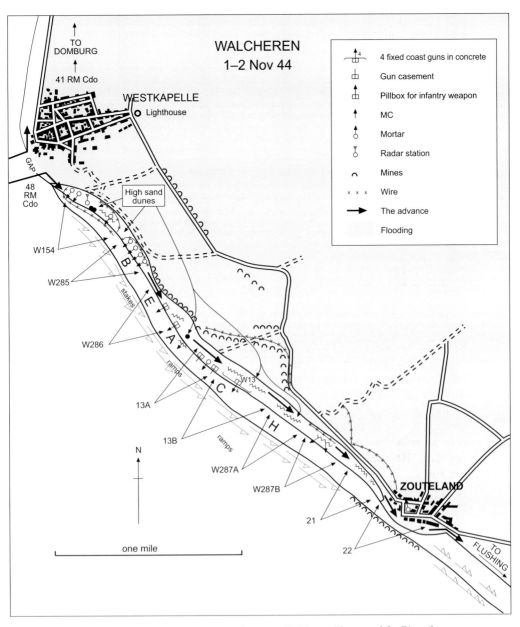

German Defences Along 48 RM Commando's Sector on Walcheren (*Courtesy of Geoff Linnell*)

Up with Mackenzie was Col Moulton. He came following on as X Troop had moved off, dodging enemy shells and surviving a near miss. The Colonel now spoke with the troop leader and told him to press on while the going was good to take the next strongpoint before the enemy could get himself organised. Maj de Stacpoole and Y Troop would follow through as soon as they arrived.

With the leading wave was RSM Colin Travers, who remembers his arrival on Walcheren: 'I travelled over with HQ Troop. We had some small tracked Weasels with us, but they were horrible things that nobody liked. We were loaded up to the gunnels with small arms and mortar ammunition. In my Weasel was myself, the driver and the orderly room sergeant. We seemed to be under fire all the way in, but we were not hit. We drifted into a small inlet and we had a dry landing. I remember the dunes were very high and we couldn't see anything of the leading troops because they had pushed on with their attacks. My first job was to look for the Colonel and to arrange for ammunition to be got up to the forward troops.'

The initial wave was now ashore and the second wave was starting its final approaches. On board the landing craft carrying Captain Linnell's machine gunners was an American reporter, Tom Bernard from *Yank* magazine, and he relayed his experiences to his readers:

> From the matchbox of a bridge we could see that the chaos, the fires, the shellbursts on or near the shore were not all caused by our ships. There were more bursts at sea than on land, and just as many fires. To the left of the gap we watched one of our many flak ships armed with two-pounders and 20 mms, tackle a line of five or six pillboxes atop the dyke. Red tracers streaked landward for a few minutes. Then the LCF (flak ship) disappeared in a mighty blast of fire and smoke. Later, we learned she had taken a direct hit in her magazine, suffering severe casualties. Eight knots was the speed of our LCT and, as the bursts around us increased in number and nearness, we felt as if we were riding the shell of a snail. The Jerry gunners were trying to get the exact range of the line of LCTs. First, the third craft ahead of us squeezed between two near misses and rocked drunkenly. Then a string of six explosions ran along our starboard side, showering the decks with spray and sending fragments pinging against the side. Four more rounds pounded off port and shrapnel rained down on the bridge.

The next salvo of enemy fire straddled the craft as it neared the beach, one shell scoring a direct hit on the Buffalo containing Capt Linnell: 'I had my elbow over the driving compartment looking through my binoculars at the shore. We were hit by a large shell that came straight into the driving compartment and I was blown to the back of the Buffalo. I think that I was saved by my machine gun slide rule that was hanging in front of me across my chest, for a large piece of shrapnel had virtually destroyed it. The two men in the front of the vehicle, the driver and the wireless operator, were killed.' Linnell lost his beret and all the hair from his head was burned off in the blast. 'It was the first time in many years I had no moustache. No one recognised me!'

In the back of the vehicle was Donald Nicholson and he remembers the explosion:

The Buffaloes had started up their engines when suddenly the men in my Buffalo were thrown about, many of them injured, two seriously, and in the immediate confusion this caused we realised we had received a direct hit. A shell had penetrated the armoured front of the driver's cabin and shell splinters had ripped through into the open well at the rear where men, weapons and equipment were being carried. Our padre, Revd Maurice Wood, appeared on the scene to give assistance. In the meantime the LCT ramp had gone down and the remaining Buffaloes began evacuating the vessel. Fortunately, our Buffalo was one of a pair behind all the others and did not impede the exit in any way.

The enemy shell had exploded just in front of the bridge and Tom Bernard was hit by the blast, as he later told his readers:

The quartermaster flew back catching me amidships and catapulting me against the after bulkhead, where I hit the deck, but hard. Flames licked up the front of the single porthole through which the quartermaster steered his course. Smoke, lifting in gusts, swirled past the port, obscuring his vision. The stern and side of another LCT loomed out of the murk. Staccato orders were piped down the tube from the bridge. The scream of shells increased in violent crescendo, but they all burst astern. The ramp dropped and the first Buffalo waddled off on to the sand. Shell fragments flicked at the stern and the sickening odour of cordite mixed with burning flesh swirled back from the tank deck.

Force T carrying 4 Special Services Brigade approaches Walcheren on the morning of 1 November, 1944. The commandos are all wearing their green berets; the men in the one-piece tank suits, who manned the Buffaloes, are from the 11th Royal Tank Regiment. (*Imperial War Museum, A26266*)

With the ramps down, unloading took place at lightning speed. In moments the tracked vehicles loaded with men and equipment had all roared off on to the beach. His job complete, the craft's skipper ordered the boat to be put astern and gradually began to pull away, much to the annoyance of several of its passengers, one of whom was Capt Linnell: 'To my surprise the LCT quickly began to reverse off of the beach and I and two of my men had to scramble ashore, taking with us what parts of the machine guns we could salvage. When I got on the beach I found that we had only recovered two machine gun tripods, which were of no use on their own. I was in a state of shock from the explosion, had no men or weapons landed so I helped move the other Buffaloes along the coast.'

Inside the blasted Buffalo, Donald Nicholson was trying also trying to salvage something from the wreckage: 'While the wounded were being attended to attempts were made to start unloading the Vickers MMGs, but before we had a chance to run them ashore the ramp was raised and the LCT started backing off the beach, to the dismay of our padre and those of us who were still able to carry on. At great risk to himself the padre insisted on being lowered into the water to enable him to strike out for the shore and rejoin the Commando. Mercifully, although having on his back a rucksack full of hymnbooks, he survived.'

Revd Maurice Wood recalls why he had to make this unorthodox exit from the craft: 'I just had to get ashore, for I was the only Church of England chaplain sent on the operation. My batman, Bill Price – a fine Welsh rugby player – dropped me over the side and then threw my lifebelt after me and I made for the beach as best I could.'

This second wave of landing craft was hit harder than the first. A and Z Troops came ashore in the face of heavy and accurate shellfire. Meanwhile, up ahead, the sweep along the dunes was continuing. With the radar station captured, X Troop was ordered to continue its move southwards and take W285, the next German strongpoint. Lt Phillips later recounted this phase of the advance:

> On leaving the radar station we were in the open of course, only the undulations of the dunes providing partial cover. We stumbled forward through the thick sand, leapfrogging over short distances as planned in a series of frontal rushes with the half-troop roughly in line abreast across the top of the dune, Bren guns on the flanks and automatic weapons in the centre. In this way we quickly overcame the next German strongpoint, taking about a dozen prisoners. There had been one or two casualties, and I had lost my runner – he turned up later saying he had returned to the beach with one of the wounded; a practice strictly forbidden!

The main enemy retaliation was concentrated on the area near the landing places. Heavy shellfire fell among the beachhead knocking out a number of the amphibious vehicles and causing numerous casualties. The Germans had woken up to the landings and had located the main assembly areas. They now began to put down accurate and sustained counter-fire. Most of the enemy small-arms fire was still coming from along the dunes, while the artillery fire whined across from inland.

There were three ways forward along the spit of land over which the Commando now had to advance: along the landward side across the face of German shellfire, along the shoreline in the teeth of a welter of small-arms fire and across the top of the dunes where every man became silhouetted against the skyline. Each route forward was equally deadly, as was just remaining on the landing beach. In fact the whole of the lodgement was under enemy observation and lacked any real cover. There was no hiding place on Walcheren as Lt John Square soon discovered: 'We landed on the beach into the usual confusion. Nobody knew what to do with us, so all we could do was just find the best cover and lay down until we were needed. Soon afterwards I was hit on the back with a great clod of earth thrown up from a mortar bomb. I felt a little shocked, but was immediately relieved that I was not hurt. Then Captain Nuttall came up and we moved out along the dunes.'

Out at sea the duel between the naval Support Squadron and the still-lively German coast defences continued. Throughout the morning, support craft came in perilously close to shore to give covering fire to the commandos and often paid for their boldness with terrible casualties. Making its way out through all of this mayhem was the landing craft carrying Capt Linnell's destroyed Buffalo. Donald Nicholson describes the scene on board and the action for which he was later awarded the Military Medal:

Flames were billowing out from underneath the driver's cab of the Buffalo. With everything else going on no thought had been given to the fate of the driver. I climbed back on to the Buffalo, then opened and quickly slammed shut the driver's hatch on top of the cabin. Inside was a raging inferno incinerating the driver and his wireless operator. Flames then started to engulf two Jerry cans of petrol and boxes of ammunition in the Buffalo. With the safety of the vessel and those on board at stake, these were hoisted up to the side of the craft where Colour Sergeant George Over promptly pushed them over into the sea.

The LCT was now under way back to Ostend. As Signaller to the Vickers MMGs I decided it was time to try and make contact with 48 Commando HQ. I took myself high up on the stern of the vessel and although locked in to the right radio frequency, was unable to make any contact whatsoever. I was joined for part of the time by Marine McArthur. My unsuccessful attempts were interrupted by a massive heaving of the ship. We had struck a mine and the back of the LCT had broken. Many of my comrades on the lower open deck were thrown into the water, some suffering broken legs and ankles. Colour Sergeant George Over had both ankles broken. Marine McArthur who had been with me shortly before had completely disappeared and was not seen again. Those of us who were uninjured went to the aid of those in the sea and hauled them back on board.

The LCT was now sinking and our fate seemed uncertain. Then quite unexpectedly a small vessel appeared already heavily loaded down with badly injured marines and naval personnel. My immediate thought was that if anyone else boarded her she should sink, as she was so low in the water. However, her valiant skipper took us all on board and headed back to Ostend. We were surrounded by many badly burned men, laid on their backs wherever there was room. Some of them were vomiting and although we could do nothing my fear was that they could drown in their own vomit. Mercifully the sea was calm. Had it been otherwise many could have been washed overboard, and all of us might have perished. I shall always be thankful to that skipper whose courage and humanity eventually brought us back to Ostend without further mishap.

Back on land the marines gradually moved along the sand dunes, edging their way towards Zoutelande, with the great strongpoint of W13 barring their way. Harry Lane in Z troop went along the coastal route, moving forwards at the top of the beach: 'Sergeant Joe Telford told me and about six others to go over the dunes and try to advance along the shore. We scrambled over the sand and tried to edge our way forward, but in doing so we exposed ourselves to the naval craft offshore. They must have taken us for Germans because everyone seemed to be firing at us.' Jock Mathieson took the route along the top of the dunes, but found it difficult and tiring: 'The sand was very deep and loose making it very hard to move. We seemed to have to drag our feet along making it very slow going.' Tony Pratt recalls the strength of the German resistance: 'The fire was coming down the length of the dunes at us, from the direction of Flushing. No sooner had one strongpoint been captured than fire started up from the next one.'

Once X Troop had captured W285, Maj de Stacpoole moved through its position with Y Troop to attack W 286. This strongpoint also fell without too much difficulty, giving up many German prisoners in the process. Then it was on to the main objective, the heavily fortified coastal gun site W13. Unlike the previous two strongpoints, W13 proved to be a very different proposition. Maj de Stacpoole rushed the wired perimeter of the site with his men, trying to preserve the momentum of the advance. They opened up with a hail of small arms fire but were stopped in their tracks by the naval gunners who manned the post. Maj de Stacpoole was shot dead, many other marines were hit and the attack halted. News was passed back to Moulton that the strongpoint was too well defended and would have to be invested with a much larger force supported by heavy weapons.

The Colonel signalled to Mackenzie to close up to Y Troop and hold the ground that had been already gained, keeping the battery under fire to occupy the German defenders while he formulated a plan for the capture of W13. Moulton's main problem was that the attack could only be made on a narrow front; the water on both sides of the long spit of land left few opportunities for manoeuvre. There was only room for one troop to make the assault and this could only be from one direction, along the dunes. All of the enemy's firepower could be concentrated at the northern edge of the strongpoint, for the defenders knew that this was where the attack must come from. Z Troop under Capt Nuttall was now selected to make the assault.

Moulton did have a small piece of luck, however, for on the left flank some way back from W13 there was a narrow spur of sand dunes running a short distance out into the flooded hinterland. If Capt Flunder could get his A Troop on to this spur, the attack could be supported by some flanking fire to occupy the enemy as the battery was rushed by the main assault. The range would be rather long, but at least some covering fire could be offered to Z Troop. The Colonel knew in his heart that this fire would not be enough and he had to get some extra support, but radio contact with the Canadian guns over the Scheldt was out, and the naval Support Squadron offshore had by this time moved away. HMS *Roberts*, however, was still on call via Capt Davies, the Artillery Bombarding Officer attached to the

Weasels and Buffaloes landing from LCTs near the gap at Westkapelle. These vehicles are supporting 41 RM Commando, which landed to the north of the breach in the dyke. 48 RM Commando landed to the left of this picture. (*Imperial War Museum, B11646*)

Commando. Moulton now requested him to contact the battleship and range her guns on the German battery. With this under way, the Colonel moved back down the dunes to get in contact with the Canadians.

The Support Squadron had withdrawn having fired off all of their ammunition. They had had a very difficult day. Three of their craft had been sunk offshore trying to silence the guns of W13, one of them being knocked out of the water at almost point-blank range, just 300 yards off the beach. Now, just at the moment when their aimed fire was most needed to support the assault, the two surviving gun craft and the one remaining flak ship turned out to sea and retired.

Radio communication along the dunes was proving very difficult, as Dennis Smith explains:

My radio set let us down. I was asked to call for supporting artillery fire, but could not raise anyone on the new set. Everyone was getting agitated, so was I. I was getting flak from the

Colonel because we needed heavy support for the next attack on the German battery. I was supposed to be working back to a set with our brigade HQ who were coming in after us, but I couldn't make contact. We didn't know if they had arrived or if their set had gone. I thought that I might get a better signal if I could get my aerial over the top of the sand dunes. So I carefully made my way up the dunes, which were about twenty to thirty feet high, and put my aerial over the top, all the while trying to keep myself below the crest. The movement was immediately spotted by the enemy and bullets quickly began to whizz round the top of the aerial. Then there was a blinding flash followed by loud explosions as a cluster of mortar bombs fell around me. I received several shrapnel wounds to my arm and legs. My frustration of not being able to get through to brigade had caused me to be hit.

Back at the landing beach Moulton was able to make contact with brigade and organise some heavy support for the attack on W13. He was promised a timed programme from the guns of the Canadian 3rd Medium Regiment on the southern bank of the Scheldt and a low-level ground attack to be made on the coastal battery by the RAF. Both were arranged to arrive just before the assault went in at 1600 hours. In the meantime, Moulton ordered as much relief as possible to be got up to the leading troops. This was not an easy task as RSM Colin Travers recalls: 'Because of the loose sand and the exposed nature of the dunes, everything had to be moved forward by hand. It was a case of getting carrying parties together to get the stuff moving. Everyone gave a hand, including myself. Things were rather sticky up ahead and the Colonel came back and urged me to get as much stuff forward as quickly as we could.'

Roy Dewar and his Bren gun group were with Z Troop as it inched its way forwards along the dunes towards W13. He remembers reaching a particularly high dune which barred their way:

A Jerry sniper was waiting for us to show ourselves over the top where we would be silhouetted against the skyline. He was pitched only about 100 yards away and could have picked us all off one by one, so we radioed back and asked for some mortar fire to be put down on his position. A few moments later bombs started to come over and landed all around us. We radioed back and asked for the range to be put up about 100 yards only to be told that the mortars hadn't fired yet. We realised then that the enemy had spotted Z Troop and had our advance covered.

With news that he and Z Troop were to make the assault on W13, Capt Nuttall called an 'Orders Group' to explain the attack to his men. He grouped his officers and NCOs around him in a hollow formed by the dunes. Ernie Taylor was close by, up with the leading troops: 'We were on the top of a high crest on the dunes, about 150 yards from W13. Captain Nuttall and our officers were in a group about thirty yards behind us. Suddenly three or four mortar bombs exploded among them, throwing bodies all around.'

Lt John Square was the senior subaltern with Z troop and recalls the mortar fire:

Bombs started to drop among us. At first I thought the fire was coming from our own side which had happened before, but it was enemy fire which bracketed us. Lieutenant Lindrea crouching beside me was killed. I was wounded in my leg, I remember it felt just like a savage kick from an opponent when you are playing football. All around me was complete shambles; virtually the whole of the group had been killed or wounded. Captain Nuttall was very brave, he was bleeding badly, but tried to patch himself up. I was evacuated back to the landing beach.

Harry Lane was quickly on the scene: 'It was a terrible sight, it looked as though the troop had lost all of its officers. Bodies were lying all around. In front of me was Lieutenant Lindrea who had been badly wounded. I tried to pull him down into some cover, but as I put my arms round his chest to drag him down I felt that there was nothing there. His front part had been shot away. He gave one last gasp and a groan and died in my arms. Then more shells started to come over. There was a tremendous explosion and I felt a sudden searing pain as some shrapnel hit me in the head and back.' Ernie Taylor saw Capt Nuttall try to get to his feet with the help of a rifle. He shouted to the officer, 'Are you all right Sir?' but got no reply. Then the next salvo of mortars came over. This time they were ranged a little further over to the left, fortunately missing everyone.

Bert Skinner managed to escape this mortaring: 'Captain Nuttall had sent me with a Bren group up to Y Troop and when all of the officers and senior

A view from inside a tank landing craft that has touched down on Walcheren. A Buffalo is descending the ramp and Weasels are lining up to disembark. (*Imperial War Museum, A26268*)

NCOs were killed or wounded by the mortar fire, I, a mere Corporal, was left as second-in-command of the troop! A little later we were all split up among the other troops; I was attached to A Troop.'

Further disaster was not far away, for enemy mortar bombs now began to fall among X Troop. Close by Tony Pratt, Capt Mackenzie was hit by a deafening explosion. 'I saw him go down on his hands and knees and thought he was dead. He had been hit in the eye and in the chest and was badly wounded. He was taken back and died a little later in hospital in Belgium. He was a real gentleman to us, we all used to call him "Mac".' Other mortar bombs eliminated more key personnel. Capt Davies and his telegraphist were also hit, their deaths severing all contact with the *Roberts*.

Not far away Lt Hedley Phillips was with his half-troop and he recalls the mortaring: 'I was on the landward side of the approaches to the battery and, due no doubt to the deadening effect of the sand, only suffered one fatal casualty. For the time being we were not aware of what was happening elsewhere.'

The padre, Revd Maurice Wood, later came across one of the worst losses to befall the Commando, as he later explained:

I had gone to the dressing station expecting to find Michael Winser, our doctor, but when I arrived I discovered that he was absent. He was last seen going over the dunes with his medical rucksack and the orderlies at the aid post were getting a little worried for he had been gone for some time. I went to look for him and had only gone a fairly short distance when I came across his body. He was lying with his medical orderly close to Captain Davies, who was also dead. All of his medical equipment and bandages were strewn around him. He had obviously been tending to the Captain when he had been hit by a mortar bomb which had dropped beside him. He showed no visible signs of injury and lay there as though he had just fallen asleep. It was a very great shock to us all to lose such a fine man. He was one of the finest doctors I have known. He was only a year older than me, but I regarded him with something close to hero worship. He was just great; all of our men loved him. He was in every way estimable.

CHAPTER FIFTEEN

The Battle for Walcheren

The close nature of the battlefield on Walcheren caused a great number of casualties. Fire seemed to come at the Commando from all directions. This was not surprising, for the enemy could be found on three sides of 48 Commando's front. Behind it, 41 RM Commando was clearing Westkapelle and the coast to the north. German fire aimed at that unit 'spilled over' on to 48 Commando's territory and caught its marines in the rear. On the landward flank, artillery fire from the other side of the island raked the left-hand face of the Commando's advance. In front of them was W13 and the strongpoints beyond, as well as heavy-calibre German weapons outside Zoutelande and Flushing. Even on the shoreline in the lee of the dunes, small-arms fire caught the commandos in enfilade.

All the wounded were brought back under great difficulties to the landing beach, where efforts were made to evacuate them. One of these unfortunates was Lt John Square: 'When I arrived back on the beach I was dragged behind a dune and the padre came round to see me and gave me a cigarette. We were being mortared and bombed all the time. I was taken off on a Buffalo out to a landing craft and taken back to a hospital in Ostend. I remember that there were many German prisoners on the LCT and they kept coming up to me while I lay there on a stretcher asking for cigarettes.'

Signaller Dennis Smith had been wounded while trying to raise brigade on his wireless:

My wounds were not all that serious and I managed to slide down the dunes and make my way to the dressing station back along the beach. I found that our MO had been killed and the medical orderlies there were very busy. A corporal dressed my injuries and told me to go further back to the beachhead and await evacuation. I thought that the landing site was probably the worst place to be as it was still under a good deal of fire, so I made my way back to my section and joined another signalman. I scrapped a hole in the sand and stayed there for two days while things sorted themselves out.

Z Troop had been left without any officers or senior NCOs so it was temporarily deemed to be out of action. Its men were split up and joined other troops until it could be reorganised and re-officered. Capt Dunn's B Troop was now told it would have to make the attack on W13. It did not, however, have much time to prepare for the assault, for the Spitfires of the RAF and the massive shells of the naval support from the monitor were soon to be screaming overhead, as Lt Evan Thomas recalled: 'When we got

The breach in the dyke at Westkapelle. 48 RM Commando advanced along the long spur of dunes, moving from right to left. The German coastal battery W13 is at the top left. (*Imperial War Museum, C4673*)

this order, we were almost 600 yards behind the assembly area and had to make a mad dash across the soft sand of the dunes to get into position before the bombardment.'

H Hour was quickly approaching for the start of the attack on W13. Lt Hedley Phillips in X Troop was still oblivious to what was happening and continued to hold his position on the left flank watching the strongpoint, as he explains:

I was quickly made aware that the CO had drummed up some support, because a flight of Spitfires came across at low level and dropped some bombs among us! Happily the sand had its effects again and apart from the concussion there were no casualties. Almost immediately afterwards we heard the noise of several trains approaching. This was the unmistakable sound of 15-inch shells in flight. We later learned that they had come from the monitor *Roberts* and they landed right in the middle of my half-troop position. Again the soft sand saved us, but our ears were ringing and I was practically deafened. Just then a runner from our troop sergeant major arrived to tell me the news about Mac.

On the extreme left flank the Bren guns of A Troop were also harassing the German defenders. Among the gunners was Bert Skinner, late of Z Troop:

> I brought my Bren group into a position in the front of the attack line, where I made a basic error in indicating a target for the Bren gun. I used a tracer round and gave the order to fire as indicated. The response from the enemy was immediate. We were bracketed by mortar bombs and, as usual, Jerry was right on target. An officer of one of the other troops arrived and ordered a ceasefire and told me of the Colonel's plan for air support. Almost immediately it arrived, as several Spitfires unloaded their 250-lb bombs on our target, followed by an attack with rockets by a couple of Typhoons.

Along with the dramatic bombing and shelling by the Royal Navy and the RAF, the Royal Canadian Artillery added their weight of fire to the deluge of high explosive being concentrated on the German coastal battery. The 5.9-inch guns of the Canadian 3rd Medium Regiment were sending salvo after salvo on to the bunkers and casemates of W13. This bombardment lasted for a full fifteen minutes and as it stopped, the 2-inch mortars of B and X Troops joined in with smoke and HE. From the spur on the extreme left, the Brens of A Troop now raked the area. Then it was time for the assault.

Lt Evan Thomas was in the van of this attack:

> I was to lead the troop with half our men, and Teddy Dunn and the rest would follow hard on our heels. Dead on time the barrage stopped and we went 'over the top'. It was the second time that day that I had led B Troop in a major attack and the second time that day that our troop had led the Commando. As the smoke cleared we found ourselves in among a collection of concrete bunkers, most of which were empty, although we did pick up one or two dazed prisoners. Teddy Dunn and the rest of B Troop came through us and we gave them covering fire as they veered off to the right to capture the battery command post, together with the battery commander and his second-in-command.

Among the marines in the assault was Sgt Joe Stringer:

> This was the nearest I came to the First World War type of fighting. Our attack was confined to the centre of the dunes, a single stretch of ground with water on both sides. The plan of attack was straight through the minefield and barbed wire. We ran through the minefield, but were lucky that the strong winds had blown away the sand covering the mines and they were mostly visible to us, but many of our weapons suffered from the blown sand which seemed to clog everything. There was little artillery support from the mainland at this time. I approached the barbed wire with Lt Albutt alongside me. His tommy gun jammed just as a German jumped up in front of us. The Lieutenant just threw his gun at the German, but I shot him. We cleared the wire by stepping on top of Dougie Gray who had stumbled on to it when he fell. He was very useful and the last man dragged him off when we had all got through.

Dougie Gray recalls the speed of the assault: 'We moved forward like a rugby pack. At the wire I got snagged trying to get through and fell over, allowing some of the others to run through it and over me. I was pulled off as the troop surged forward. We were a ferocious sight, with our commando cap comforters squashed on our heads and our faces fierce and blackened.'

The first building to fall was the command post to the right of the breach in the wire. The steel door was blown and a few hand grenades were thrown down the steps, prompting the Germans inside to come out with their hands raised. Once through the wire the marines of B Troop spread out, employing the tactics they had rehearsed over and over during their training on the dunes at De Hann. Following close on their heels were the men of X Troop. First one gun emplacement was cleared and then another. Buildings and bunkers were all blasted and sprayed with fire if the occupants showed any signs of resistance. There were few German heroes inside W13 that late in the day. The enemy garrison had endured non-stop bombardment from the early hours, suffering the effects of almost the whole range of Allied weaponry available: rockets, shells, bombs and bullets had all rained down on them relentlessly all day. Once the commandos were inside the perimeter, the enemy knew that all was lost and only death or surrender awaited them.

Helping to clear the gun casemates was Ernie Taylor:

> I stood with my back against the concrete side and threw a Mills 36 grenade through the entrance. I waited for a while then threw in a 69 concussion grenade followed by a 77 phosphorus one. After the smoke had cleared I entered the passage and got into the main opening. There were two Germans dead near the entrance, both with their legs blown off. In the main chamber by the gun, the gunner was sitting dead on the gun-seat and his two loaders were lying dead on the floor beside him. Just as I was about to leave the bunker a head appeared out of the basement and a tall German shouted 'Nix shoot!' I levelled my tommy gun at him and said 'OK Fritz', and beckoned him up. He showed me a picture of his wife and his little girl. Just then another German came up from below covered in white dust and offered me a jar of cherry brandy.

Whenever they could safely do so, the men of strongpoint W13 just gave themselves up. George Hawkins witnessed at first hand the fatal resignation of the enemy troops as he later recalled: 'I asked one German officer why they had surrendered with so many guns and so much ammunition still intact. He replied, "What would you have done when hordes of mad soldiers with green berets came screaming at you?"' The death and devastation suffered by the enemy was clear to see, as Tony Pratt remembers: 'The insides of all the bunkers of the strongpoint were full of German bodies. Most of them had been killed by the bombing and the naval bombardment. I recall one immensely thick casemate made from solid concrete had a crack about a foot wide running down its side. The blast that did the damage had killed everyone inside.'

The size of the strongpoint was surprisingly large and while the main buildings had been quickly captured, there were still remote areas that needed to be rooted out. Y Troop was sent through along the seaward side to clear the far end of the battery, where some defiant gunner was still firing occasional bursts from a light cannon. Closer to hand, Sgt Joe Stringer found that there were still many Germans still alive, as he explains:

> We had just settled down after the capitulation of the battery when an English-speaking German came towards us from below the dunes on the left-hand side. I took him to Captain Dunn and he asked if our Medical Officer could go and treat their wounded. By this time in our MO was in fact dead, killed in the earlier fighting. We said no he couldn't. If they wanted medical treatment then they must surrender to us first. Dunn then sent me with this German

to bring the prisoners in. I wasn't very pleased, I thought why doesn't he send one of the officers, but I suppose he was testing my worth, because he had only promoted me twenty-four hours earlier. I went with the German on the understanding that if they touched me, our troop would mete out gruesome punishments on all of them. Our Captain used very strong and forceful language when explaining this to the German. We went off with a white flag into the German trenches. The enemy troops looked rough and very tired. The heavy shelling from the warships had demoralised them. Their guns seemed to have been completely destroyed during the bombardment, even their lighter canons and anti-aircraft weapons were smashed. We approached their officer, he saluted and shook my hand after the other German had spoken to him and explained the situation. He then shouted an order to his troops in the trenches all around and they threw down their weapons and we then proceeded down the dunes to this blockhouse. An awful sight greeted us, everywhere around there were dead and wounded men. Some were on stretchers but most were lying on the ground. They were in a terrible state. Those that were able gathered up the wounded and carried them back to our lines. I walked them in and handed them over to other marines and they were sent back to a holding area on the beach.

By the time the battery had been made secure it was quite dark. It had been a long day for the Commando and everyone was tired, worn out, cold and hungry, but there was still work to be done. Moulton ordered a screen to be set up in front of the battery to warn of any counter-attack. The next strongpoint, W287, was only 800 yards away and was still held in force by the enemy. The marines of A Troop were brought forward and given the task. Bert Skinner was among them: 'We moved up to the battery site and went into a casemate just as night fell. There were no torches and it soon became pitch black. We placed sentries 500 yards out beyond the strongpoint with a Bren group in a central position. At 0200 hours it was our group's turn to go out and man the Bren. I took our own gun with us as I had ordered my men to clean the sand off of it and change the barrel, so I knew that it would fire OK. We then spent the loneliest two hours of our lives out in the blackness with every sound magnified and every nerve straining.'

The advance along the dunes had outstripped the means of forward supply. The Buffaloes and Weasels did not prove to be of much use carrying stores. They had all been left far behind as they could not get forward along the difficult terrain. Some had hit mines and burned out, others were stuck in the sand and some were swamped. The inland route was impassable because of mines and movement by the tracked vehicles along the shoreline attracted accurate enemy artillery fire. To get supplies forward, the marines had to rely on the old-fashioned method of humping them by hand. All those men who could be spared were put to the task and the commandos struggled through the soft ground throughout the night to resupply the head of the line. Signaller Sgt Percy Bream was one of the rear party that night:

German prisoners had been brought back to the beach and were herded together before being sent back over the Scheldt on landing craft. There were quite a few of them. That night we had to carry all the ammunition and food along the beach up to the forward troops. Everything had to be manhandled and this was hard work walking through the loose sand. When this was finished we found we could not dig in at all for the night, the sand was too soft. Every time you tried to scrape a hole the sand would cave in; it was impossible to get

Inside the German coastal battery W13 looking towards Westkapelle, showing the vast area covered by the strongpoint. The concrete casemates holding the guns are to the left. The bunker in the centre houses a searchlight which can be moved out into the open on rails when required. (*Imperial War Museum, BU1277*)

below ground to any depth, all you could do was try to pile it up around you. There was no cover, but even though it was November, I don't seem to remember it being very cold. Perhaps we just had too much on our minds and were too exhausted.

At 0630 hours the next day, just before it got light, Capt Dan Flunder and A Troop resumed the advance. After a brief struggle they stormed their way through strongpoint W287 with little trouble and pushed on towards Zoutelande. The original plan was that 48 Commando would lead the attack up to Zoutelande and then 47 RM Commando would pass through and take the village. Lt Col Phillips and his 47 Commando had landed behind 48 Commando the previous day and spent the night waiting on the beach in the rear for the order to move forward. They were now impatient to get to grips with the enemy. Brig Leicester came forward to Moulton to see how things were progressing, only to learn that A Troop was making such good progress that its marines were at that moment in contact with the enemy in

Zoutelande. 47 Commando were now sent forward to take up the advance. When Lt Col Phillips and his men actually got to Zoutelande at the end of the morning, they found A Troop had not only taken the village but had advanced out the other side and had secured the dunes looking towards Flushing close by battery W11. The marines had found a path through the protecting minefields into the village and had captured a small central redoubt. The speed of its action had demoralised most of the enemy into surrendering. The troop took almost 200 prisoners. As Moulton later explained: 'It was a notable feat for a single troop with little mortar support and was a triumph for Dan Flunder's methods. If anyone had the hardihood to shoot at A Troop, down the troop would go, and a few minutes later their opponent would find himself being shot at from several different angles, with A Troop coming closer the whole time.'

Bert Skinner was with A Troop in this advance: 'On the second day of the operation we assaulted and captured the small hamlet of Zoutelandee right on the coast road. Originally the village had been given to 47 Commando to attack and their CO was apparently a bit miffed about our taking it! 47 came forward and passed through us to invest the next battery. A Troop were detailed to support their attack and their CO was a bit terse with Capt Dan Flunder who had led the assault on Zoutelande!'

With the baton now passed to 47 RM Commando, Moulton's men could stand down and take stock. They spent the rest of the day in the dunes. Although the enemy had been cleared from its sector, the Commando was still under occasional artillery fire, as was the landing beach close by the gap. Battery W11 continued to fire throughout the day, even while 47 Commando was attacking it. An LCT approaching to beach by the Westkapelle gap was hit by the German guns and sunk. This closed the beach for a while, cutting it off from resupply. Brigade organised an air drop much to the surprise of Moulton, for he and his men had plentiful supplies at their disposal from the stocks left by the Germans. That night, in a wooden hut complete with bunks, the Colonel recalls dining on Spam fried in German spiced oil, German bread, German tinned pears and German cocoa. After his supper, Moulton was interrupted by Brig Leicester, who told him that 47 Commando had not taken W13 and that he would have to send a troop over to Zoutelande to assist in a fresh attack the next day.

Lt Col Moulton chose A Troop again. Dan Flunder got a chilly reception when he reported to 47's HQ. They had not forgotten that his troop had captured their primary objective unaided. Flunder was ordered to take his men over to the left 500 yards to the front and provide flanking fire for the attack. A Troop advanced without support. The commandos established themselves in a group of cottages overlooking the battery with the enemy being completely unaware of their presence. From this position, Flunder's marines could look right into the centre of the German strongpoint. The troop vented its feelings by opening up with a furious broadside which startled the enemy. This was the signal for the attack to begin and 47 Commando put in a perfect assault, taking the battery and destroying the guns. By midday, Lt Col Phillips's marines had pushed on to meet 4 Commando at the gap close by Flushing, thus linking together the two landings.

Meanwhile, fighting was continuing elsewhere on the island. Supported by Lt Aldworth's mortars, 41 RM Commando resumed its push along the northern coast; the Canadians and 52nd Lowland Division continued their epic struggle to link Walcheren to the mainland and clear the north bank of the River Scheldt; but for the moment, 48 Commando could take some respite from the battle.

'The next day we buried our dead in the dunes by the Kerke at Zoutelande,' recalls Bert Skinner. 'A combined thanksgiving service was held in the church with the local civilians. Common hymns were sung in both Dutch and English and the service was led by the local pastor and Revd Maurice Wood.' The official history recounted the mood of the people: 'It was a really moving service; the locals turned out in their best national dresses; the children wore orange ribbons and the Dutch flags were flying everywhere.'

On 5 November the Commando was ordered to cross the Westkapelle gap and support 41 Commando in their attacks to the north. 4 Commando had already been moved over to Domburg and a plan was evolved for the capture of two German strongpoints, W18 and W19, near the northern tip of Walcheren. The brigade reserve for this operation would be 48 Commando. The attack was scheduled for 8 November, but 41 Commando made such good progress on the previous day that W18 was taken and W19 outflanked. The Germans were cracking and early on 9 November the enemy commander of the island negotiated the surrender of all his troops.

Just before this general surrender, a more local capitulation of the enemy was arranged. Since the death of Capt Mackenzie, Evan Thomas had been promoted to captain and had taken over command of X Troop. On 9 November, Thomas and his men were in the line close to Domburg. Two German officers walked into their positions carrying a white flag. Capt Thomas remembers this meeting:

At about 3 a.m., when we were waiting for the 'off' at 5.30 a.m., the two enemy officers were brought to me and the senior of the two (I think he was a Lieutenant Colonel) explained in fairly good English that he wished to surrender himself and his men. But, he added, military protocol required him to make the formal surrender to the senior British officer in the area. I contacted Moulton on the radio and he ordered me to hold the Germans and that he would bring up Brigadier Leicester to do the honours. For me, holding the German colonel in my Troop HQ – a half demolished cottage – was slightly embarrassing. The German colonel was dressed in a crisp tailored uniform, liberally sprinkled with insignia and medal ribbons, which he wore over highly polished jackboots. Needless to say, there was an Iron Cross at his throat. I, on the other hand, was in a loose fitting camouflage smock over my battle dress with no badges of rank – an anti-sniper precaution – and my boots and trousers were covered in mud and sand from the long march up from Zoutelande. Conversation was difficult, but knowing that many of the German troops on the island had served on other fronts, I asked the colonel if he had served on the Eastern Front. He was pacing up and down the room with his hands behind his back and he did not reply. Instead, he walked to the end of the room, turned round and held up both hands. All his fingers and thumbs had been amputated at various joints, a grim souvenir of the harsh Russian winters. I was speechless. Fortunately, a few minutes later, Brigadier Leicester appeared and took the Germans off of my hands. I had led 48 Commando ashore at Westkapelle and by a fluke was present at almost the last act of the invasion.

All the fighting was now over, but the north-east side of the island had not been cleared up and Moulton was ordered to send a party up to Veere to determine what the enemy were doing there and to make contact with 52nd Division, who had attacked around the eastern side of Walcheren. A Troop was selected and Capt Flunder was told to take a patrol through Oostkapelle and Serooskerke to Veere and meet up with the Lowland Division.

The whole of the inland part of the island was under water ranging in depth from three to ten feet, so the patrol was carried forward in Buffaloes. The patrol set off at 1215 hours and reached Serooskerke without incident, collecting nine German prisoners on its way. Bert Skinner was in one of the four amphibious Buffaloes: 'I was with my Bren group and Lance Corporal Ernie Taylor was with his group, we were now both with A Troop after Z Troop had been spilt up. We were in the second vehicle which was almost full.' In the first Buffalo was Harry Timmins: 'Four Buffaloes were needed to take us over the floods. The Troop Commander, Captain Flunder, myself and a few other men were in the first to lead the way. It was limited to carrying just a few of us in case it got blown up. The second Buffalo was quite full with about twenty-nine men inside. The third one was empty just in case we picked up any German prisoners and the fourth contained only about eight or nine men.' The patrol made its way through the buildings of Serooskerke along streets that were almost totally flooded, then set off for Veere. The first of the Buffaloes pulled out of the town along a side street and then slipped into much deeper water, looking for the turning that led to the main road to Veere. Well spaced out behind came the other three vehicles.

Jack Desmond was also on the patrol that day and recalls the journey:

We had tossed up as to who would go in the first Buffalo in case of mines and our section lost, as always. We started off and stopped in Serooskerke at the school house and took some German prisoners which we put into one of the Buffaloes at the rear. We carried on through the village and came to a crossroads which we couldn't actually see because the whole area was under water. At the crossroads there was a man in a boat. He directed the driver to go straight up and then turn sharp left to keep to the road. By the time the second Buffalo had come up, the man in the boat had moved and the Buffalo behind us cut the corner to join us.

Bert Skinner in the second Buffalo also recalls the man in the boat:

As we went along the street a Dutchman in a small dinghy was rowing after us shouting something. We turned on to the main road and the next thing I recall was a huge explosion as our craft blew up. We had run into an 11-inch shell fixed to a post and rigged up just under water as a mine. Ironically, immediately before the explosion our officer, Lieutenant England, had received a radio message to say the enemy on the island had capitulated. He said, 'It's all right lads, they've packed it in.' He was killed in the next instant, together with eighteen other men. The remaining nine marines in the Buffalo were all wounded by the explosion, including myself. As the shell exploded I remember the full ammunition box on

A German prisoner compound dug among the sand dunes near the Westkapelle gap.
(*Imperial War Museum, BU1280*)

the port Browning MG going skywards, it came down and hit me on the head and injured my left wrist. When I came to, I was under water outside the craft with my webbing caught up in the wreckage. My No. 2 David Rowley cut my straps and released me, his first words were 'They've killed Bill,' meaning Bill Bean my No. 1 on the Bren. They were both ex-7th Battalion men and were close friends. They had served together for three years. We were taken back to Serooskerke town hall where they cut my coat off me as they thought I had been badly wounded. The man standing next to me had his head blown off and his blood had saturated my Denison Smock.

The incident was a sad blow to the Commando, coming, as it did, at a time when the fighting on the island was all over. Dougie Edwards of A Troop recalls the aftermath: 'The actual task of collecting the dead and treating the wounded is thankfully blotted out from my memory. This was without doubt the worst incident of the war for me, but the memory of those mates and their faces will last for ever. We had only just been laughing and celebrating with the local villagers on their liberation.'

The loss of life in the explosion was greater than the numbers suffered in the whole operation. During the fighting the Commando had lost six officers and six other ranks killed, fifty-seven men wounded and twenty-one missing. With the explosion at Serooskerke, the operations on Walcheren had reduced the total strength of the Commando by 40 per cent, almost comparable to the losses on D-Day.

Sgt Percy Bream lost two signallers in the explosion and his experience of what followed was repeated by other sergeants and officers in other troops: 'I went with Major Sanders to identify the dead. One of them was Signaller Colin Skelland. Back at the beginning he had failed the course at Achnacarry and was to be sent back to his unit, but Lieutenant Ronnie Grant relented and accepted him into our signals group. He got married just before we left for France. I identified him from his service watch that he had on his wrist. I had the number of it recorded and knew it was his. You could just make out his features; he was very badly knocked about.'

The dead were buried in Domburg cemetery and then, a few days later, the marines of the Commando retraced their steps and marched the 15 miles back round to Westkapelle, through Zoutelande and on to Flushing, where landing craft ferried them over the Scheldt to Breskens.

CHAPTER SIXTEEN

The River War

The Commando arrived back from Walcheren and was given ten days in De Hann to reorganise and re-equip. Reinforcements arrived to make up the losses suffered on the operation and 48 RM Commando built up to a strength of 26 officers and 376 other ranks. This was an improvement in numbers compared with pre-Walcheren, but was still short of its original pre-D-Day complement of almost 500. This shortfall reflected the continuing crisis felt by the whole of the British Army at that time; there were just not enough men available. All units everywhere were short of strength and had been since the invasion. Drastic steps had been taken to alleviate this problem, including the disbandment of whole divisions, but the fact was that the prosecution of six years of war by Britain and her Commonwealth had exacted a great toll on her fighting forces. The bottom of the manpower barrel had been scraped and was found to be empty. Until the war was over 48 Commando would have to remain in the line.

Some of the marines coming to the Commando were those who had been wounded in the earlier fighting. Wherever possible, it was the policy of the Royal Marines to let casualties return to the unit in which they had previously served. This contributed to the friendly spirit of comradeship that was found in the Commando. A few of those now joining 48 were marines who had served elsewhere and had transferred to the commandos for a change, some were volunteers, some had been 'coerced'. One of these was Derek Turner. Although he never actually volunteered for the commandos, his sergeant had ordered him and a few of his mates to take 'one step forward' when asking for recruits. Turner remembers his arrival with the Commando:

I presented myself to the RSM, a much decorated man, whose response to my name, rank and number was a sharp, 'Are you eating?' Swallowing half a biscuit I denied the accusation and was sent off to join S Troop, the heavy weapons Troop. We were in civilian billets at the time and the first time me and another newcomer, Ginger Forbes, met our other Troop members was on a cold and clear winter's day. We arrived at the cookhouse/storeroom to find about twenty men sitting around on ammunition boxes enjoying a breakfast of tinned bacon and beans. Heads nodded a welcome, but we soon realised that the friendship of these men would have to be earned. They had lost many friends on D-Day and more on the Walcheren landings. Just then a jeep arrived outside with a screech of brakes carrying the Troop Commander, Captain Linnell. His jeep was something different, for his driver had built a wooden body on it complete with doors, which transformed it from a draughty open truck into a strange looking saloon car. Quick to spot the new arrivals he returned our smart salutes and told us that one salute in the morning would last all day.

Marines of 48 RM Commando clearing a minefield on the enemy side of the River Maas during a daylight raid. (*Imperial War Museum, A28408*)

One of the new officers to arrive was Lt David Ellis and he joined Y Troop and its commander, Capt d'A. Hosking. 'I arrived in the Commando with five other 2nd lieutenants, all of us fresh from training at Achnacarry. My troop officer was Captain Hosking, a giant of a man who had played rugby for England a few times. He weighed about seventeen stone and his main delight was to "bear hug" me into submission for whatever reason. Most of the time he succeeded (I being less than thirteen stone) but I could run faster.' These new officers were fortunate that the Commando was now engaged in fairly quiet activities, so they could assimilate themselves into the unit without too much risk.

The Walcheren operation marked the last full engagement by the Commando. It was not employed in any of the future battles which brought about the end of the war. This did not mean, however, that it spent the remaining months of the conflict in reserve or kicking its heels in the rear, for it was soon back in the line defending the area to the north between the River Scheldt and the River Maas. Allied strategy had dictated that the land to the north of the Maas in Holland would be left in German hands while the main offensives against the enemy took place in the east. It was thought that little would be gained by attacking into the Netherlands and capturing ground for the sake of it. The Germans there would be contained, harassed and kept unsettled by British and Canadian troops with a taste for making trouble.

In December, 4 Special Service Brigade changed it title to the more suitable 4 Commando Brigade. Just before this change it had been given the area captured in the Walcheren operation to hold against the enemy. North Beveland was held by 4 Commando, 41 RM Commando was in Walcheren, 47 RM Commando held the mainland north of the Scheldt and 48 RM Commando settled itself on South Beveland, with the town of Goes as its base. There followed a period in the line through a particularly cold spell of winter weather.

At first it was thought that the enemy would not possibly wish to retake the land north of the Scheldt. The whole of the area was low and flat and very wet, and it would take a major offensive to dislodge the Allies to regain the vital Scheldt waterway. Intelligence suggested that the all of the Nazis' effort and resources were being tied up in trying to stem the British and American drive to the Rhine, as well as holding back the Russians on the Eastern Front. This view changed in late December when von Rundstedt launched his major offensive through the Ardennes and pushed the Americans back towards the Meuse. The attack came as a complete surprise to the Allies. At the same time, reports were received that the enemy was also concentrating several divisions north of the Maas. It looked as though a major attack to retake Antwerp might be launched to tie in with the push through the Ardennes.

In response to this threat, X, Y and Z Troops were moved eastwards to Oosterhout and placed under the command of 47 RM Commando, who held a long section of the front line along the River Maas. Other help for 47 Commando in defending the sector came in the shape of anti-tank and armoured car troops, and there was a Polish armoured regiment in reserve, but the main hope of stemming any German attack relied on the barrier formed by the flooded ground and the River Maas itself. During this period the remainder of 48 Commando held its positions on South Beveland and was ordered to maintain a flying column ready to move should any German parachutists land in the area. Lt James Dick, the MO, later recalled this 'flying column':

> While we were stationed in Goes our primary duty was to act as a mobile rapid response force to be used in the defence of Antwerp should the Germans try to retake the city. We were all on immediate call if the code word was given. The Commando had six armoured cars attached to emphasise the mobility of this force. I remember one night when the code

word was flashed to all units. I rushed around with my sergeant collecting our gear and then set off in the direction of Antwerp. Halfway there the recall was given and we trooped back again. The signal had, in fact, been a trial run – not the real thing. Just as well perhaps, because every one of the armoured cars had broken down within a few miles of setting off.

Although the winter was bitterly cold, there was some comfort to be had from the fact that the marines were living in houses when out of their immediate defence positions. Nonetheless, it was a miserable time for them in the damp, waterlogged areas so often covered in thick frosts and snow. So cold was it that there was some concern that the water obstacles separating them from the enemy might become ineffective by being frozen over.

The three troops with 47 Commando held a section of the line opposite Keizersveer on the River Maas. Capt Evan Thomas and X Troop were sent to the area near Oosterhoute:

My troop was ordered to organise a second line of defence on the banks of the small River Donge. There we set about constructing a strongpoint. It was very cold and all the ponds froze and so did parts of the river. Digging slit trenches in the frozen ground with picks and shovels was almost impossible and we had to enlist the help of some Royal Engineers who had a pneumatic drill. Looking north from where we were, we could see the exhausts of the V2 rockets when they were launched by the Germans against London from sites in the Utrecht area. A minor chore for us was to plot the bearings of these vapour trails for the RAF. Armed with three or four of these bearings they could find the site of the launch and make an attack. But they had to be quick for the Germans didn't stick to one site for very long.

X and Z Troops had a fairly quiet time with 47 Commando, but Y Troop was close by a stretch of no-man's-land between a side-water of the Maas and the river itself. This territory was not held by either side, but both sides frequently sent patrols across to investigate. One fighting patrol carried out by Y Troop, led by Capt Hosking, had the misfortune to clash with a German patrol. A vicious firefight took place with the German patrol being backed up by mortar support. The enemy was beaten off by concentrated light machine gun fire and grenades, but not before Hosking and two others had been wounded. Marine Relf was posted missing. He was in fact captured by the enemy and made a prisoner of war, the only prisoner lost by the Commando during the whole of its history.

Marine Richard Cannock, one of the Commando's drivers, was normally employed providing transport between HQ and the forward troops, but on this occasion he was doing his turn out in no-man's-land. He later recalled carrying out this patrol and trying to get back to friendly lines:

When Captain Hosking was wounded, along with Sergeant Jones and our Corporal, he asked me if I could lead the patrol back. I did, but went slightly astray in the black night. When I got to where I thought our lines were, I spotted the glow of a lighted cigarette. I walked in that direction until I heard a voice shout, 'Halt! Halt!' The voice had an accent, but it was not German or Dutch, of this I was sure. I gave the password several times and always got the same reply, 'Halt! Halt!' After a while Geoff Hosking came up and asked about the hold-up. I tried again, but the reply was the same. By this time the Captain was getting annoyed (we had no idea then how badly hurt he was) and he shouted out, 'Shoot the bastard!' The immediate reply was 'No don't shoot, pass friend.' I don't remember what unit we had arrived at, but the sentry was a Belgian Army private who was obviously terrified that we were a German patrol. While the wounded were being treated, the officer in charge of this unit put me in touch with our HQ and I reported what had happened. As we left our houses in Raamsdonk I remember Sergeant Jones saying to me, 'Well done son!'

Shortly after this patrol returned, Lt David Ellis was ordered to take the remainder of Y Troop out into this no-man's-land to reconnoitre the area. He later described his experience:

I mustered about twelve other ranks and set out to perform a sweeping patrol to within sight of the river and then return. The snow was about two feet deep and difficult to move in, but it did enable us to advance in a diamond formation very quietly. The main trouble was the clinking of the metal of our guns and equipment as we moved. I decided, with the advice of one of my sergeants, to proceed in bounds of about 100 metres at a time and then to stop and listen and wait. It was very cold, but I was sweating profusely inside. On one of these stops a noise was heard away on our left flank. We dropped down and were well concealed in our snow suits, witnessing a large German patrol passing quite close to us. I lost count of the number of the enemy when I got to forty and they were still going by. After a safe period of time, we got up and continued our sweep to the river. Then we returned to our own lines. Looking back, I think that if we had been spotted and had opened fire I am sure we would have suffered heavy losses, even though we had a high proportion of automatic weapons with us in the shape of Bren and Thompson light machine guns.

On 10 January 1945, X, Y and Z Troops rejoined the Commando at Goes. The remainder of the month was spent holding its positions in South Beveland. In February, the Commando resumed the offensive. It had been exercising various techniques since the Walcheren battle and had recently concentrated on specialised training for raids across the enemy river line. Occasional raids on to the island of Schouwen had been made by 4 Commando and now this programme was to be taken up by 48 Commando. The neighbouring island of Overflakkee was also targeted. The object of these sorties across the narrow channel which separates Schouwen and Overflakkee from the mainland was to keep the enemy alert and to determine the identity of the German units garrisoning the islands.

These raids were given the code-name 'Incalculable'. During the end of February and the first eighteen days of March five raids were made against the two islands and three others were planned but cancelled. The marines were carried over to Schouwen and Overflakkee in landing craft assault (LCA), provided by the Royal Navy under the control of Capt Pugsley and Naval Force T. There were several problems to be faced, three of which were outlined in the Commando's official history:

Firstly, strong tidal waters and shifting sand made navigation difficult. Considerable use was made of direction beacons to overcome this, but the slow running of the craft, necessary to ensure silence, increased the time of the sea trip and the effect of the tide. Secondly, the time which could be spent ashore depended on the moon and the tide, as many of the channels were only safely navigable around high tide. Thirdly, the interior of the islands was flooded and all movement was necessarily along the dykes. These were heavily mined so that progress along them was slow. Even so casualties were inevitable.

Lt Col Martin Price and two naval officers direct the embarkation of marines during Operation Bograt. (*Imperial War Museum, A28412*)

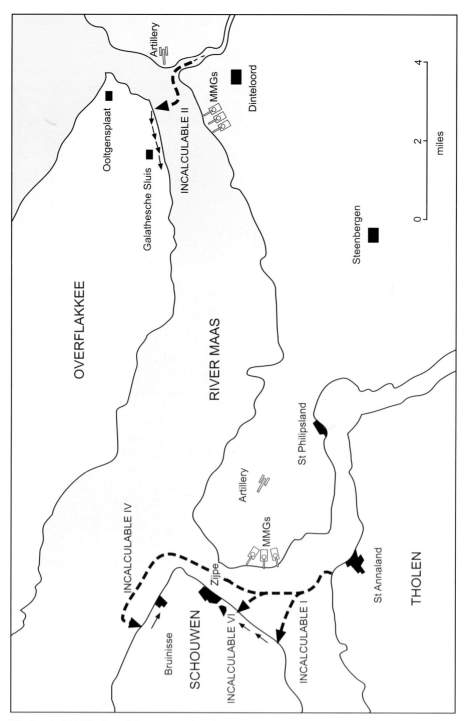

The 'Incalculable' Raids on Schouwen and Overflakkee

The enemy was very careful at night and usually lay low within his defensive positions along the dykes. If the Commando wished to capture any Germans it would either have to go into their positions and pull them out, or lay a trap to snare them if they ventured out on to the dykes. Either way it was a game of cat and mouse. The Germans didn't need to take risks and they could lie up behind a defensive minefield during the hours of darkness. Whereas the commandos had to venture out across the water and advance through the pitch-black night, across unmarked minefields to penetrate the enemy defences, all the time trying to be as silent as possible to gain the element of surprise.

Each of these raids was carefully planned so as to be ready for any eventuality. They had naval parties to man the landing craft and establish a beach group on the far shore to organise the landing and embarkation. The patrol itself was usually of troop strength. It would land from LCAs, carry out its objectives and then withdraw into the protected base held by the beach group for its return. On the home side was a forward HQ with a raid commander who controlled the operation. This was usually Lt Col Moulton.

The locations of the landings on the enemy islands were selected so as to be within range of supporting fire should it be needed, as Capt Geoff Linnell later explained:

> The points at which the raids were carried out were never more than 4,000 yards from the nearest part of our own territory, so that they could always be covered by medium machine gun fire and mortars, in addition to the field artillery support. Good communications were very important. The general set-up was to have a combined forward HQ on the home side of the river, with the CO, the artillery Forward Observation Officer and the naval representative in communications with the craft and the beach party by means of a 510 VHF radio set. This was a most useful set. The raiding party itself took an 18 or 38 set netted to the mortars, machine guns and the Tactical HQ controlling the support fire. If this link failed, fire could be called down via the naval set. In practice it all worked well.

The first raid was 'Incalculable I' carried out during the night of 4/5 March. A Troop, under Capt Flunder, landed unopposed on Schouwen and advanced 2,000 yards along the dyke towards Zijpe. The marines came across several German positions but all were deserted. After four hours ashore the raiders met no enemy and so withdrew to the LCAs for embarkation. There was only one casualty during the sortie when one of the commandos stepped on a *Schu* mine. These were small wooden boxes filled with explosives buried just below the surface capable of blowing a man's foot off if he should step on one.

'Incalculable II' took place on the night of 10/11 March. It had been planned for the previous night, but the navigator of the LCAs lost his way in the darkness and the patrol was forced to return. The next night Z Troop, commanded by Maj Nuttall, was ordered to cross over to Overflakkee and land on its south-east coast. It was known that there were some of the enemy in the area as German troops had been seen working there for several days. Intelligence suggested that they were constructing defensive positions.

Z Troop embarked at 2120 hours and slipped as quietly as possible down the narrow waterway from Sas Van Dintel and out across the tidal reaches of the Maas over to Overflakkee. The marines landed forty minutes later without incident and climbed up the dyke to start their raid. Maj Nuttall split his troop into two groups. A small party under Lt Mackinnon waded across some flooded ground on to the next dyke inland and moved parallel to Nuttall's main group towards Galathesche Sluis. The main group with Lt Prendergast in the lead soon ran into a huge minefield laid across the dyke. They made slow progress through the obstruction as it seemed to continue interminably along the raised earthbank. When they finally reached safe ground, 300 yards later, the length of the minefield outstretched the amount of white tape they had with them to mark a safe path through it. Nuttall and his men continued their probe forward in the dark and arrived at the *sluis* where they found a thick wire entanglement surrounding a pillbox. This was the enemy's main defensive position at the *sluis* and was manned by a small party of Germans.

Maj Nuttall quickly evolved a plan of attack. A small party would cut their way through the wire with explosives, followed by a direct assault on the concrete pillbox in the centre of the compound. Lt Mackinnon would cover the far side. Roy Dewar and a few others moved up to the wire, and he recalls what happened next: 'We had got close up to Jerry's position quietly and they did not know we were there. It was pitch dark as I went forward and had just about got to the wire when I stepped on a *Schu* mine. There was an explosion and I lost my foot. The others that were OK rushed up with a Bangalore Torpedo and pushed it through into the wire and ignited it. The explosion cleared only part of the wire so the rest had to attack the remainder with wire cutters.' Nuttall and the others kept the enemy position under fire while the wire was cleared. The Germans in the pillbox returned this fire and soon some stick grenades began sailing over into the marines. Maj Nuttall was one of the first through the wire and charged at the pillbox firing his Thompson sub-machine gun through its opening. Cries of 'Kamerad' quickly went up and a wounded German emerged with his hands held high. Inside he found another of the enemy also wounded. Both were able to walk so they were seized and taken back as prisoners.

The rest of the enemy who were manning the position ran out through the back and made their escape, passing Lt Mackinnon's party coming down the dyke towards the rear of the position. Shots were exchanged, one German was hit, but the others escaped. By this time it was 0125 hours and time was running out; the LCAs were set to pick up the troop at the landing place at 0200 hours. Maj Nuttall therefore fired the recall signal which instructed the commandos to withdraw to the river-bank. To keep the enemy from following too closely, the major called for a barrage of machine gun fire to be laid on the German position. Four of Linnell's Vickers machine guns fired many thousands of rounds across the river at uneven intervals to help persuade the enemy not to follow Z Troop.

Disaster then struck the troop as it traced its way back through the long minefield to the landing craft. The commandos were carrying Roy Dewar and the wounded Germans with them along the narrow dyke and the leading men lost their way through the untaped section. Very soon a large explosion erupted as one of the men stepped on a mine, shattering his lower leg. With great difficulty the wounded marine was put on a stretcher and then, as Lt Prendergast came forward to help to lift it, he too stepped on a mine. Another explosion and another lost limb. The narrow path through the minefield and the awkwardness of the stretcher parties led to even more casualties. Before the troop had managed to extricate itself from the obstacle, a further four men had had their feet blown off. One of the unfortunates who was wounded was a sergeant from 30 Battalion Royal Marines, who had joined Z Troop just for the raid to gain active service experience in offensive operations. Most of the marines now became involved in carrying their injured comrades. The seven wounded men, plus the two enemy, had to be got back through the minefield, along the dyke and down to the landing craft. The move to the beach was agonisingly slow and dangerous, and all the while the tide was on the turn and starting to go out. Embarkation had to be at 0200 hours.

Details of the troop's misfortunes were radioed back to HQ and Capt Pugsley gave permission for the naval craft to remain until 0300 hours, but Sub Lt Lee in charge of the LCAs on the beach estimated that he could probably wait until 0400 hours for Z Troop to embark. The painfully slow progress of manhandling all of the injured men back to the craft seemed as though it would take all night. At one point it looked to Nuttall as though he would have to let the landing craft return without his whole of his troop, but just as he was going to radio back that his men would have to dig in and remain until the next night, the last of the stretchers was brought down from the dyke. At just after 0400 hours, the LCAs withdrew from Overflakkee with Z Troop on board.

Bert Skinner was waiting for his troop to return to the friendly shore: 'I remember Lt Prendergast being among the injured. He was newly arrived in the Commando. He left 48 Commando as a corporal much earlier in the campaign and returned to England to get a commission. My job was to meet the returning troops in early hours with hot tea and three gallons of navy rum. They had had a rough time of it, but I could find no takers for the rum! This was unbelievable to an ex sea-service marine such as myself.'

Also at the harbour was Lt James Dick, the Medical Officer:

I was waiting with my medical orderlies to deal with the casualties, one of whom was one of my own men who had been a stretcher bearer on the raid, a lance corporal called Tug Wilson. I said to him, 'Are you all right Tug?' And he said, 'No, I've been hit in the stomach,' adding, 'Am I all right down there?' I had a look and could see this black object buried in his right groin. I couldn't think what it was so I grabbed hold of it and slowly eased it out, to discover that it was the heel of the boot of the leading stretcher bearer who had been in front of Tug and who had trod on a *Schu* mine. I assured him that his injuries had not inflicted any untreatable damage and saw him off in the ambulance. One reaction from the wounded men interested and surprised me; not one of them wanted, or would accept, brandy, but all wanted cigarettes.

One of the prime reasons for carrying out the raid was to collect enemy prisoners. Among those waiting for these to arrive on the jetty was the Intelligence Officer, Lt Harold Smedley: 'My role was to collate any information that we obtained. Any Germans that we captured were sent back to brigade to be interrogated.' Geoff Linnell remembers seeing the Intelligence Officer on the dockside that night: 'He was resplendent in arctic clothing and a fur cap, looking for all the world like a polar explorer waiting to receive the two prisoners, both miserable specimens, both very frightened. One was an infantryman from 346th Division, whose platoon had moved out some days before and left him behind; the other was a grounded sailor who had arrived the previous day and had never ventured outside his dugout.' Not a very impressive catch.

That same night, another raid was also taking place out in the wetlands of the Maas, this time against the island of Schouwen. This was 'Incalculable IV' and was carried out by A Troop and led by Capt Dan Flunder. The troop had been out the previous night to Schouwen and had landed on the dyke north-west of Bruinisse. The marines had advanced over 1,200 yards along the dyke but did not make contact with the enemy and withdrew. The next night Flunder and his men landed further down the dyke and began their advance to contact. Harry Timmins was on that raid and recalls the patrol.

March 10 was my twenty-second birthday. We blacked our faces, wore felt bottomed boots and tied down anything on us that would rattle. We boarded the LCAs at St Annaland and made our way towards Schouwen. As we neared the shore the engines were shut off and very slowly and quietly we drifted until we touched the beach. The ramp was dropped and the section I was in stealthily got out and went 200 yards along the dyke to take up a defensive position. Lieutenant Collins came through us with the rest of the patrol. They moved off until they came to some barbed wire surrounding a house. They made a gap through the obstacle and advanced to a slit trench containing two Germans. Lieutenant Collins called on them to surrender, which they did, but a third German saw what was happening and threw several hand grenades, which killed the two captive Germans and injured Lieutenant Collins and his batman, Marine Coleman. This alerted the main body of the enemy and the whole group came under sustained German machine gun fire. Even though he was wounded he still ordered his section to retire. A brave attempt to rescue Lieutenant Collins was made by Sergeant Brownfield, but he was hit in the face by grenade fragments and temporarily blinded. The fire was so accurate that the officer and his batman had to be left behind. We gave covering fire as Lieutenant Collins's section withdrew through us to the beach. Meanwhile, the enemy had sent up flares and they could see us and the boats. We began to get a bit worried and, although there were no more casualties, our boats looked more like overgrown colanders with so many bullet holes in them. It was later learned that both Collins and Coleman were killed, although they were only wounded when we left them, so we can only guess the truth of what happened to them. We do know that the Germans hated our green berets and called us gangsters.

Several other raids were made on the two islands while the Commando manned this sector of the line, but all failed to capture any more of the enemy and had to be withdrawn. Some further casualties were suffered from *schu* mines. There were also casualties from friendly fire, as Lt James Dick, the Commando's MO, later recalled:

Maj Wall and Lt Kingsley after they had been rescued from the Biesbosch during Operation Bograt. (*Imperial War Museum, A28398*)

One night I got a call to come up to a Troop HQ. When I got there I was told that two of our patrols had fired at each other, thinking they were facing a German patrol. When I examined the wounded, one was dead – his throat cut by a bullet – and the other two quite badly, but not fatally, wounded. The problem was how to get the wounded men back to base. We had no ambulance as such, we normally used stretchers tied to a jeep's frame. We could not use the lane we had used to the Troop's HQ, because of deep ruts and holes in the track. The only road of any use ran along the raised river bank in full view of the Germans. It was finally decided that when it got dark the Troop commander would open fire with everything he and his men had, forcing the Germans to keep their heads down, while we made a dash for it, keeping a tight hold on our patients.

Cpl Fred Wyatt of S Troop did not go over the river on any of these raids, but his experiences on the friendly shore supporting them were often more hazardous than being on any patrol, as he later explained: 'Our mortars and machine guns were set up near the river bank. When the patrols radioed back for support we had to open up with our weapons. The minute we did this, the Germans could see the flashes from the mortars and replied in kind. They were often very accurate and we were kept on edge the whole time. Each time a patrol asked us for supporting fire you knew that you would become a target and we couldn't stand down or move until the whole patrol had returned back across the river.'

More raids were planned to advance along the islands, but were all later cancelled for various reasons. Lt Col Moulton would not allow a raid to take place unless every eventuality had been covered and all necessary steps had been taken to prevent discovery or casualties. The Commando's history sums up the usefulness of these sorties into enemy territory: 'These raids, although they produced little tangible result, kept the enemy incessantly on his toes, and provided valuable active service experience to the Commando, of which nearly 50 per cent had joined since Walcheren and had seen no fighting. In addition, much information was gained which would have been useful had it ever been necessary to assault the islands, and, still more important, the enemy was prevented from finding out how thinly our front was held.'

CHAPTER SEVENTEEN

The Last Patrol

On 14 March a great change took place within 48 RM Commando; Lt Col James Moulton was promoted to brigadier and moved to take over 4 Commando Brigade from Brig Leicester, who had been posted to a command in the Far East. Moulton had raised 48 RM Commando from scratch, trained it and fought it, making the unit very much his own. His men had grown to respect him and to have trust in him and his methods. They also had a great affection for their commander.

Moulton was replaced by Lt Col Martin Price, another Royal Marine officer who had seen a good deal of active service. Price had been second-in-command of 47 RM Commando and had seen earlier action in the Madagascar operation in 1942. It was difficult for Price to take over the unit which for so long had identified itself with Moulton. His personality was such that he often appeared to be pedantic about regulations and aloof in this manner, but he had proved himself in battle and was a fearless leader.

By mid-March everyone was expecting that 4 Commando Brigade would be involved in the next great amphibious battle, the crossing of the River Rhine, but this honour went to 1st Commando Brigade, who had been withdrawn back to England for rest and retraining after Normandy. In fact, 4 Commando Brigade was doomed to spend the rest of the war on watch along the River Maas. On 25 March the Commando was moved to the line of the Maas north of s'Hertogenbosch and put under command of 116th Brigade Royal Marines, to continue with the policy of the containment of the enemy-held side of the river and harassing him at every opportunity.

The Commando held a 10,000-yard front along the Maas in a section of the river which was very open. With the enemy just 200 yards away, safe movement could only take place at night. Three troops were held in the forward positions, while the other two were in reserve. The troop positions were located in the villages of Empel and Bokhoven, and in an ancient fortification called Fort Crevecoeur. In support of the Commando was a squadron of Polish tanks and a half share in a field battery. The enemy opposite were fairly active. The Germans had already managed to send one patrol over the river and were thought to be planning more sorties into the British lines. During daylight they shelled the area and at night engaged in frequent firefights across the river. In reply, the Commando shot up anything that moved and often lay in wait to catch unfortunate Germans who strayed along the roads in their rear.

Y Troop boarding assault landing craft in preparation for Operation Bograt.
(*Imperial War Museum, A28403*)

The front here was static, but the clashes of arms were frequent, as Bert Skinner recalls: 'Bokhoven itself was on an island approached by a Bailey bridge. I got to know this bridge very well as I had to take a jeep over it every other day. Jerry had a fixed line on it and every trip was accompanied by bullets all round.'

On 7 April, the Commando was on the move again, this time along the Maas to the west to take over a stretch of the river around Kapelsche Veer from a Polish battalion. It was while the Commando was in these positions that Jimmy Wood won a Military Medal and emulated the achievements of his father and uncle who had also won MMs in the First World War. He rescued a patrol when it got into trouble after it had run into tripwires, setting off flares and lighting up the night sky. He later explained: 'The enemy were waiting for us and opened up with machine guns pinning down the whole of the sub-section. They made the mistake of using tracer and I set up the Bren and fired long bursts straight down the line of their fire. I must have been spot on, for it shut them up very quickly.'

Among the equipment left in the area of Kapelsche Veer by the Poles were four immobile Sherman tanks. Bert Skinner recalls his involvement with two of these armoured hulks: 'Their guns and the turrets were still working. One day the second-in-command of the Commando, Major Wall, came up with some ammunition for both tanks and, spotting my gunnery badge (from my service at sea), ordered me into one of the tanks and got in the other himself. After banging away for half an hour he took his leave of us. This firing had rather annoyed our opponents over the river and they stonked us unmercifully for the next two hours. Of course I got the blame for it!'

While in these positions, Capt Linnell made good use of the long range of his Vickers machine guns in S Troop, as Derek Turner recalls:

We seldom actually saw the enemy. Usually it was the noise of his bullets and the shells passing by that announced his presence. One spring afternoon we had two machine guns in operation to assist a marine battalion to hit a target their weapons would not reach. My gun was ranged on a large clearing through which a path meandered. Using a marine in a forward observation post to observe the fall of shot, we covered the area. Some time later the forward marine informed us that a six-man German patrol was entering our target area. When they were out in the open, I fired a long burst lasting four or five seconds which sent around sixty bullets into an area maybe sixty by thirty feet. Four of the patrol dropped immediately and were presumed killed. The other two decided to make a run for cover, but the second burst I fired brought down number five. The last remaining survivor had by now reached the surrounding trees and although I expended the remainder of the belt of ammunition, he craftily waited until each burst of fire ceased and gained another ten yards! Strangely, although number six discarded his rifle in his retreat, he clutched a parcel under his right arm while in full flight. Maybe it was his washing or a parcel from home. The five men who dropped were still there when we withdrew.

On 15 April the Commando came back into 4 Commando Brigade when they took over another stretch of the Maas between Willemstadt and Geertruidenberg. It held a particularly long front of over 35,000 yards with some help from other units. The unit took under command the partly trained and equipped 1 Belgian Fusilier Battalion and 600 Dutch volunteers, most of whom were no more than civilians. In support, one battery of field guns was available on call. The Commando's role here was to remain in reserve while the Belgians and Dutch held the line. It helped and advised these units where it could and organised raids across the river into an area of waterlogged islands known as the Biesbosch.

After a few days the Dutch reported that the Germans were evacuating the Biesbosch. Lt Col Price decided to send a patrol across to Steenen Muur in the heart of the islands to test the report for himself. A patrol went out under the command of Maj Wall on 20 April which contained Lt Kingsley and a sub-section of X Troop, together with a guide and an interpreter. The group crossed over the Maas into the network of islands carried in two dories, each of which towed a three-man canoe. These light craft were used to preserve silence in the approach.

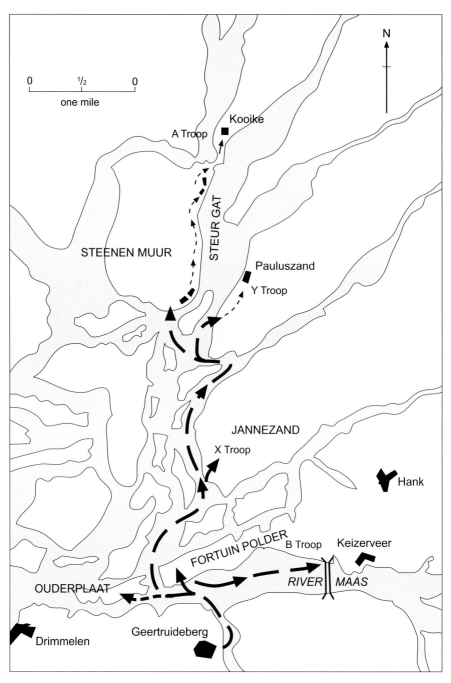

N

0   ½   0
one mile

Kooike

A Troop

STEUR GAT

STEENEN MUUR

Pauluszand

Y Troop

JANNEZAND

X Troop

Hank

FORTUIN POLDER

B Troop

Keizerveer

RIVER MAAS

OUDERPLAAT

Drimmelen

Geertruideberg

Operation Bograt

A line of LCAs loaded with the marines of 48 RM Commando makes its way through the Biesbosch during Operation Bograt. (*Imperial War Museum, A28402*)

The plan was to land the patrol on Steenen Muur near a group of houses. Maj Wall and his men would then reconnoitre the area and determine if the houses were clear of the enemy. If they were, Wall and the bulk of the patrol would withdraw while Lt Kingsley and two marines would lie up during the day watching for the enemy and then be withdrawn the following night. The first part of the plan went well: the patrol was landed at 0210 hours, it advanced to the houses in the north of the island, which were found to be clear of the enemy, and the dories were called forward for the Major and his group to withdraw. However, it was a dark night and the dories never met the rendezvous with the major. The patrol searched all night, but the dories could not be found. It was now daylight and at 0630 hours Maj Wall sent part of the patrol back to the original landing place to see if the boats were there. They were not. Three-quarters of an hour later a German bicycle patrol approached from the direction of Kooike and was beaten off by the commandos, leaving two of their men dead. At 1130 hours a further patrol was sent in search of the dories. This group ran into three more Germans, one of whom was shot dead and the other two were captured. The prisoners confirmed that their unit was pulling out of the Biesbosch, but the withdrawal was far from complete. Maj Wall decided that as the Germans were now becoming too alert, and as he had completed his objective and captured prisoners, he would withdraw to the southern end of Steenen Muur and try to arrange an evacuation. This was completed a few hours later and the patrol spent the whole of the day hiding from the enemy. At about 1700 hours a German patrol approached the marines' positions and opened fire. In the short action that followed, the prisoners were killed. The German patrol then withdrew. It was obviously becoming dangerous to remain, so Wall elected to try to escape by island-hopping southwards back towards the mouth of the Biesbosch. His Dutch guide said that he knew of a ford across to the next island of Ambatchen to the south. After nightfall, the patrol ditched all of its equipment and set off. To their dismay, it proved impossible to get off of the island, although the Dutchman crossed by waterlogged boat and was not seen again by the patrol.

The patrol moved back to the original landing place and Maj Wall instructed Lt Kingsley to lie up there for a further twenty-four hours, while he, his batman and the Dutch interpreter tried to get off the island by swimming across the main channel. Wall and his two companions attempted the crossing but were swept down the Steur Gat, landing up on the German-held mainland near Pauluszand. On reaching the shore they found refuge in a farmhouse where they stripped off their wet clothing and took warmth and shelter in some hay in the barn.

Back across the River Maas, Lt Col Price was becoming concerned at the disappearance of the patrol. Communications with Maj Wall and his party had terminated just after they had sent a message that they had landed safely. The naval radio operator with them had lost his set in the water. All through 21 April, the Commando's HQ waited for some news. None arrived, so at 1620 hours, Capt Flunder's A Troop and Capt Square's B Troop crossed the Maas and landed at the edge of the Biesbosch on the two islands of Ouderplaat and Fortuin Polder and held the entrance to the inland waterway that led up to Steenen Muur. Both landings met no opposition, but found that the dykes alongside each waterway were heavily sown with mines. B Troop were approached by an enemy patrol which withdrew after it had opened fire.

The rest of the night was quiet. No news had arrived from Maj Wall's patrol who had now been out for over forty-eight hours. At 0200 hours, the officer commanding the dories returned, explaining that he had been unable to find Wall's patrol at the rendezvous, had hidden up during the day and, after visiting the rendezvous again that night to find no one there, had decided to return across the Maas. On hearing this news, Brig Moulton

The lost patrol from Operation Bograt after its return. Back row: Cpl Gardiner; Marines English, Edwards, Thorp, Sharp; Sgt Workman. Front row: Marine Costain, L/Cpl Tickle MM (RAMC). (*Imperial War Museum, A38399*)

ordered Price to arrange for the immediate occupation of Steenen Muur and to rescue the lost patrol. The whole of 48 RM Commando was to be put into the operation, which was given the code-name 'Bograt'.

At 1300 hours the next day, all the troops of the Commando swung into action. B Troop was to continue its occupation of Fortuin Polder at the mouth of the Biesbosch to create a diversion for the enemy; A Troop was to be withdrawn from Ouderplaat and landed near Kooike to hold the north of Steenen Muur, while X and Y Troops were landed en route: X Troop on Jannezand and Y Troop across the Steur Gat at Pauluszand. All of the troops were ordered to sweep along the dykes and find the lost patrol.

As soon as the main body landed on the Steenen Muur they met with success. Lt Kingsley and his party were found near the original landing place. They were cold, wet, tired and hungry. Of Maj Wall's party there was no sign. X Troop now began their search of the island for them and across the waterway Y Troop did the same near Pauluszand. Present in Y Troop was Lt Hedley Phillips and he remembers the operation: 'We landed on the right flank of the Commando. After the troop had established a defensive position, I took a section of ten men to patrol forward and clear a group of houses and farm buildings.' One of these men was signaller Tom Clarke, who recalls:

> We approached the farm, which had a huge barn alongside it, and while the other chaps walked towards the house, I made for the barn. The barn was enormous, with a large opening and a huge haystack at each end. I went cautiously inside checking each stall in turn and passed right through and out the far side. Close by was a small shed, which I checked and found it to be all clear. There was nobody about, so I went back into the barn and had just got back to the entrance when the other lads came in. I spoke for the first time saying, 'It's all clear, there's nobody about.' Then there was a scuffling noise up on the haystack and a voice called out in English to us. It was Major Wall and his party and they came sliding down the hay towards us. I was very relieved they were not Germans!

All three of the men were stark naked. After the events of the day before, they had stripped off their wet clothes and were drying them in the hay.

Meanwhile, two other troops were in action. Maj Flunder's A Troop had met with a German patrol at Kooike but the enemy turned tail at the sight of the band of commandos moving towards them and escaped, and Capt John Square, now commanding B Troop, was in the south of the Biesbosch carrying out his own operation, as he later recalled:

> My B Troop had taken up positions on the German side of the River Maas to reconnoitre the factory at Keizersveer. A patrol cleared the mines on the river bank, but as it was a tidal river we found later our 'safe' route lined with white tape had been covered by the river. So I sent for our landing craft and landed a patrol by the bridge at Keizersveer which captured some Germans and killed one of the defenders. But from then on a very large calibre gun fired at the bridge every few minutes. So every time we heard it fire the LCA was manoeuvred out of danger. I interrogated one of the prisoners and told him to escort me up to the factory through any minefields that were there. He was a very obliging chap and led me to the top of their positions by a bunker. I asked him who was inside and pulled a pin on a grenade ready to throw it down the steps. He screamed at me saying it was full of ammunition and just then I dropped the pin of the grenade. Unable to make safe the grenade

Lt Hedley Phillips (with pipe) gathers with other Royal Marines to discuss their raid into the Biesbosch after Operation Bograt. (*Imperial War Museum, A28409*)

without it, we, the captured and the capturers, spent the next few minutes groping about on the floor looking for the pin. The German positions were excellently sited and I decided that we would hold them for the night. We had a good look around the factory which was empty and found a Russian machine gun which we kept. I was then told by the artillery officer who was with us that he could not raise anybody on the radio set and that we would not be able to call down any counter fire if we were attacked. That made me feel rather vulnerable, but fortunately we were soon recalled by Commando HQ and withdrew back across the river. We went back in the landing craft in high spirits, with all my chaps singing like mad, thankful the operation was successful. Inside the craft were four enemy prisoners sitting in the bottom of the boat looking quite dejected, two dead Germans on stretchers and a captured Russian machine gun as 'booty'. Lt Col Martin Price was in charge of the Commando for the operation. He had told me that I was not to take any casualties in the raid.

With the objectives of the operation now achieved, the whole Commando could withdraw back across the Maas. Operation Bograt had killed seven of the enemy, wounded four more and taken four prisoners, with many others probably wounded during the exchanges of fire. There were no casualties in the Commando. Information later received learned that the enemy was in a fine state of panic when he learned that hundreds of commandos were loose on his side of the river.

Operation Bograt was the last great exploit of the Commando, for a week later an order was received to cease firing, except in unusual circumstances, in the whole of the Netherlands district. The next day, a truce was declared and on 4 May the Germans in the north-east of Europe capitulated to Gen Montgomery. The war was over.

It was a great relief to each man to know that he had survived the war, none more so than Tony Pratt and he had a very good reason for feeling that way: 'Throughout the war I never really felt that I would be killed, but when the war ended I was very relieved to think that my mother would not get another of those telegrams such as the one that came when my elder brother was killed in the RAF.' With the war ended, thoughts now turned to home. The marines felt that after all the promises that had been made and broken, surely it was now time for the authorities to keep their word and return the Commando to England. In fact preparations were actually begun to do so, but again someone had other ideas. On 26 May 48 RM Commando was moved to Minden in Germany and brought under the control of the Allied Naval Commander Expeditionary Forces (ANCXF). Its first task was to supervise the eviction of 300 German families from their homes to make space for the ANCXF to establish its HQ. Sgt Joe Stringer remembers this task: 'We had to move people from their homes and cordon off areas for our forces. Minden was a lovely town with apparently no war damage. There was no fraternisation at that time and this was strictly observed. The Germans were not particularly friendly towards us. It was as though Minden had missed the worst of the war.' When Adm Burrough and his staff arrived, the Commando's main role was security, being responsible for the Admiral's personal protection and that of his HQ.

In June a request was made for reinforcements to join 1 Commando Brigade in the Far East to continue the war against Japan. On 25 June a draft of 6 officers and 102 other ranks left to join 45 and 46 Commando on their journey to India. Fortunately, the war with Japan ended by the time they had arrived.

As the months of the summer dragged on, there was still no prospect of going home. More jobs were found for the Commando in Germany. In August it supervised two displaced persons camps and an ex-POW camp. Lt David Ellis recalls the inmates of these camps:

> The displaced persons were mainly from Estonia, Latvia and Finland and had been used as virtual slaves by the Germans. They were very tough characters and we had them housed in Nissen-type huts in guarded camps, mainly to keep them from harming the local population. They had two main vices: first, they often broke out of the camps and raided German farms, bringing back the dead carcasses of sheep, pigs and goats, and second, they would insist on making stills and distilling a strong alcohol made from potato peelings. They housed these stills in holes underneath the huts. We had great fun in finding them and smashing them up.

After this period the Commando was involved in a series of moves around northern Germany carrying out various occupation duties. By this time some of the longer-service men were beginning to be released back to the UK. This trickle grew until 27 November when the Commando handed over its commitment to 607th Regiment Royal Artillery and set off for home. The marines arrived at a hutted camp at Horsham and each was gradually awarded three weeks disembarkation leave. Finally, only the rear party was left and on 31 January 1946, 48 Royal Marine Commando was disbanded.

BIBLIOGRAPHY

Yank Magazine, vol. 3, no. 24, USA, 1944

Dunning, J., *It Had To Be Tough*, Durham, 2000

Edwards, Cdr K., *Operation Neptune*, London, 1947

Gale, Lt Gen R.N., *With the 6th Airborne Division in Normandy*, London, 1948

Howarth, D., *Dawn of D-Day*, London, 1959

Ladd, J.D., *The Royal Marines: 1919–1980*, London, 1980

Linnell, G., *48 Royal Marine Commando: The Story 1944–46*, privately published, 1946

Moulton, Maj Gen J., *Battle for Antwerp*, London, 1978

——, *Haste to the Battle*, London, 1963

Portugal, J., *We Were There: The Army*, vol. 4, Canada, 1998

Ryan, C., *The Longest Day*, London, 1960

INDEX